M12-R
#983

CW00970145

STORMY APPLAUSE

STORMY APPLAUSE
MAKING MUSIC IN A WORKERS STATE ★

ROSTISLAV DUBINSKY

Hutchinson
London Sydney Auckland Johannesburg

Copyright © 1989 Rostislav Dubinsky

All rights reserved

This edition first published in 1989 by
Hutchinson

Century Hutchinson Ltd, Brookmount House,
62-65 Chandos Place, London WC2N 4NW

Century Hutchinson Australia
20 Alfred Street, Milsons Point, Sydney, NSW 2106

Century Hutchinson New Zealand Limited
PO Box 40-086, Glenfield, Auckland 10, New Zealand

Century Hutchinson South Africa (Pty) Ltd
PO Box 337, Bergvlei, 2012 South Africa

British Library Cataloguing in Publication Data
Dubinsky, Rostislav
    Stormy applause: making music in a worker's state
    1. Chamber music ensembles. String quartets. Borodin
    String Quartet, history
    I. Title
    785'.06'247

    ISBN .i.0-09-174257-9

Printed and bound in Great Britain by
Courier International Ltd, Tiptree, Essex

To Luba, my wife

Contents

PROLOGUE 3

QUARTET 7

COMPETITION 14

ORCHESTRA 24

STALIN'S DEATH 34

BORODIN 45

GOING ABROAD 60

EAST GERMANY 72

FINE ARTS 85

FIRST QUARTET RECITALS 92

OLYA 104

MOLDAVIA 113

SIBERIA 123

LET'S WALK 140

LUBA 145

CONTENTS

OH, AMERICA! 158

WACO, TEXAS 180

CALIFORNIA 196

BACK HOME 213

SCHNITTKE 220

CRACK-UP 226

GOING WEST 236

OISTRAKH 262

ROSTROPOVICH 275

SHOSTAKOVICH 278

THE END? 285

EPILOGUE 292

A Note to the Reader

With my heart beating a little faster than normal, my hands a bit colder than usual, with not exactly a comforting feeling in my stomach, I take the first steps to the stage. I hear applause, sometimes stormy applause. I bow deeply to the audience and take my seat . . .

Touring all over the world, I have experienced this moment about three thousand times. To describe all my concert trips I would probably need a second life. So in this book I tell only the most interesting ones, with a few episodes shifted slightly in time. This is especially so in the chapters about the Borodin Quartet's first trip to America. True as these stories are, with almost word-for-word conversations, I still don't call this book a memoir. For me it's not simply a piece of personal history but a story about a political regime which corrodes people the way rust eats into iron. The Soviet people have never been permitted to be truly themselves. They are brainwashed from childhood. When they grow up, they go on living by political slogans. The slogans glorify the Communist Party and its "great and beloved" leaders—leaders who sooner or later become enemies of the Soviet state. They die or are dismissed, but the slogans remain forever. "Glory to the Communist Party, which leads the Soviet people from one victory to another!" Stormy applause. "Long live the Communist Party—inspirer and organizer of our victories!" Stormy applause. "Long live . . ." "Long live . . ." We lived long enough to realize that these "victories" gradually brought the whole country to the brink of catastrophe.

So, no applause, please. Never applaud political slogans. Only applaud in a concert hall—and only if you like the performance.

STORMY
APPLAUSE

Prologue

Aɴᴛɪ-Sᴇᴍɪᴛᴇs have always found grounds for persecuting Jews. And if no rationale was to be found, they did without one. There were, however, periods of relative calm and governmental show in the Soviet Union. In 1935, when Soviet violinists won two prizes at the Wieniawski International Competition in Warsaw, all the world's newspapers carried the photograph of Stalin smiling at fourteen-year-old Busya Goldstein. Like Hitler, Stalin himself cherished the dream of wiping out all Jewry, yet he later rewarded the Jewish boy with a medal, a car, and an apartment. This had a stunning effect on the whole country. Then, in 1937, at the Ysaÿe Competition in Brussels, five top prizes went to Soviet violinists, and of those five musicians, four were Jews. The Soviet newspapers gasped with delight! This opened unlimited possibilities, which Jewish parents hastened to exploit, nourishing a whole new wave of *Wunderkinder*.

The Second World War began and ended. Interest in the Soviet Union increased enormously, and the first trickle of curious tourists gradually became a powerful stream. Russia now understood the value of her Russianness, and the Jews had become expendable. At the 1945 Moscow musical competition, the "mistakes" of the recent past were rapidly "corrected." Some twenty Russian-Jewish violinists were swept

3

out of the contest after the first round, Leonid Kogan after the second, and only Yulian Sitkovetsky managed to reach the finals.

I was among those who found themselves out of the game after the first round, but unexpectedly, several Russian musicians from the Moscow Conservatory petitioned for fairness. The higher-ups apparently decided not to get into a fight with the stubborn Russian intelligentsia (which, according to the elegant expression of Lenin himself, "is not the brains of the country but its shit"), and I was allowed to play in the second round. The audience understood that it was only a temporary reprieve and gave me a long farewell ovation.

That same evening, Sitkovetsky came to see me in the dormitory, together with the stupefied Kogan, and after them, as if after a two-headed comet, a tail of student violinists. Struck by the news of the contest results, they stood around in the corridor near the lavatories, not knowing what to do next, until a girl's clear voice rang out above the crowd: "Hitler is dead, but his deeds live on!" And at once the crowd began to disperse. The students' mass protest, having arisen spontaneously, quickly disappeared. The youth of the U.S.S.R. do not protest for long. They don't know how to protest, for they were never given a chance to learn.

Lisa, the girl who had shouted that Fascist version of the Soviet slogan "Lenin is dead, but his deeds live on," was a pupil of Abram Yampolsky, as were Kogan, Sitkovetsky, and I. We were all surprised that she got away with this outburst, and we often remembered it as a part of the competition. But that time and that competition vanished in the past, and not long before her graduation in 1948 Lisa was arrested. It happened on January 15. I remember the date because the day before we had stood together near the conservatory in a dense crowd. All Herzen Street from the conservatory to the Jewish State Theater was packed with people. It had been announced that on January 13, in Minsk, Solomon Mikhoels, heart and soul of the Moscow Jewish State Theater, had suddenly died of a stroke.

It was a strange crowd. Thousands of silent people stood in the streets, caught by one disaster and fearing another.

"I don't believe he died without help," said Lisa.

"Quiet," I said. "Nobody believes that, but be quiet."

"We all looked forward so much to the end of the war, hoped so much . . . But the war goes on against our own people."

"Quiet," I repeated.

"They killed him . . . I know it. They killed him because he was human, and because this human dared to be a Jew . . ."

"Please be quiet."

"Quiet, quiet . . . To be scared even after death. That's what they want from us."

She burst into tears.

We stood there an hour and then said goodbye. I didn't know it was for good. The next day she was arrested.

Soon afterward, as if by a strange coincidence with Mikhoels's death, the Jewish Theater was closed down. Then, the only Yiddish newspaper, *Der Emes* ("Truth"), was banned. The campaign against "cosmopolitanism" had begun, bringing with it the newly coined expression "rootless cosmopolitan." Not quite understanding what these words were supposed to mean, people would substitute the simpler word "Jew" for them. One after another, university doors closed to young Jews. At the conservatory several Jewish teachers were fired and Russians were invited to take their places. Mendelssohn's portrait disappeared from the walls of the conservatory's Bolshoi Hall. Jews were gradually prevented from taking administrative jobs, then any kind of work at all. Newspapers encouraged people to insult Jews with impunity. Officially, anti-Semitism was against the law—there was even a specific article forbidding it in the Soviet constitution—but no one ever thought of enforcing it. Jews lived in a state of growing alarm. The climax of the campaign came when Jews started to be jailed for "cosmopolitanism" and "bourgeois nationalism."

Many years later an old lady stopped me on the street. "Can I have a word with you?"

"Certainly."

"Somewhere private?"

I looked closely at her face and understood: she was "from there" and she was not that old. "There is a small park nearby and no people at this hour, only trees."

She smiled with just her eyes and nodded.

As soon as we found a place to sit down, she said, "Lisa sends you her love."

"Really? Oh, thank you! How is she? And how are you?"

"I'm already back, as you see, but she is still there."

"How many years was it? For you and for her . . ."

"I got ten; she, fifteen."

"Oh, my God!" I said. "Well, how is she?"

"It's better now, she plays in an orchestra. But in the beginning it was bad, especially in the winter, cutting wood . . . From despair she worked like a crazy woman, to make the time go faster."

"My God!" I repeated.

"But I'm here with a message for you. She wanted me to tell you what I saw on the thirteenth of January."

"The thirteenth of January?"

"Yes, back in 1948 . . . It was in Minsk, late at night. I woke up because two men were talking loudly under my window. It disturbed me. I got up, came to the window, and knocked on the windowpane . . . And at that moment I saw a truck. It was headed straight for them. They shouted and ran. The truck chased one of them and crushed him against the wall of a house."

"And this was . . .?"

"Mikhoels," the woman said.

"So that's how it was! Lisa was right. What happened next?"

"Early in the morning they arrested our whole street. They took everyone, even the children."

"Damn fascists! And we were surprised at the Germans!"

"Lisa asks you to go to the crematorium for her on January 13 and put flowers on his grave. I hope it is not dangerous for you . . ."

"I certainly will," I said.

She stood up. "There is one thing more Lisa asked me to tell you. You see . . . she has a different name, but she is one of Mikhoels's nieces. As a matter of fact, the whole Mikhoels family was arrested, even his distant relatives."

The woman turned away and left before I could say a word.

Quartet
1949

THE BEETHOVEN QUARTET was formed soon after the October Revolution. Its four members were Russians. Growing up in Moscow in the 1930s, I learned their names in early childhood, even before I knew what a string quartet was. The names Dmitri Tsiganov and Vasily Shirinsky (violins), Vadim Borisovsky (viola), and Sergei Shirinsky (cello) were always on concert posters plastered all over the city. The quartet played everything, but preference was noticeably given to Russian music.

The quartet's audience, built up in the early twenties, almost disappeared in the late thirties as a result of Stalin's mass suppression of the Soviet intelligentsia. After the Second World War, when at a grand Kremlin reception Stalin drank his famous toast to the Russian nation, taken as a signal to start an anti-Semitic campaign, a large number of Russians, more chauvinists than music lovers, congregated around the Beethoven Quartet. The "Beethovens," as they were usually called, were now at the top of the Soviet musical establishment. As trusted members of various committees, always sensing the way the wind was blowing, they easily created the necessary majority, acting jointly like a battering ram. The Soviet government appreciated their services and generously rewarded them with all the titles and decorations possible, in spite of the fact that they were not Communist Party members.

7

In the late forties, to be a Communist differed entirely from what it had been earlier. The romantic flame of revolution had long ago died out, grand expectations seemed illusory, and instead of high ideals people again began to think of how to accommodate themselves to the new order. The new, worldly Communist soon learned that if he paid membership dues on time, attended without question all Party meetings, said only what was printed in *Pravda*, and never voiced his own opinion, he could survive and even make a nice living.

Many people followed this strategy, and somehow everyone understood why. Even when the best Soviet musicians were joining the Party, we knew that it was the only way to gain the confidence of the government, without which no concert tours abroad, no professorships in the conservatory were possible. The leading musicians were simply invited to join the Party, and then all choice vanished; to refuse would be suicidal for one's creative life.

I remember talking to a schoolmate, a very good violinist with a promising career ahead of him, who had just become a Party member. I asked him why he had done so, and he answered frankly that he had been strongly advised to. I then asked what his own opinion was.

He smiled. "I certainly have an opinion of my own, only now I don't agree with it."

Now you are a real Communist, I thought.

I reminded him of a wartime story we had both enjoyed, about soldiers who wrote just before a battle: "If we die, consider us Communists! If not, don't!"

But he pretended not to remember and hastened to leave.

We never talked again; when I saw him in the conservatory, he preferred not to notice me.

Well, I thought, he'll find some other friends to talk to. There are a lot of Communist Party members in the country, some twenty million. He'll be all right.

This happened when I was twenty, the year I graduated from the Moscow Conservatory and together with three classmates of mine formed a string quartet.

In our quartet all four of us were Jewish, though the cellist, Valentin Berlinsky, was Jewish only on his father's side. His passport said he was Russian. That was his choice, because in the postwar Soviet Union the word "Jew" had become somewhat taboo. Free of the stigma of being branded a Jew, Berlinsky, who had been a member of the Young Communist League, the Komsomol, joined the Communist Party. This gave him a noticeable advantage over the rest of us: in the conservatory he was given a Stalin scholarship, and after the conservatory he found himself an *aspirant* (a postgraduate fellow). Besides permitting a well-paid idleness, this fellowship had the strong psychological boost of governmental support. Young Jews, especially non-Party members, could not even dream of it. They could only shrug their shoulders and say that their access to the fellowship had been cut off on the eighth day after their birth. Berlinsky's political activities took up a lot of his time. Apart from frequent Party meetings, he could always be found in the conservatory's Komsomol committee room. The room would be locked, as if important questions were being discussed there, until late at night, when the door would fly open and all these "Party VIPs" would come out with red faces, talking and laughing louder than usual. Our cellist would be with them.

But I did not fully realize how much he was with them until one night when we were rehearsing in the conservatory. We were playing that incredible D-minor Mozart quartet, where each phrase speaks more movingly the more simply it is played. We argued about the tempi and discovered that all four of us felt the music differently.

"The music doesn't move . . ."

"It shouldn't run away."

"It's allegro moderato . . ."

"But still allegro!"

"With moderato . . ."

"But allegro . . ."

That led us nowhere. After a while Berlinsky said, "If only we could play for Comrade Stalin . . ."

I thought he was joking and was ready to laugh, but he continued quite seriously. "Everything would become clear. We would have no doubts."

Suddenly I did not feel like laughing anymore. "You don't really think he knows the right tempi of this particular quartet?"

"He knows everything," Berlinsky said solemnly.

I looked around and saw the frozen faces of Vladimir Rabei, our second violinist, and Rudolf Barshai, the violist. When Stalin's name was mentioned, the best thing to do was to maintain a reverent silence.

"Okay," I said at last. "Let's go home. We'll try again tomorrow."

We walked out of the conservatory. At the entrance, two workmen were pasting up a fresh poster: NEW WORKS OF SOVIET COMPOSERS. The names of Tikhon Khrennikov, Dmitri Kabalevsky, and the Beethovens, freshly painted in big letters, were gleaming in the streetlights.

"Interesting," Berlinsky said. "We should attend. I'm going to."

He looked at me.

"I don't know yet," I said

"You'd better go."

"Why? To listen to that crap?"

"You don't have to listen. Just be there. The Beethovens have already noticed that you don't go to their concerts."

"So many people will be there! How will they know if I'm there or not?"

"Come backstage."

"I never know what to say there."

"You don't have to say a thing. Just go around and shake everybody's hand."

"And if I didn't like the performance?"

"That doesn't matter."

"They're clever people. They'll see I'm lying."

"They will thank you for coming."

"The hell with them! I won't go."

"That would be a big mistake."

Berlinsky turned and left without saying goodbye. The other two didn't say a word. I didn't know whose side they were on. I waved to them and started to walk home.

I felt lousy. The rehearsal had reached a dead end and tomorrow . . . What should I do tomorrow?

Barshai caught up with me and took my arm. "Relax," he said.

"Oh, shit!"

"Take it easy."

"It's fine for you to talk! You didn't say anything, as if it didn't concern you."

"What could I say? He's right."

"You followed me to tell me that?"

"No . . . There's something more interesting . . . Did you know that yesterday was Borisovsky's birthday?"

"I didn't."

"You didn't? The whole Beethoven Quartet calls it 'Violist Day,' as if it's a national holiday. Musicians come to pay their respects, and he notices who appears and who doesn't. Well, I came fairly early, but there were already some violists from the State Orchestra at the entrance, and we went upstairs together. Borisovsky met us very warmly, as if we were his best friends. We each drank a glass of vodka to his health . . . But this morning in the conservatory he said that the first to congratulate him were the Jews of Moscow."

"Great," I said. "Just great!"

"But listen," continued Barshai. "There's more. A crowd started to gather. His favorite, Galina Matrosova, came with her whole quartet. Borisovsky kissed them all, nodded in my direction, and said that in the other quartet, ours, he is appreciated by only twenty-five percent. Once everyone had had a drink, he picked up his instrument and started imitating different performers. That is his best show! Everyone laughed till they cried, but he said seriously that the Beethoven Quartet always followed the great Russian traditions of the Maly Theater, and that all those modern tricks only foul up real Russian art. He hunched his back, played a tune from a Tchaikovsky concerto in the style of a provincial Jewish wedding, made a mournful face, and sobbed. There was a roar of laughter, and he said, 'All that is alien, not Russian . . . not ours.' He looked at me and added that now a lot of people crawl into music by non-musical means. How about that?"

Barshai stopped and turned to me. "Well?"

"Well," I said, but I didn't know what else to say.

We went on. Barshai squeezed my elbow. "Our cellist spends a lot of time in that Komsomol room."

"I know."

"They mostly drink vodka there and . . ."

"I need a drink right now."

". . . pretend they are awfully loyal."

"A lot of people do that."

"It's just a sham."

"A good way to repay the Stalin scholarship and Aspirantura, isn't it?"

"And his cronies, let me tell you . . . By the way, they're all Russians. He even considers himself Russian."

"Don't worry. He still plays like a Jew."

"Have you noticed how he shows his passport? As if he's better than us."

"He is better. His passport says he's Russian."

"Russian, my ass! The passport doesn't matter—they'll hit him for his face. Like all of us."

"Listen," he continued, squeezing my elbow harder. "Back there, outside the conservatory, I didn't want to interfere in your argument about the Beethovens. But I'll tell you—he's right. When everyone everywhere lies, it's not a lie anymore. It's just a new life-style, a new morality. He got the idea and there's your result: he's doing fine. But you and I, we won't get anywhere. And the quartet won't either."

"So what? You want *me* to join the Party?"

"Why not?"

"Why don't *you*?"

We reached my street and stopped. I could see he wanted to say something else.

"Yes?" I said.

"No . . . nothing."

"So long, then?"

"So long."

The next day I brought a metronome with me to rehearsal. The problem of the tempi in the Mozart quartet had to be solved somehow. Berlinsky was still angry. He sat tensely, and painstakingly did only what was required of him.

When I thought the music started "breathing," I asked, "So, how do you like this tempo?"

"It's all the same to me," he answered.

I asked the others. Both answered simultaneously.

"Too slow!"

"Too fast!"

"Beautiful!" I said. "Shall we try playing something else?"

No one answered.

"Does anybody think it's a good idea?"

"I don't care," Berlinsky said finally. "I have to go. I have an important meeting to attend."

We split up and didn't meet for several days. It was our first "ideological" quarrel. To redeem myself, I felt I had to go to the Soviet-music concert, go backstage to see the Beethovens, and smile. I rehearsed this scene carefully in my thoughts, and on the day of the concert I dragged myself to the conservatory concert hall. During the intermission, I trudged backstage. The Beethovens were putting away their instruments. I went up to each of them and each one shook my hand. They smiled and thanked me for coming.

As I left, I ran into Berlinsky and Barshai.

"So? You didn't die, after all? What time tomorrow?"

"As usual," I said.

When at our next rehearsal we tried the Mozart quartet, any tempo I started playing was suitable for everyone. We were friends again and played the whole quartet with pleasure.

"Oh, what divine music!" Berlinsky cried.

"Heartbreaking!" Rabei echoed.

"Simply impossible to play," Barshai joined in.

"Yes, it should be banned, shouldn't it?" I said.

Competition
1950

W<small>E</small> B<small>EGAN</small> the next year by busily preparing for the International Quartet Competition in Prague. One day, on my way to rehearsal, the neighbor's six-year-old boy suddenly rushed at me. He kicked my violin case, shouting, "I'll kill your Jewish violin!" and ran off. Passersby looked at me; some of them laughed. They, of course, would repeat this at home as the latest Jewish joke. I ducked into an alley, went an unfamiliar way, and was late to rehearsal. I apologized and tried to start playing, but the phrase "I'll kill your Jewish violin!" kept running through my head.

Berlinsky looked at me curiously and then stopped playing.

"What's going on? What's wrong with you?"

"Sorry," I said, and told them what had happened.

"It's nothing. Just a childish trick. I wouldn't pay any attention."

"But it's strange. A little boy, where did he get it?"

"Probably from his parents," Rabei joined in. "Typical scene: the whole family is at the dinner table; mother feeds her brat with a spoon; father drinks vodka, gets drunk, and swears at the Jews. One of the first words that kid learns is 'Jew.' No wonder."

"Then he grows up," continued Barshai, "turns into a copy of his father, makes new kids, and first of all passes on his 'love' for the Jews."

"And there are plenty of them, fathers and their offspring!" concluded Rabei.

"I don't agree," said Berlinsky. "It's dangerous to generalize. And anyway, our job is to play, not to talk. The competition is getting close!"

"That's just it," Barshai answered spitefully. "Are you sure that there won't be people like that bastard's father in the jury at the competition? Imagine, we come out to play and they see these very same Jewish violins. Of course, no one will kick our instruments, they'll even smile at us, but who knows which is worse! Before our rehearsal I stopped off in Borisovsky's studio. He and Tsiganov were listening to the women's quartet. You should've seen how graciously they bowed to me. The more they smile, the less hope we have."

"Did you hear the girls play?" I asked.

"No, they stopped when I came in."

Rabei winked at me. "They don't even have to play. They have such good names: Matrosova, Kaverzneva, Karpova . . . To the officials they'll sound like the sweetest music."

"Which you can't say about ours," I said. "What if we tried changing them? Just a little. For instance, not Barshai but . . . say . . . Barinov."

"No way. They don't change Jewish names nowadays. The composer Solomon Kaganovich already tried to do it. His pseudonym is Lev Solin, and he wanted to make it legal. He was refused everywhere, even though he got as far as the main militia office in Moscow. Some general received him, listened attentively, and said that a name could be changed only if it sounded offensive. 'For instance,' the general said, 'if your name was Mr. Stinker, or even better, Stink Kiker, that would be fine.' "

"What a swine! A real fascist!"

"I don't believe that happened," said Berlinsky. "To hell with your discussions."

He started to put his instrument away.

But Barshai was still furious. "Four quartets are trying out for the competition, and only two will be sent to Prague. The girls definitely go, no matter how they play. The Leningraders are all Jews, so we're even with them. The Georgian quartet, I think, is no threat. It's Prague, after all. We have a chance."

"The girls and us?" Rabei said. "That means two quartets from Moscow. What about the other cities, and republics, and national culture?"

"We'll have to play well," Berlinsky repeated, "and talk less."

We went outside. The streetcars had already stopped running. Berlinsky and I set off along Herzen Street toward the center of town, passed the beautiful Manezh, came out on the Bolshoi Kamenny Bridge across the Moskva River, and approached the shapeless dark-gray government building.

"Some building," I said.

"The residence of our leaders," replied Berlinsky.

"Looks like a pile of coffins."

"Oh, shut up!" He glanced behind us. "You sure found a good place to philosophize."

We drew even with the entrance. From the shadows a man's figure came toward us. "You guys have a light?"

"Sure." Berlinsky reached into his pocket, lit a match, and offered it to the stranger. In the light of the match he stared at us and suddenly drawled with surprise, "Je-e-ews . . ."

"Yes," I said. "Jews. So what?"

He gave us an evil look. "Your time is running out." He spat and left.

On the corner where we parted, Berlinsky stopped. "Listen . . . tomorrow at rehearsal . . . about this . . . don't . . . better not."

I didn't answer. I was shaking all over. A kind of animal rage rose toward my heart and rattled in my throat. This was the enemy. Face to face! I felt I could kill him. Easily.

The next day at rehearsal Berlinsky kept looking at me imploringly. I said nothing.

The competition was approaching and the jury had been announced: the cultural tsar Anisimov himself as chairman, the Beethoven Quartet, director of the Moscow Conservatory Alexander Sveshnikov, professors David Oistrakh, Evgeni Gusikov, Sergei Aslamazyan, musicians from Leningrad and some "neutral" cities, officials from the Ministry of Culture—altogether twenty people.

The program for competition had been set a year in advance. Together with a free choice of classical works, one Czech composition was required for everyone—Leoš Janáček's second quartet, "Intimate Pages."

Brought up strictly on the classics, we were not ready for this quartet. Janáček's highly individual style was for us as strange as a foreign language. Measure by measure, page by page, this remarkable quartet opened up for us a new world of sounds, colors, and rhythms, and gradually seemed like the inflections of speech. We felt as if we had started speaking Janáček's language without a dictionary.

Moscow Radio became interested in Janáček's quartet and invited us to perform it on the air. When we came to the studio, however, we discovered that the broadcast had been canceled.

"I am very sorry," the program director told us. "It's not my fault. But don't be disappointed. You can play something else."

"Something else!" I almost screamed. "So many people wanted to hear Janáček for the first time in their lives."

"That's just the trouble. The interest was too great."

"But why? What did they say?" Rabei asked.

"They said, 'We will wait until the competition.' "

"And then?"

"I don't know. They didn't say."

We looked at the program director. She looked back at us. We all knew that Mahler and Bartók were not performed, that for Ravel special permission was required, that Shostakovich and Prokofiev were banned as "enemies of the Soviet people." But Janáček? Now they were frightened of Janáček!

A week before the competition it became known that Janáček's quartet had been removed from the audition program. It was hard to cope with. We practically stopped working and just talked, sitting in our places with the instruments in our hands.

"All right, then. Here they'll get by without Janáček. But what will they do in Prague?"

"They banned Janáček here, they'll ban it there," Rabei said. "Don't worry!"

"It's none of our business," commented Berlinsky nervously.

"What the hell, whose is it, then?" Barshai cried out. "Do you really think that they are always right?"

"This talk won't do us any good."

"And what should we do? Pretend that nothing is going on? Or refuse to play as a sign of protest?"

"*That* will make them very happy!"

"Oh, stop it!" Berlinsky said. "I can't stand it any longer."

The last few days before the audition I couldn't eat, I felt so nauseous.

And on the very last day the news came that Oistrakh was sick and would not be on the jury.

The day of the competition came. We were to play first, after us the Leningraders, and the women last. The Georgians, we were told, would not be coming to Moscow.

We were announced. Applause was not allowed and it was unnaturally quiet in the hall. We bowed into the emptiness and took our places. I lifted the violin . . .

From the balcony, where the jury was sitting, a familiar voice reached us, "I not only can't listen to them, I can't stand the sight of them!"

The voice belonged to the director of the Moscow Conservatory, People's Honored Artist of the U.S.S.R., Stalin Prize laureate, Alexander Sveshnikov.

There was laughter in the jury. I remembered that meeting at night by the bridge and "I'll kill your Jewish violin!" With despair, eyes closed, I waved my bow . . .

How we played I'll never know. When we finished, the hall, as before, was quiet. We rose, bowed once more into the silence, and walked offstage. My heart was pounding. As if in a dream, I heard the announcement of the next quartet, the Leningraders, their non-Russian-sounding names . . . I felt nauseous again.

Berlinsky gave me a close look. "Come on. Let's go." I followed him mechanically. He took me to the Komsomol committee room, locked the door behind us, opened the safe with another key, and pulled out a bottle of cognac. He poured two glasses.

"We should have a drink."

"How did we play?"

"All right, I think. The Beethoven was good. Especially the beginning. You were great . . . Only pale as"—he searched for the right word—"as shit!"

We drank.

"Well, now? Feeling better?"

"Probably," I said.

He put the bottle back in the safe. "I want to hear the girls play."

"I'd like to sit a while. May I?"

"Slam the door shut behind you," he said, and left.

I sat still, thinking of nothing.

Someone knocked at the door. It was Andrei Gorbatov, my regular chess partner. "Berlinsky told me you were here . . . Shall we play a game?"

He was almost a professional and always won. I was glad when I could manage a draw.

"Sure," I said. "The best thing to do."

We set up the pieces. He won. "Another one?" he offered.

"No, Andrei. I've got to go back to the hall."

"What's going on there?"

"The audition."

"Oh yes, the competition . . . Listen, tomorrow we're all getting together. Will you come?"

"Definitely," I said. "I've got to win a game sometime."

When I got back to the hall, the women were already playing, furiously waving their bare arms. I didn't recognize the music right away—it was the rarely played Taneyev second quartet. But their manner of playing was familiar, even though I was hearing them for the first time. It was (as we called it) a "coarse-ground" style. It came into fashion in Moscow after the war, when traditional playing was branded "non-Slavic" (read "Jewish"). This new style neglected everything that is so attractive in quartet playing: flexible ensemble, refined phrasing, variety of colors. In their place there was something else, insolent and smug. You wanted to cover your ears.

I saw Berlinsky in the audience. We caught each other's eye and shrugged our shoulders . . .

Later that evening we were all standing in the foyer awaiting the results. Upstairs they were still busy. Then we saw Professor Aslamazyan coming down the stairs. Passing Berlinsky and me, he paused for a second. "It's all right," he whispered. "You are the best."

Professor Gusikov then walked by, but returned to counsel us, "They couldn't do anything. The way you began Beethoven . . ." He rolled his eyes and spread his arms.

I turned to Berlinsky. "Well, congratulations, old man!"

He shook my hand firmly.

"Let's go," I said. "It seems clear now . . ."

"It's still better to wait. To be sure."

"Then let's wait where there's something left in the bottle."

Everything repeated itself: Berlinsky unlocked the door, opened the safe, pulled out the same bottle of cognac and glasses. He poured. I raised my glass.

"To the quartet!"

We clinked glasses standing and drank up. Now the cognac seemed tastier.

"Good . . ." I said.

Berlinsky looked warmly into my eyes.

"You see now? I was right. We have only to play well. They are all musicians and surely know what is what. They need the first prize in Prague and they know that the girls won't do it . . ."

"Good," I said again. "And we'll play Janáček there."

"And how!"

He took the bottle and carefully shared out the last drops. I felt the warm glow of the cognac dissolve the tension of the last few days.

"Listen, are we really going? I can't believe it somehow . . ."

"I was sure of it from the beginning," Berlinsky said. "Whatever they say about the Beethovens, they are still good musicians. I'm sure our Beethoven impressed them. They understood that . . ."

There was a loud knock at the door. He opened it and we saw Barshai.

"Celebrating already? Isn't it a bit early?"

We stared at him.

"Everyone has left already," he continued. "I caught Aslamazyan

in the bathroom. In strict confidence he told me that after the voting
Anisimov announced a break. That's when Aslamazyan and Gusikov
came down and congratulated us. But Anisimov and the Beethovens
remained upstairs for a consultation. When everyone got together
again, Anisimov made a speech. About how the Ministry of Culture
and the conservatory serve Soviet art, that their aims are mutual, that
in the future there will be other competitions and, therefore, a mutual
understanding is required . . . on and on, the same old stuff. In short,
he suggested a new vote. Everyone got the message: now the girls get
first place and we're second."

I looked at the empty cognac bottle.

Barshai continued: "Good old Gusikov didn't agree, Aslamazyan
supported him, but the Beethovens did their job."

"That doesn't matter much," Berlinsky said. "We're going, and that's
the main thing. It will all be decided in Prague."

"That's true," I added. "What difference does it make now? They
selected two quartets and that's it. Why did they bother to change our
places? They need the first prize in Prague, not here."

"It's strange. Very strange."

The next morning I was still asleep when my door was flung open
and in came Barshai. He sat heavily on the corner of my bed.

"It's bad," he said in a gloomy voice. "We've been cheated." He
turned away. "Now it's clear, this second vote. This morning there
was a third one. Anisimov called the jury together again, but this time
he spoke about the friendship between all our nationalities."

I was not fully awake yet.

"Which nationalities? Russians and Jews?"

He gave me a wild look. "After this speech, Anisimov declared that
the selection of quartets would be changed slightly. Instead of us—
the Georgians."

"How come? They didn't even play."

"Why should they, when they have Mikhail Chiaureli?"

"That lousy film director?"

"That lousy film director makes movies about Stalin, drinks wine
with Beria, and, by the way, is the Georgian first violinist's uncle.

One phone call and that was it. The Georgian quartet was recommended to the Ministry of Culture; no audition for them. Anisimov and the Beethovens knew about it from the very beginning."

"What about the jury?"

"Gusikov, Aslamazyan, and the others were simply fooled. The main thing was to drag those girls into first place, which they did with the second vote. And now it's all honest: the jury selected the two best quartets. As for the Georgians . . . Well, that's an order from above . . . And Anisimov thanked everyone and shook everybody's hand. A clean job!"

"Where did you get all this?"

"Yesterday all Moscow was talking about us, and Oistrakh was looking for us all evening. I've already phoned him. I thought he wanted to congratulate us. Far from it! He didn't even mention the competition. He invited us to play the Chausson concerto with him and Oborin. He said they would change the program and print up a new poster. 'Right now,' Oistrakh said, 'I just want your names to appear on posters. Give my regards to the whole quartet.' I understood everything. That's why he wasn't on the jury—he didn't want to be mixed up in this dirty business."

"Does the quartet know?"

"Yes, I phoned them."

"And?"

"We have to go to the ministry. All together."

"Should we?"

"Yes! They should know . . ."

"Know what?"

"Get dressed!"

We all met at the entrance with the black marble sign: U.S.S.R. MINISTRY OF CULTURE, COMMITTEE OF ART. We went in and started up the stairs . . . No one knew what to do next. We looked around perplexedly.

"No use," I said. "No one is going to speak with us. Let's get out of here."

We headed downstairs. Toward us, climbing energetically, came the Georgian quartet, and in front, the bulky Chiaureli in a wide black jacket. A Stalin Prize laureate's gold medal glittered on his chest. We moved aside. They passed us without saying hello and disappeared behind the minister's door.

We went outside and stood for a while. Berlinsky wanted to say something, but his voice failed. He waved, turned around, and went away. We watched him leave and then set off our different ways.

I headed for the conservatory. The news had already spread. The students avoided me.

In the foyer on the second floor people were playing chess, and there was a crowd around the tables. I saw Andrei Gorbatov and nodded to him. We sat down to play.

It felt good to look at the board with its black and yellow squares and rows of waiting pieces. Here was an age-old, solemn order and rules that held for everyone. There were no exceptions. Everyone was equal before this ancient judge of wisdom.

Andrei was not lucky at first, and I got an advantage. Some spectators started coming up to our table, and soon we were surrounded. At one moment I played badly, and there were disapproving voices.

Andrei waved his arms. "Looks bad, old man! You can see I'm behind in development, you have more space. Just the time to attack and strangle! Strangle," he giggled, and added, ". . . the Jews."

"You are drunk, Andrei," I said.

"Not really," he answered, without looking away from the board.

It suddenly became silent. I got up.

"Where are you going?" shouted Andrei. "Wait! You have a winning game here!"

"Black resigns," I said.

For several days our quartet didn't meet, and we didn't call each other. A few weeks later, in the paper *Soviet Art*, there appeared a photo of the women's quartet. They had won first prize in Prague.

Orchestra

1952

PREPARATIONS for the first International Youth Festival were proceeding apace. Music had been given a principal role, and so the Moscow Conservatory became the center of events. A Youth Symphony Orchestra was hastily formed from the very best students, and rehearsals were filled with genuine enthusiasm, kindled by everyone's hope of going abroad for the first time.

As orchestra members we were all called to the Central Komsomol Committee to fill in a special biographical form. No one dared to be late and we all dressed up, white shirt and tie. We were put at separate tables. An attractive blonde with a Komsomol emblem pinned on her breast walked around, placing a thick questionnaire before each of us.

Everyone's head lowered. It became as quiet as a funeral. The girl stood by the doorway watching us. I caught her eye and she smiled. I opened the questionnaire.

. . . Name . . . Year and place of birth . . . Nationality . . .

My response, "Jew," looked strange on the paper, as if it were in another language.

. . . Membership in the Komsomol . . . Party . . . Other groups . . . No . . . No . . . No . . .

. . . Conviction, prosecution, sentence, reprimand . . .

No . . . No . . . No . . . Not yet, I thought.

. . . Everything about parents . . .

They wanted to know more about them than I did. I left a few questions unanswered.

. . . Everything about the parents of the parents . . .

. . . About near and distant relatives . . .

"As if in a Russian folktale . . . deeper into the forest."

I looked around. Heads were still in the same position, eyes glued to the papers.

I stared at the girl until she saw me and walked to my table.

"Excuse me," I said. "What is meant by 'social background'? . . . And also here . . ."

But she didn't look where I was pointing. Instead, she turned back to the first page and bent over. Her glance stopped at the line "Nationality" and my answer "Jew." She bent down even lower, nearly touching my ear with her lips, and in a barely audible whisper said, "Don't fill in any more . . . Hopeless . . ." Then she straightened up and asked in a loud voice, "So what do you find confusing here?"

With just my lips I answered, "It's all clear now. Thank you very much."

I folded the papers, stood up, and walked slowly to the door. In the doorway I glanced back. The girl was looking at me, and as soon as our eyes met, she turned away.

The Youth Orchestra rehearsed the next day at seven o'clock in the morning. By a strange coincidence, all the first violinists were Jewish, with the exception of the freshman Nebitov, who sat at the very end. The concertmaster, Yuli Reyentovich, tuned the orchestra and we waited for the conductor, Kiril Kondrashin. Some time passed and he did not appear. Reyentovich stood up, raised his violin, and began the virtuoso finale from Tchaikovsky's Fourth Symphony, which we were preparing for the festival. He was answered by the percussionist. Several violinists picked up the next passage; the woodwinds joined in. The air was filled with the melody of Russian folk song, and by the time we reached the dance motif, the whole orchestra was playing. The

triumphant sound filled the Bolshoi Hall of the Moscow Conservatory.
When the music ended, everyone jumped up and applauded. Reyentovich was surrounded and congratulated from all sides.

Kondrashin was still not to be seen. Reyentovich left to find out
what was the matter. He was gone a long time before returning to
announce that today's rehearsal was canceled and that we would be
informed about the next one. Unwillingly, everyone started packing
up. It seemed a pity to leave the hall, having just witnessed genuine
musical inspiration.

After the hall had emptied, I sat for a while onstage, holding my
violin. It's surprising how solemnly calm it is in an empty hall. And
how everything changes when you come out on the same stage under
bright lights, before a full house.

When I went out into the conservatory's courtyard, a number of
musicians were still standing in small groups, talking. I saw Rabei and
waved to him, and we walked on together. About Rabei I knew only
that he had been born somewhere near the Lithuanian border. His
whole family had been shot by the Germans at the very beginning of
the war, along with the other Jews of the town. Luckily Rabei had
come to Moscow as a youngster before the war. Here he had finished
school and then entered the conservatory a year ahead of me. In his
home, Russian, Polish, and German had all been spoken; he himself
had a wonderful gift for languages and spent quite a bit of time translating poets I had never even heard of.

We wandered to the Moskva River, leaned on the stone balustrade,
and looked down. The running water put us in a philosophical mood.

I said, "You don't think this cancellation of the rehearsal has anything to do with yesterday's questionnaires?"

"Anything is possible."

"Did you answer all the questions?"

"Sure. I wrote 'Not married'; about the parents and all relatives,
'Killed by the Germans.' They're not interested in dead people. And
about myself, not much to write yet. Oh, by the way, what happened
there? I saw how that blonde was whispering something tenderly into
your ear, and you disappeared right after that."

"Yes, a wonderful girl!"

"Met her already? Congratulations!"

"If only!" I told him the story.

"Did she really? Right there? That's something! But that's it for the orchestra. For us, anyway."

My arm had fallen asleep and I stretched.

"Listen . . . how did Pushkin put it? 'Leaning on the granite . . .' "

"That's from *Onegin*," he replied, reciting:

> *"His soul full with deep compassion,*
> *His hand the granite leant upon . . ."*

"Very nice," I said.

"It's strange that you remembered Pushkin right now. The other day I started translating *Onegin*. Want to hear some?"

"Of course."

He recited in English, very expressively:

> *"I know: life is short and boring,*
> *But to prevent my dying soon*
> *I must be sure every morning*
> *To see you in the afternoon."*

"Beautiful!" I said. "I don't know the language, but you've got the rhythm and rhyme. Wonderful!"

He was very pleased.

"Have you thought of taking up translating seriously? You do it so well."

"I'd like to. But where would I get time for that?"

"Give up the quartet," I suggested.

"I will," he said, not looking at me.

"You're not serious, I hope?"

"I am. I've been thinking of it since the competition. Of course, a competition is a competition, somebody wins, somebody loses. To lose in an honest contest is no disgrace. But what they did to us was not a real contest. We lost before the competition."

He continued bitterly. "The trouble with us is that we have lost ourselves. We aren't Jews anymore, but they wouldn't allow us to become Russians, and they never will. We are threatened again by physical destruction. This time not by Germans but by Russians."

I looked around, but we were alone.

"Recently I was at the Polish Radio. Brought them two translations from Mickiewicz. In the corridor I ran into Kalinenko. He was the one who took Janáček off the air. I didn't want to stop, but he held out his hand and asked how the quartet was. . . . For a moment I thought that he was really interested and said that we have no concerts and that a few radio broadcasts would be quite helpful. He interrupted me and said, 'My dear friend, do you really think that your names could be broadcast across the whole country?' "

"Did he actually say that?"

"It even seemed to me that he sympathized."

"And what did you say?"

"What can you say to that? It's the government speaking!"

"Oh, mighty government! Better tell me what you are going to do about the quartet and everything . . ."

"You heard about my folks. They were all killed in one day. But I still have an uncle who lives in Tashkent. He speaks Uzbek, the Uzbeks consider him one of them, and he is content. I had invited him to join me here in Moscow, but he answered that he was in no hurry to meet his Maker."

"Wise old Jew. As if he knew that Hitler's ideas would be repeated here."

"It was possible to escape from Germany . . . But from the Soviet Union . . ."

"They don't permit us to live here and they don't allow us to go there. There is no way out."

"There is one," he said. "Poetry and translations."

"And a string quartet," I added.

"Not for me. I've had enough of it."

"I'll be missing you," I said.

"Are you trying to make me cry? Let's go."

*   *   *

Rehearsals of the Youth Orchestra did not resume for several days, and the conservatory buzzed like a disturbed beehive.

Those questionnaires, filled out in secrecy, became a matter of common knowledge. As if a conspiracy had been uncovered, we learned that the conductor, Kondrashin, was a Jew on his mother's side, the violinist Igor Bezrodny on his father's; and the parents of the "Russian" violist Yura Nikolaevsky both turned out to be Jewish. I had never kept my Jewish origins a secret and did not feel guilty about my nationality. But it was becoming less and less pleasant to attend the conservatory. I decided to go there one last time to say goodbye.

I walked around the first and second floors and then up to the quartet studio. The room was empty; the chairs and music stands stood in their usual places. I sat in "my" chair, but this whole farewell suddenly began to feel as grim as a funeral. Nevertheless, I went up to the fourth floor, to the chamber-music studio, and immediately regretted it: Matrosova was leaving from Borisovsky's adjacent studio. We met face to face.

"Oh, hello," she said. "It's been some time since we last saw each other."

"Yes, since the competition . . . How is your quartet?"

"The quartet? It doesn't exist anymore."

"Why not?"

"Why should it? We showed everybody that we were the best. What else was there to prove?"

We started walking together down the stairs.

"To be honest, we had no intention of continuing with the quartet. There is so much other work. I'm Borisovsky's assistant now, exams are coming soon, and then there's the Youth Orchestra, and I'm the leader of the viola group."

I could not remember seeing her at the orchestra rehearsals.

"The Youth Orchestra? We haven't had any rehearsals for days now."

She burst out laughing. "You think so? We rehearse every day, or, rather, every night."

"We've been told nothing."

"Naturally. All the strings are new."

"How come?"

"Well, now! The orchestra is meant to travel abroad."

"So what? What was wrong before?"

"Are you pretending or do you really not know?"

"Pretending," I said.

"Well, that's better."

"Who is sitting next to you?"

"At first it was Nikolaevsky. But just think of it, what impertinence! Borisovsky treated him like his own son, but Nikolaevsky turned out to be a Jew! He was hiding it so cleverly!"

How could I listen to all this and calmly keep up the conversation, as if it had nothing to do with me?

"Is he still in the orchestra?"

"Are you kidding? Of course not!"

"And anyone . . . I mean . . . anyone from . . ."

"Oh no, nobody."

We came down to the lobby.

"Well, I've got to go now," Matrosova said. "So long."

I found myself standing just opposite the cash box. The small window was open, and behind it I could see our cashier, Yakov Aaronovich, who knew all the students by name. He smiled, and I walked up to shake his hand.

"Hello, hello there," he said. "You don't have to explain anything to me. I know. And what can you do? You have to sit very quietly these days . . . Well, how is your health?"

"Not too bad."

"Thank God for that. And sit quietly . . ."

I went out into the courtyard. It was warm. The trees were already showing their first tender leaves. Some students were sitting by the Tchaikovsky monument on the stone steps.

Brushing me with her violin case, Professor Galina Barinova ran by, then turned back. "Oh, it's you! I wanted to phone you . . . Walk me to the Arbat metro, will you?"

"With pleasure. Let me carry your violin."

"Thanks. You know, I was remembering you the other day. How you, Kogan, and Sitkovetsky played at my place for Jacques Thibaud. You were wearing short velvet pants. I even remember that you played the Wieniawski polonaise. Thibaud liked you very much then. Listen now . . . My student Nebitov told me how all of you were filling out forms. What happened there? Why was he called out urgently in the night for the orchestra rehearsal?"

"I've just learned that rehearsals have started up again. But without those who were filling out the forms that day. Except for Nebitov."

"I wonder why."

"You really don't know?"

"I have no idea."

"The new orchestra doesn't have a single Jew."

"That's impossible!"

"Everything is possible nowadays. Even an orchestra without Jews!"

We came up to the metro. Taking back her violin, she shook my hand.

"I hope you aren't right. But . . . In any case, you yourself shouldn't worry; we like you . . ."

She gave me a wave and disappeared.

The Youth Orchestra went on tour and returned. Before leaving, the string section was strengthened with a few Jewish players. From our quartet that honor fell only to Barshai. The trip abroad affected him so much that he could talk of nothing else, and he told anyone who would listen how the train came up to the border, how everyone was quiet when they passed the neutral zone, how they all became cheerful right after that, and then about the festival—the confusion of different languages, and how some girl, a Czech or maybe a Pole, fell in love with him.

The quartet had a few sessions left before summer vacation, and during the last one Rabei announced his decision to leave. He explained that it was for personal reasons only, and to show that he had no bad feelings, he shook all our hands in turn.

"Send me your translations," I said. "Even from Chinese."

He forced a smile and left.

*   *   *

It's amazing how fast news spreads through Moscow. Even faster than jokes. The phone started ringing early the next morning as violinists called, offering to take Rabei's place.

They all said the same thing: they had already played in a quartet and loved it. They all swore that they didn't drink, except for New Year's Eve and on birthdays, and even then only a little, and that they had very agreeable personalities.

Even old Professor Gusikov called and invited us to come to his studio. When we arrived he came to the point right away. "I have just the right person for you: honest, serious, accurate. He is never late."

"Does he play at all?" I joked.

Gusikov shook his finger at me. "He is exactly what you need. He has just finished his fellowship and is not working anywhere yet. My advice is, give him a try."

"We certainly will," Berlinsky said.

"Do some reading first, then take any Beethoven quartet. Two or three lines from each movement, but very detailed, just as you work normally."

"It's a very good idea," I said. "Thank you very much."

We stood up and walked out into the corridor. Gusikov followed us but stopped in the doorway and beckoned us back.

"One other thing," he said, lowering his voice to a whisper. "He is Russian, and a Party member." He then hastily closed the door.

"How about that!" I said. "Some old man! Can you imagine him taking the risk to say that?"

Berlinsky shook his head. "He shouldn't have. 'A Russian, a Party member . . .' It's none of his business."

"Why not?" Barshai countered. "He knows the situation. Do you?"

"Still, we need a good musician first of all."

"Bravo!" I said. "Precious words!"

"A Russian, a Party member, and a good musician . . ." Barshai smiled ironically. "A rare combination."

I saw that they were ready to start a quarrel.

"Look," I said. "We have about twenty people to audition. Let's give everyone a try."

"Right," Berlinsky agreed. "To play together, to talk things over and then decide."

"I suggest we begin tomorrow."

"Very well. We'll make it fair."

Barshai called me the next morning.

"Everything is all set."

"What is all set?"

"He has agreed."

"Who?"

"Alexandrov."

"Alexandrov who?"

"Yaroslav Alexandrov, the Russian and the Party member."

"Hold on . . . We have to try him out first."

"Why? He has such credentials," Barshai giggled.

"You can't decide it by yourself."

"I didn't. In fact, it was your bosom friend Berlinsky who arranged it all. Got his phone number, met him already this morning, and the two of them came over to my place. We agreed."

"I object!"

"Well, it's your one vote against two of ours."

"Hadn't we decided to make it fair?"

"You still haven't learned."

"I don't understand . . . Berlinsky was talking so enthusiastically about the open audition."

"That was yesterday. Today he understands that words are one thing and real life something else. He knows that a Russian is not a Jew. Do you?"

Stalin's Death
1953

ON THE SIXTH of March 1953, at five in the morning, the telephone rang. The neighbors didn't bother to answer it; they knew it was for me. By the time I had walked the full length of the corridor, it had rung several more times. I picked up the receiver and heard the voice of Alexandrov.

"You know why I'm calling so early . . ."

"Has the inevitable occurred?"

"Yes. Vice Minister Kholodilin himself called me; they need a quartet. I'll let you know when and where. Be ready. Tails and black tie."

"I don't have a black one."

"Get one! Make it yourself. I'll call back."

Five minutes later the phone rang again. This time it was Berlinsky. "What do we play?"

"Beethoven would do, but . . ."

"Yes, I understand."

"Are you in your tails?"

"I am. But I don't have black studs."

"Studs also? I didn't know."

"We should hang up. They'll be calling any minute."

Alexandrov called as soon as I hung up.

34

"Are you ready? Leave now. We'll meet in the Composers' House, and go from there to the Hall of Columns."

"Why the Composers' House?"

"Oh, you don't know yet . . . Prokofiev died."

"My God! When?"

"Last night. At the same time."

"What a nightmare . . ."

"Kholodilin said to bring Tchaikovsky."

"For whom?"

"Both."

"That's no good," I said. "Prokofiev didn't like Tchaikovsky."

"Want to call the vice minister yourself?"

He hung up.

The streets were still dark. I passed Pushkin Square and through side alleys went right to the Composers' House. In the lobby several composers were standing in a circle, smoking. I shook everybody's hand. In the hall the chairs had all been moved to the back wall and a closed coffin stood alone in the center. A funeral wreath leaned against the piano on the stage.

Kholodilin appeared.

"Hurry up!" he said, looking at his watch. "Where is the quartet? We've got to hurry. It will be difficult to get through."

The rest of our quartet arrived together.

"It's already impossible to get through the center of town," Alexandrov explained. "We had to go around."

"Get your instruments ready," Kholodilin hurried him. "What are you playing?"

"You suggested Tchaikovsky."

"We also have Beethoven," I put in.

"Tchaikovsky is good," Kholodilin said. "Sit wherever you like. We'll begin right away."

The wreath was laid on Prokofiev's coffin. Everyone in the hall, including the workmen, stood silently. Kholodilin gave us a nod and we began the slow movement from Tchaikovsky's second quartet.

We had played about half the movement when Kholodilin stopped us. "Enough, fellows. Time to go."

*   *   *

The streets were filled with people heading toward the center of the city. At Pushkin Square we could get no farther because of the crowd. "There's nothing we can do," Kholodilin said. "Let's wait at the Radio Club. I'll call the police."

We waited a long time while Kholodilin kept running from the street to the telephone. Finally about twenty policemen, all large men, appeared.

We went out and encountered a wall of people. Firmly linking their arms, the policemen formed a ring around us, stepped back a little, and with a running start pushed into the crowd. We moved forward a few meters and came to a stop. The three largest policemen stood at the front. "On three!" one of them said. "One, two, three!" and the three of them drove a wedge into the crowd. The rest rushed behind them, pulling us along. The front troika worked like a machine: half a step back, "One, two, three!," a strong thrust forward into the crowd, a pause, and then another half step back . . . Their faces streamed with perspiration.

We were a tiny island in a boiling human sea. Cries and swearing blended into a single constant roar. Several times we were crushed by the crowd. We held our instruments tightly to our bodies and swam with the current. At one point we were pressed to the wall of a building. Kholodilin shouted something, but his voice could not be heard. The policemen "braced" their legs against the wall and pushed us into the crowd with their backs. Now they were driving a wedge with five people working at once.

All the side streets were full of people fighting their way into the mainstream. We managed to cross Moskvin and Stanislavsky Streets. There were still a few blocks to go. The policemen worked twice as hard . . .

And suddenly it became quiet. We were brought into the stage entrance of the Hall of Columns. I fell to the floor, exhausted. Kholodilin leaned against the wall, breathing heavily. He wiped his forehead, looked at us, and asked, "Still alive? Then let's go."

We climbed up the long stairway to the hall. Next to me, holding his chest, walked the composer Mikhail Rauhverger.

"Are you feeling bad?" I asked.

"No, no, it's all right . . . May I lean on your arm? What a misfortune! To think that a week ago we were sitting together at the table."

"At the table?" I asked him, amazed. "How come?"

"At his place. He was showing us his latest composition."

"Oh, you mean Prokofiev. I thought . . ."

"No, no, of course I meant Prokofiev. I wanted to ask you, why did you choose to play Tchaikovsky? Please understand me, I like Tchaikovsky very much, but Prokofiev . . . You see, his taste was different."

"I know," I said. "But we were told what to play."

"Even at the funeral?"

"At the funeral, before it, and after."

He smiled. "Oh, I see."

The State Orchestra was already seated onstage with their conductor, Alexander Gauk, standing on the podium. More musicians crowded quietly backstage. Kholodilin stood up on a chair and looked around above everybody's heads.

"Where is the quartet?" he demanded.

We pushed through the crowd.

"Get up onstage. Sit down and watch Gauk. You begin as soon as the State Orchestra finishes, and continue until the Bolshoi Orchestra takes their places. Then I'll tell you what to do next. Go on."

We sat up in the corner of the stage. I glanced at Gauk and gave him a slight nod, but he did not respond. A look of horror was fixed in his eyes.

In the center of the hall, surrounded by three rows of guards, was Stalin's body lying in an open coffin. From behind a curtain a group of people emerged and proceeded to the coffin. I recognized Beria, Molotov, Kaganovich, Malenkov. David Oistrakh walked past us, violin in hand, and stood next to Gauk. Oistrakh raised his violin, Gauk his baton. The hall was filled with the sounds of Tchaikovsky's "Sérénade Mélancolique." Oistrakh played with a deep expressive tone.

And with the music, a river of humanity flowed into the hall. There was loud sobbing, cries, and howling. A woman fell to her knees and exclaimed hysterically, "They didn't spare you! Beloved! . . ." Two guards lifted her and stood her on her feet, but she fell again. She was carried out of the hall.

We saw a tall gray-faced man walk up to Oistrakh.

"Suslov," Alexandrov whispered to me.

Oistrakh, still playing, bent over and was told something. His playing sped up, becoming lighter and less expressive. All-powerful Suslov returned to the honor guard.

We kept our eyes on Gauk. He conducted the last chord and held it a long time, signaling us with his frightened eyes. I raised my violin and nodded back. We began to play Tchaikovsky's second quartet, for the second time that morning, as the orchestra players quietly left the stage. A short time later, the stage began to fill with the players of the Bolshoi Theater Orchestra. The new conductor was terrified as well. I turned to him and he immediately started the orchestra, without giving us time to finish.

Since we had no further instructions, we sat at our places listening to the music. When the orchestra stopped, a piano started up from the other corner of the stage. The violinist Pavel Mirsky, holding his case, walked up to the edge of the stage and stopped, looking sadly at the coffin. Two men in identical suits immediately ran up to him, tore the case away, pinned his arms behind his back, and dragged him away. After the piano, a choir sang, then Oistrakh, Lev Oborin, and Sviatoslav Knushevitsky played the first movement of Tchaikovsky's trio.

At three o'clock the government leaders appeared again. In the same order as before they proceeded to the center of the hall and surrounded Stalin's coffin.

I put my violin into its case.

"Don't go too far," Alexandrov said. "They could call us any minute."

I walked into the foyer and saw Oistrakh sitting by the window. I paused and bowed from a distance, but he held out his hand. There was a free seat next to him, and I sat down.

"I heard this is your second funeral today."

I nodded.

"How was it there? Many people?"

"About fifteen."

"So few? Prokofiev picked the wrong day to die."

We spoke quietly to the strains of solemn music from the hall.
Musicians walked by us and bowed to Oistrakh. Oistrakh nodded back
to each of them. When Berlinsky and Barshai passed, Oistrakh followed
them with his eyes.

"How is it with the new one?"

"He is all right," I said cautiously. "Very punctual, perhaps too
much so for a musician. Looks at his watch often."

"And how was his predecessor?"

"Oh, that one didn't even have a watch. He could work for hours.
I think he quit the quartet because he was so dedicated to it. The
competition broke his heart."

"I remember that competition," Oistrakh said thoughtfully.

"It was a difficult time for us," I responded. "You kept the quartet
from falling apart by inviting us to play the Chausson concerto with
you. Our names on your posters were a real challenge to the authorities.
Not many people would have dared to do that."

"That was all I could do for you then. But . . . thank you, I didn't
know . . ."

"Oh no! We have to thank you."

Despite the difference in our ages, a certain trust was growing between us.

"And what about your concerts now? Do you have anything?"

"Nothing definite."

"I happen to know that the ministry needs a quartet, a young quartet
especially for tours abroad."

"We probably wouldn't suit them."

Oistrakh was silent for a while, then turned away from me. "At least
half of the quartet must be Russian. There's no decision yet, but the
quartet's name is already chosen."

"A name for a nonexistent quartet? What is it?"

"Tchaikovsky . . . The Tchaikovsky Quartet."

"I understand," I said. "It's a sort of a banner now. The sign of the
times . . . I'm not even surprised when . . ."

"And you're right," Oistrakh interrupted.

For some time we listened silently to the music.

"The main thing is not to lose your identity and to continue working," Oistrakh said. He looked me in the eye and smiled. "You have a quartet. That is such joy! You can forget everything else in the world. I'm playing a lot of chamber music these days. Tomorrow we were going to give the first performance of two trios, Sviridov and Babadzhanyan, but because of the mourning all concerts have been canceled."

"For three days?" I asked.

"Yes, three days."

"And we have to stay here?"

"I'm afraid so."

"It's a pity we don't have a chess set," I said. "I was in such a panic this morning that I forgot everything."

"I have a pocket set," Oistrakh whispered.

"Do you think?"

"We can cover it with music."

He placed the small chess set in the score of Babadzhanyan's trio. I called my moves in a whisper, and he carefully moved the flat pieces. He played very well; the time was unlimited, and the mournful music pleasant.

Lev Oborin brought us back to reality. He bent down to Oistrakh and said, "Babadzhanyan is beside himself. He says you have been studying the same place in his trio for two hours now."

He looked at the music. "Oh, that's what it is! Very ingenious. Bravo!"

"How are things in there?"

"About the same as before. It's impossible to get out. I'm hungry. Whatever there was in the buffet is all gone now."

I remembered that I had eaten nothing since early morning.

"Do we play again?" Oistrakh asked.

"Not today."

"And the quartet?"

"I really can't say. If they don't bother you, that means you're not needed."

"Who's playing now?"

"The Radio Orchestra just finished. Now the Beethovens are on."

"Well, then?" I turned to Oistrakh. "Shall we finish studying the rest of the trio?"

"Why not? Only let's turn pages from time to time . . ."

We played several more games. Gradually it grew darker and more difficult to see the pieces.

"Shall we stop with this one?" Oistrakh suggested. "I think we've spent the day very fruitfully."

"Thank you," I said. "And not only for these chess games."

Oistrakh smiled gently. "Don't take it too hard. And here come your friends now."

Berlinsky and Barshai walked up to us. "Excuse us, David Fyodorovich, we have to talk to our violinist."

Oistrakh nodded. "I understand. In our trio we can never get everyone together. In a quartet it must be even harder."

I got up. We walked away and stopped in the corner. Berlinsky nervously lit a cigarette.

"Barshai's leaving the quartet," he said. "He's found a better one. We don't suit him."

"That's not quite right," Barshai interrupted. "I only said I was invited to join a new quartet."

"And you agreed!"

"Yes, I agreed."

"What quartet?" I asked.

"You see"—Barshai turned to me—"when I was abroad I was asked why our quartet didn't come. And what could I say? That we're not allowed out of the country? Nothing will work out for us."

"What has to work out? We're a quartet already."

"A dead quartet! With no concerts and no future."

"And how about your lovely words? That a quartet is already a treasure by itself, that it's enough to sit down to play Mozart or Beethoven and you're in another world, and so on . . ."

"I can repeat those words."

"And you're leaving?"

"Yes," Barshai said. "We've already been given a name and offered trips abroad."

I remembered Oistrakh. "Yes. Of course. The Ministry of Culture and the Tchaikovsky Quartet."

I pulled Berlinsky by his arm. "Let's go . . . There's nothing to talk about."

Public access to Stalin's body had ended for the night, but we remained in the Hall of Columns. Backstage and in the foyer, in chairs and on the floor, wrapped in overcoats or just in their tuxedos, people slept. Carefully avoiding the sleeping bodies, I walked through the foyer and came to the front stairway. There, too, people were sleeping, but there were a few free steps. I sat down, leaned my back against the handrail, and closed my eyes. I immediately saw that morning's crowd, with myself in the middle of it, being swept in one direction, then another. People with distorted faces stretched their hands toward me, grabbed my violin, reached for my face and hair. Someone behind me grabbed my shoulder and started to shake me. The violin slid out of my hands and fell in the mud. Immediately people stepped on it, there was an unbearable noise; I tried to bend down, but they held me and shook me . . .

I opened my eyes. Alexandrov stood above me, shaking me by the shoulder.

"You sure know how to sleep! I've been trying to wake you up for five minutes now. We have to go. They're starting again. We play before the orchestra comes."

I straightened my back and got up. "Did you sleep?"

"Not a wink. All night Kholodilin and I were making a schedule. Let's go."

Carrying our instruments, we came out onstage and sat down. We played, the orchestra took their places, we finished, and while the orchestra began playing, Kholodilin left us the day's schedule on Alexandrov's music stand. We were to remain onstage and fill all the gaps between the orchestras. They changed, but we stayed. Over and over again, we played Tchaikovsky's Second Quartet. Everything began to appear unreal, repeating itself as if in a strange dream. And again, as on the day before, people walked in with their heads bare, looking at the coffin with the same expression of grief and humility.

Toward evening I fell asleep with my violin in my hands. Alexandrov nudged me. I fell asleep once more and he nudged me again.

"Don't fall off the chair," he whispered. "We have to play now."

When it grew dark, the procession around the coffin stopped, the doors were closed, and we left the stage scarcely able to move our stiff legs. The three of us, minus Barshai, went to sit on the steps of the front stairway, where I had slept the previous night. News about Barshai had already spread and we caught some sympathetic glances. A young musician from the Radio Orchestra, Dmitri Shebalin, approached us and sat down on the steps. From his pockets he took out a bottle of wine and some paper cups and said, "Well, what are you going to do?"

"Drink," I said.

He broke into a wide smile. That was unexpected. No one had smiled here for the last two days.

"Sounds good to me," he said, filling the cups. "Would you like to give me a try in the quartet? . . . You'll teach me. Don't worry!" He smiled again and raised his cup. "Well, what do you say?"

"Why not? The king is dead, long live the king!"

"Quiet, quiet," Alexandrov said. "The king is dead, but still . . ."

The third and final day came. We still had had nothing to eat. Contact with the outside world was maintained only by those brave people who could make their way back after going out into the streets. Their tales were spread in terrified whispers. They said that people kept coming and coming, besieging trains from Leningrad and other cities to Moscow. The city itself was surrounded by troops with heavy trucks. They blockaded all the streets leading to the Hall of Columns, leaving only Pushkin Square open. Through it the stream of people was shoved into Pushkin Street and pushed into the Hall of Columns. An enormous jam developed from which there was no exit, and new people kept squeezing in, tighter and tighter. At first trucks were used to restrain the crowd. But the pressure grew even stronger and the trucks themselves were eventually swept away by the flow of people.

Late in the evening we put mutes on our instruments and began Tchaikovsky's "Andante Cantabile." We played quietly, without vibrato, the way Russian folk songs are sung. The delicate sound of the quartet drowned in the incessant noise of the slowly moving crowd. We played through to the middle and suddenly the quartet sounded louder. I looked around the hall. Yes, it was all over. The procession had stopped, only the soldiers remained by the coffin. The orchestra had disappeared. I hadn't even noticed that we were onstage by ourselves. Kholodilin walked up and said, "Another five minutes and that will be all. You can go home." We played through to the end, the last sound faded away, and we walked off the stage. There wasn't a soul to be found either backstage or in the foyer. After three days of crowds it was a strange feeling having so much free space around.

The street outside was empty, too. I walked toward Pushkin Square. The street resembled the dried-up channel of a recently flooded river. The sound of my steps echoed sharply in the stillness. All along the side streets stood trucks bumper to bumper. In the empty square the streetlights were badly bent and a truck lay on its side, the cab windows shattered, the carriage twisted off. Farther on there were two more trucks, also turned over. In the surrounding buildings, the glass of all the ground-floor windows was smashed, and in places iron gates were hanging on one hinge, squeaking in the silence. Pieces of clothing were underfoot everywhere, trampled into the dirt. It resembled a field of battle; I could scarcely believe that I was in the heart of Moscow.

Borodin

1954

THE EMERGENCE of the Tchaikovsky Quartet deprived us of whatever hopes we might have had. We still had no name, no visible future, and no definite present. We had no concerts and made ends meet by playing at funerals.

The old mansion on Vorovsky Street described by Tolstoy in *War and Peace* as the Rostov house now housed the Union of Soviet Writers. All the members of this union, as a rule, were accompanied on their "last journey" by the music of a string quartet. There were plenty of Soviet writers; very small, old chaps, they tended to die pretty regularly. We would sit in a far corner of the hall and play the slow movements from Mozart's and Beethoven's quartets, which we interpreted as either a solemn procession behind the coffin or as the eternal peace of the future life.

These funerals turned out to be excellent practice for performing slow music. Moreover, we were paid cash, strictly forbidden in the Soviet Union. As our fame as "wonderful gravediggers" spread, music lovers from all over Moscow would gather at these funerals. They would stand so motionless and silent that it often seemed that the only living thing present was the immortal music. Many people told us that these funerals had become a place of purification for them.

After every funeral, the secretary of the Writers' House would approach us with tears in his eyes and shake our hands, saying that he hoped to hear us again soon. Trying not to smile, Shebalin would accept the envelope with our pay and say solemnly that it depended entirely on the "brother writers." The secretary would agree, adding that, unfortunately, he could not give us a precise schedule for the future, since everything was in God's hands, but he nevertheless hoped to see us again.

We would leave the funeral inwardly reassured. Shebalin, slapping the pocket of his jacket contentedly, would invite us to a restaurant to share a glass of wine.

"Why not? There's plenty of time until the next funeral."

"Sure. Let's sit and talk about music."

"And the frailty of this life on earth."

Although it was not as enjoyable as playing funerals, we sometimes introduced the work of young Soviet composers. The composers, as a rule, did not appreciate interpretation of their music. The more accurately the score was performed, the better. They all liked fast tempi, and because we could play their music as fast as they wanted, they said that we were a great quartet. To which I always wanted to reply that we could play even faster.

We were paid for these recitals, too, though not as well. But for us there was no hint of real concerts, to say nothing of concert tours. All that was reserved for the Tchaikovsky Quartet.

The Tchaikovsky Quartet was to go on a tour abroad, but first the Ministry of Culture had requested an audition, because the group had yet to play together in public. The Beethoven Quartet, as always, was on the jury. Unexpectedly, after the audition, Tsiganov said that although these young people were unquestionably talented musicians, they were not yet a professional quartet, and he, personally, would refrain from sending them abroad. The other Beethovens supported him. A hot argument ensued with the Ministry of Culture's officials, until Anisimov pointed out that the government had already made the decision to send the quartet on tour. Tsiganov then asked what the purpose of the audition had been. No one could answer him.

And so the Tchaikovsky Quartet left for Hungary, while we were left to play a new "masterpiece" by some Stepan Akimov or Akim Stepanov—or, as Shebalin would put it, "making candy from a piece of shit." After the performance, Vasily Shirinsky of the Beethoven Quartet came up to us and said that our playing was so understandable that he didn't even need a score to follow us. He added a few more compliments and mentioned that he himself had recently written a quartet. Berlinsky immediately stepped on my foot and replied that we would play it with pleasure. By some strange coincidence, the music was in Shirinsky's briefcase and he ceremoniously handed it to us. After observing all this, Tikhon Khrennikov, head of the Composers' Union, walked up to us and said that it was the first time he had seen such cooperation between quartets. Shirinsky smiled amicably and replied that he had always had the highest regard for our quartet and that the Composers' Union should invite us to do steady work. Khrennikov said that that was a good idea.

Shirinsky winked at us and whispered, "Don't waste this opportunity."

We exchanged quick glances.

We had become accustomed to feeling guilty about our quartet. The very fact that we went on working irritated the Ministry of Culture. But perhaps with the quartet's personnel changes the official attitude toward us would also begin to change. Now there were three Russians in our quartet, two of them Party members and one, Shebalin, in the Komsomol. I myself was, as before, both Jewish and "non-organized," but Berlinsky told me once that that was even better for the quartet, because in each collective there should be people led by the Party. I replied that that suited me well and gave me the freedom to say whatever I liked, since the whole responsibility would fall on my Party colleagues. But Berlinsky retorted, "Don't make an idiot of yourself more than is necessary, and even better, shut up."

We left the Composers' Union and walked silently for a long time, until Berlinsky recited a Russian proverb: "A poor peace is better than a good fight."

He had said what we all were thinking, but proverbs pronounced too seriously often sound sanctimonious. I was not much surprised when Shebalin joked, "An eye for an eye, a tooth for a tooth . . ."

"You're a fool," Berlinsky said. "I'm serious now."

I came to the rescue with an old wartime slogan. " 'Death for death' was serious, too."

"That was then. Now it's time to make good connections."

"Forgive and forget," remarked Shebalin.

"Fascists are hard to forget," I said. "Especially our own."

"It's not their fault. Everything depends on the whole . . ." He stopped short and glanced at Alexandrov. "Anyway, Khrennikov obviously offered his assistance, and I don't think it was just by accident. It's possible they've considered us already."

"You mean the Composers' Union Quartet?"

"Yes, what's wrong with that?"

"Always playing crap," I said.

"We do it anyway."

"Because we have no choice. But once we join the Composers' Union, we'll never crawl out of the shit."

"What do you think?" Berlinsky asked Alexandrov.

"Hard to say. The danger of remaining in the shit, of course, exists, but on the other hand, support from the Union . . ."

"That's what I say! Talk to Khrennikov before he forgets. Strike while the iron is hot."

"Strike Khrennikov on the head!" exclaimed Shebalin, bursting out laughing.

"Why don't you go to the devil's mother!" Berlinsky swore.

"Quiet, gentlemen," sighed Alexandrov. "For the time being we have to play Shirinsky."

"Give me a couple of days," I said. "I'll get the score ready."

How many people can live in one room together? I had always thought that even two would be a disaster.

In the room next to mine, sixteen people lived together. The head of the family was the grandmother, who had five grown-up children, three daughters and two sons. The oldest, Victor, was married, with two kids, and the four of them would sleep on a narrow bed in one corner. The second son, Herman, would appear periodically, spend a couple of weeks at home, and then land in jail again. The three daughters from time to time would get pregnant and have babies. The oldest, Larisa, at one time even had a husband, Nikolai, but he lived with them for only a year before running off. The grandmother, Larisa, and her three children slept on the other narrow bed in another corner. The second daughter, Zina, with her three kids, slept on the table. And the youngest, Masha, slept under the table by herself, since she had no children. All the adults worked at the same factory, and they left the kids by themselves all day to crawl naked around the apartment. Food was prepared in a bucket and the smell from the kitchen was stupefying. On holidays they would all drink vodka, sing songs, and dance with just their legs while sitting at the table.

When I was practicing, the kids would crawl toward the music like insects toward light, opening my door and looking at me with unblinking eyes. Then they would crawl away again, except for one, slant-eyed Borka. He could listen to music forever. In the evening, in order not to disturb the neighbors, I would put on a heavy mute, but Borka always heard me and soon my door would swing open and his voice would ask, "May I?" He would sit on the floor near the door so quietly that I often forgot about him until he would sigh and say that he had to go, otherwise all the places would be taken. Sometimes he would fall asleep where he sat. I would pick him up and carry him to the next room. Everyone would be fast asleep, snoring and whistling, the air in the room heavy. I would lay Borka wherever I could find a place for him, and cover him with whatever was handy, someone's dress or a towel. I didn't even know which of the sleeping women was his mother. No one knew who his father was.

Even though I knew all their names, we practically never met, as if we belonged to different species. It probably would have gone on this way if Herman hadn't come back from prison.

The family did not greet him warmly. He would sit morosely for hours on a trunk in the corridor. But one morning when I was practicing, he walked into my room.

"Herman," he said, holding out his hand. "I see you're always at it, sawing at your fiddle. Ever get tired?"

"I'm a musician, Herman, it's my life."

"We had some musicians there, but we wouldn't touch them. They were very easy to scare . . . Always protecting their hands."

"Hands are everything for musicians. Even a hangnail is a tragedy."

"They were kept with the politicals. In winter they took them on a path to the woods and ordered them: 'One step to the side!' And the snow there was up to your waist! Then the chief gave them a lecture—'You think you came here for a vacation? You're sent here to be punished . . .'—and kept them in the snow for hours."

"For what? They weren't guilty of anything."

"Who knows . . ."

"Listen. I knew a violinist, a girl, who was taken from my class. She got ten years for anti-Soviet propaganda. What could she say with her violin that was anti-Soviet? Only wrong notes!"

"I wouldn't know," he replied. "Do you have any vodka?"

"No, Herman, I don't keep any."

"Any tea?"

"Yes."

"Seriously?" His eyes came to life. "Be a friend, give me some."

"I have some Chinese and some Georgian."

"Either, give me either! Can I have a whole package?"

"Of course. Here's one, unopened."

He grabbed the tea convulsively. "They would kill for this in camp! Only you . . . that is . . . Don't tell anyone, okay?"

He went to the door, but then stopped. "In the evening, how do you usually get home?"

"Sometimes by bus, but more often by metro, and then on foot along Taganka. Why?"

"Always go the same way. I'll warn the boys not to touch you."

We had a rehearsal that evening and I returned home late. Zina was standing on the stairs. Seeing me, she shouted, "Don't go home!"

I came up to her and stopped. "What's the matter?"

"It's our Herman. Got drunk again."

"Can't the man even have a drink?"

"Not him. He gets crazy right away."

"Where did he get the vodka?"

"It's not vodka he drinks. Vodka is expensive. He drinks tea."

"Tea?" I remembered how he had grabbed my package of tea. "I drink tea every day," I said uncertainly.

"That's different. There in the camp they boil up a whole package for a single glass, 'chifir' they call it. Knocks you off better than vodka."

I felt guilty. "What could happen now?"

"Anything. He can kill . . ."

"Are you going to stand here the whole night?"

"I'm waiting for Victor, to warn him. They quarreled yesterday, he and Herman."

"Look, Zina. We can't stay here all night. I'll go upstairs and talk to him. You wait for Victor out in the courtyard and watch my window. When I come to the window, you'll know the coast is clear. Hurry to your room and lock the door. I'll keep Herman away."

I went upstairs and entered the corridor. Herman was sitting on the trunk in his underwear, a raised hatchet in his hand. Seeing me, he lowered the hatchet.

"Oh, it's you. Pass, friend!"

"What are you up to, Herman?"

"Waiting for my brother. He's got to be killed."

Inwardly I shuddered. "I wanted to talk with you. We didn't finish our conversation this morning."

"We will . . . Later."

"I wanted to ask you something. Come on in and have a bite to eat."

He followed me.

"Sit down," I said. "I'll make something for supper. I have to wash my hands first."

I went out to the kitchen, came back, and as if by accident closed the door to my room. He didn't notice. I got the bundle that hung outside my window, where I kept food cool. I saw Zina in the courtyard looking up. I spread a newspaper on the table and cut pieces of bread, sausage, and cheese. Herman was watching me.

"Is it all right on a paper?"

"Cultured," he said.

I walked up to the window again, where there was still a jar of pickles. Zina was no longer in the yard. I returned to the table and sat on the bed. I thought I heard the entrance door squeak.

"Help yourself, Herman," I said loudly.

"It's damn good," he said. "But I won't stay here for anything. I'll just finish off Victor and go back to camp."

"And what's there?"

"There's life there! We decide things ourselves. If something's wrong, someone has to pay for it! Understand?"

"Have you been there long?"

"This time I got five years. A year ago the amnesty came. People were rejoicing, 'Freedom, freedom!' But what the hell do you do with it? Everyone looks at you like a wolf, even your own people. No way to get a job. The moment they see your papers, it's the end! 'Get lost!' Nothing to buy tea with! One pair of pants, but even they've got holes. No, this freedom is worse than camp. I'm going back."

There was something convincing in his logic.

"How?"

"I'll think of something," he replied.

I could see the conversation was calming him down. He even yawned.

"Victor is late. I better go and wait for him. Thanks for the treat!"

He got up and dragged himself off into the corridor. When I went to the bathroom later, he was asleep on top of his trunk, still holding the hatchet.

Herman was arrested a week later. He was sitting on the trunk when two policemen came for him. He immediately got up and left with them without saying goodbye to anyone.

After that the neighbors' door was no longer locked and the kids crawled along the corridor again. In the evening the grownups sang songs and tapped their feet on the floor.

The next day we played Shirinsky's quartet in the chamber-music section of the Composers' Union. We played the quartet through twice, and then, as was standard practice, discussion began. There was some confusion over who should speak first. The chairman asked what the performing artists thought of the work. I knew very well what I thought and therefore kept silent.

"May I?" Berlinsky asked.

"Of course. Please go ahead."

He cleared his throat and began: "The quartet by Vasily Petrovich is written in the best traditions of Russian music, which derive from Taneyev and Glazunov. The thematic material is attractive in its imagery, its development, elegant in its classical simplicity. Within the quartet there are many original utilizations of string instruments, and this is not surprising, because the composer himself is a remarkable quartet player and is wonderfully aware of the string quartet's nature. We worked at this composition with great pleasure, and I wish to thank and congratulate its author."

Berlinsky was applauded. The tone of the discussion had been set, and everyone praised the composition, congratulated the composer, and by necessity complimented the performers. The last to speak was Shirinsky himself. He thanked everyone: us for such a wonderful performance of his quartet, the audience for listening so attentively, and the chairman of the chamber-music section for the fine way the whole program was directed.

Berlinsky whispered to me, "Live and learn! This is how it's done."

Everyone got up. Shirinsky, smiling broadly, walked up to us. "Well, my friends, thank you. I didn't even suspect myself that I had written such a quartet! This definitely has to be celebrated. I invite all of you to my place this evening."

"Thank you! We'll certainly come," replied Berlinsky.

We all arrived together in a taxi. Shirinsky opened the door, helped us with our overcoats, and, rubbing his hands, took us toward the table right away.

"Please be seated."

On the table were two decanters of vodka and a dozen different hors d'oeuvres.

"Decanters!" Shebalin said approvingly. "What a lovely sight!"

"Straight from the freezer. Before it gets warm, allow me to pour you some."

He went around the table and filled up a small wineglass for everyone.

"Now to business, gentlemen!" Shirinsky said, and raised his glass. We raised ours.

"Your health!"

"Your health!"

Everyone drank except for Shirinsky, who only sipped from his glass.

"I have to take it easy," he said, pointing to his heart. "*Poco a poco.* But you go ahead, I beg you."

The vodka was excellent, the food, too. I looked at Shirinsky and somehow I didn't want to remember the past, especially since we had just brought the man happiness and he was sincerely grateful. After all, I thought, people aren't born scoundrels, something makes them that way, so they are not completely to blame. His heart is feeling it already, and man's life is short . . .

I drank another glass, then another. From a distance I could hear that Shirinsky was talking about a quartet and how it had to be lived through. "A quartet will definitely pay you back a hundredfold, but it has to be earned first. I have seen so many quartets in my life. The more successful their beginning was, the sooner they would fall apart. You've passed the beginning and haven't fallen apart. You need a name now."

"We were thinking of the name Composers' Union Quartet," Berlinsky said.

"That's not a name. It's a place to work. You need a good name."

"But how can we get one? The road to the ministry is closed to us."

"I'll teach you how. In the spring there will be a widely celebrated Glinka jubilee. Ask Khrennikov to write a letter to the minister, and we'll ask Shostakovich to sign it. He won't refuse, and after him everyone will sign. It will be difficult for Anisimov to ignore that, especially now, after giving Tchaikovsky's name to another quartet right away."

"The Glinka Quartet?"

"Well, I don't think they will give you the name of Glinka, but any other name will do."

"Glinka is a good name," Berlinsky said dreamily.

"What's wrong, for example, with Borodin? Two beautiful quartets."

"Then let's ask for it right away," I suggested.

"No, no, my dear fellow, that's not the way things are done. They usually don't give what is requested."

"And how did you get the name of Beethoven? Did you ask for Bach or for God Himself?"

Shirinsky smiled, his eyes narrowed, and a sly flame began to shine in them.

"We never asked anyone for anything. We just named ourselves the Beethoven Quartet from the very first concert. That was back in the twenties, right after the Revolution. The spirit of freedom, so to speak, was still flying over our heads. We couldn't think of a better name than Beethoven."

"And why is it so complicated to get a name now?"

He smiled again. "The Soviet regime is a peculiar thing," he said, squinting his eyes. "Some more vodka?"

"Definitely," Berlinsky said. "I have a toast." He waited while Shirinsky poured some for everyone and then raised his glass.

"Dear Vasily Petrovich, I would like to drink to you, to your health, and through you to the Beethoven Quartet, which we value very much and from which we are always learning."

Shirinsky smiled and replied, "Thank you, thank you, dear friends."

We drank and got up from the table. Shirinsky saw us to the door.

We did everything the way Shirinsky wanted us to. We made an appointment to see Khrennikov and laid before him the whole idea about receiving the name of Glinka in connection with the forthcoming jubilee. Khrennikov seemed relieved that we asked for nothing more and promised to support us with an appropriate letter.

It took him, however, half a year to compose his letter, and when we finally got it, the Glinka jubilee had already been announced. We brought the letter to Shirinsky, who showed it to Shostakovich and got his signature. After this, we could gather as many signatures as we wanted. We sent the letter to Anisimov, the Minister of Culture, and in another month he invited us to see him.

He was kindness itself. He said that he had personally watched our quartet develop, especially appreciated our assistance to young Soviet composers, agreed that our quartet needed a name, that the time for that had arrived, but . . . We had been waiting for this "but."

"But," he said, "Glinka is the father of all Russian music and his name is too great to limit it, so to speak, to the scale of chamber music alone. We are willing to give you a name. There are good names in the Russian musical heritage. Consider them, choose one, we have no objection," he concluded generously.

"What about the name of Borodin?" Berlinsky asked.

"I don't object."

Berlinsky looked at us and we all nodded.

"We agree," he said, as if he had just accepted a life sentence for our quartet.

"Splendid. Write an application and leave it with the secretary. I will sign it."

We got up and left hurriedly. In the corridor Berlinsky lit a cigarette.

"He's done us in very nicely."

"Not only us, but also Shostakovich, Khrennikov, and everyone who signed the letter."

"He probably thinks that by not giving us Glinka's name he saved the whole state from danger."

"How on earth did we dare to ask for that name!"

"The father of all Russian music!"

"Well, Borodin, then," Berlinsky sighed. "I'll go to the secretary."

He came back soon and lit another cigarette.

"Don't get upset," I told him. "We've got a name. Borodin has two lovely quartets, much better than Glinka's, which even the Beethovens don't play. Borodin has two large os, it sounds good—BO-RO-DIN — nothing to compare with that squeaky 'Glinka.' Borodin is great, and Glinka is just . . ."

"Shit!" Shebalin finished for me, and we all burst into hysterical laughter.

"We should call Shirinsky."

"Yes, he'll be delighted."

"By the way, he predicted everything exactly."

"He's been through the mill."

"He must be at the conservatory now."

"Let's go there. Just to see his reaction."

We walked up to his studio. He had some students, but when he saw us, he waved his arms and asked the students to leave.

"Forgive us for intruding," Berlinsky said.

"Why, I'm happy to see you. Do come in."

"We've just talked with Anisimov," Berlinsky continued.

"Really? Tell me all the details, please."

Berlinsky described everything, word for word. Shirinsky laughed from time to time. Berlinsky finished his story and said, "Somehow I thought they would give us Glinka's name."

Shirinsky squinted. "If you had gotten Glinka's name right now, together with the jubilee, I would've thought that I hadn't learned anything in sixty years. Well, my friends, congratulations! You got a good name and I hope it will be a successful one."

"We are very grateful to you," Berlinsky said.

Seeing us to the door, Shirinsky said, "And my quartet, thanks to you, has been lucky. They even want to publish it. You won't refuse to play it once again at the publisher's?"

"Of course not, any time."

"I thank you, and again, congratulations. We worked it out very cleverly."

As we were leaving, we could hear him laughing to himself.

The Tchaikovsky Quartet gave its first public performance in Moscow soon after returning from Hungary. It was not a bad concert, although from a professional point of view it was not a great one. The audience, however, eager for sensations, shouted and howled like crazy. The audience, it is true, had been warmed up, because there had been an announcement on the front page of *Pravda* about the concert. Mere mention in *Pravda*, especially on its front page, indicated Party approval, and the Soviet people knew only too well how to respond.

The Tchaikovsky Quartet played together two years and then suddenly broke up. We didn't know exactly what had happened. But we remembered Shirinsky's words that a quartet ought to earn its colors first.

Soon afterward, Moscow was struck by the rumor that all concerts abroad, originally scheduled for the Tchaikovsky Quartet, were to be given to the Borodins! The winds of fortune blew abruptly in our direction, and we immediately felt the change. People who only yesterday had not noticed us now stopped, smiled, and asked how we were and when we were going abroad.

And, indeed, the rumor seemed to be true. Two weeks later we were summoned to the Party Central Committee—"with your passports," we were told.

Two guards checked our pockets and gently frisked us. We gave our passports to the man on duty and were given a pass to go in. "Third floor."

Upstairs we were greeted by a young man who led us into a separate room and gave each of us a pink booklet and a white form.

"Read it carefully," he said, and went out, firmly closing the door behind him.

The booklet was called *Rules of Conduct for Soviet Citizens in the Countries of Peoples' Democracies.*

"Oh, that's where we're going," Shebalin said. "I thought we'd be sent abroad!"

"None of your idiotic jokes," Berlinsky whispered. Alexandrov supported him by raising his eyes to the ceiling.

The booklet told about the brotherly friendship between the Soviet people and the peoples of Eastern Europe, who had embarked on the path of socialism but in whose consciousness there remained memories of capitalist life, and Soviet people visiting these countries must be aware of this. The forms were noticeably thinner. There were no questions about grandparents and parents, just their names, ages, and occupations before and after the Revolution.

We filled out the forms. The young man appeared again, took them, and again disappeared.

"Now we are under the X-ray," I whispered.

"We have nothing to fear," Berlinsky answered just as softly, and held his finger to his lips.

An hour passed. We did not talk.

Then the door opened, and with a nod of his head the young man invited us to follow him. We walked through the corridor, and at the door marked HEAD OF THE FOREIGN TRAVEL DEPARTMENT he stopped, looked us over from head to toe, slowly opened the door, and announced: "Ivan Kuzmich, the Borodin Quartet!"

"Please have a seat," Ivan Kuzmich said, without looking at us.

Before him lay our filled-out forms; he looked through all of them, then raised his eyes to us, looking us over in the same way.

"The government has decided to send you to the German Democratic Republic, which will celebrate next year the tenth anniversary of the 1945 liberation. I see here that your political portfolio is quite impressive: two Party members, one Komsomol member, and one . . ." I wanted to continue for him, "and one Jew," but he said instead, "and one non-Party member. You also have a good recommendation from the Composers' Union and the personal support of Comrade Khrennikov. This will be your first trip abroad, but I hope you understand the seriousness of your task. You will be going to Berlin; the situation in that city is complicated. It is divided into four sectors. You will be meeting West Germans. Does any one of you speak German?"

"We all can speak some school German," Berlinsky replied for all of us, "but we are Soviet people, regardless of what language we speak."

I could see that this answer made an impression on the official. Ivan Kuzmich looked approvingly at Berlinsky, then at all of us, and rose heavily from his chair.

"I hope, comrades, that you will justify our trust in you."

"You can be sure of that," Berlinsky replied.

"I wish you success," Ivan Kuzmich said, and stretched out his puffy hand, which we shook with proper respect.

Going Abroad
1955

THE TENTH ANNIVERSARY of the defeat of Hitler had great political significance, and sending a string quartet to the celebration in the German Democratic Republic was not a bad idea, considering the Germans' traditional love of chamber music. At Goskoncert, which controlled all trips abroad, the program editor immediately demanded our programs for the trip.

"We have to think," I said.

"Is one day enough?"

"Yes."

Once we left the Goskoncert offices, we started fighting right away. Berlinsky said that one program should be all Russian, while I felt that Germans, even East Germans, are brought up on the classics.

"We are Russians," Berlinsky declared.

"You mean Soviets?"

"I mean what I said. We are Russians."

In music it was true; we were Russians, and would be seen abroad as a Russian quartet, no matter how many Jews played in it. But in Moscow a statement like that sounded wrong. I started to get heated and said stubbornly that on my passport it said something else.

"I know what it says on your passport," Berlinsky growled, "and you know what I have in mind. We're Russians and have to play Russian music."

"No one's arguing," I said. "In each program we should have a Russian piece."

"And I think that at least one program should be all Russian."

"What is this? Music or politics?"

"Both."

"And what do the others think?"

"The others," Alexandrov answered, "think we can do without big words and do what's needed. One Russian program won't do any harm."

"Okay," I relented. "We'll give them several mixed programs and one all Russian. They can choose."

"This program should be number one," Berlinsky insisted.

"Why? The Germans will choose what they like best anyway."

"That's their business. We have ours."

"Well, what sort of Russian program are you suggesting?"

"Borodin by all means, Tchaikovsky, and . . ."

"And a samovar on stage, and raspberry jam."

". . . and something from Soviet music: Kabalevsky or even Shirinsky."

"Why do you want so much to play shit? Here we have no choice. But abroad?"

"Even more!"

"There'd be no problem if they allowed Shostakovich and Prokofiev."

"They won't."

"What if we try?"

"Better not get them angry. They know much too well what's forbidden."

"But maybe we could naïvely toss in Shostakovich and Prokofiev between Russian and Western classics? These are different times . . . There's a thaw outside."

"Say 'spring,' or even better 'summer.' "

"The weather's changeable," I said.

"But the calendar's steady," answered Alexandrov.

* * *

That evening, while I sat at home playing solitaire with composers' names, trying to make all the programs interesting enough, Stepanida, who rented me the room, knocked on my door and came in. She worked during the day in a dairy shop and came by from time to time to bring me some milk or produce. This time she brought me some cheese and put it by the window.

"Thanks, let me pay you," I said as usual.

"Why? I didn't pay for it myself."

"How'd you get it?" I asked naïvely.

"Don't ask!"

"Oh, I see. And how about the room, Stepanida?"

"Why are you always forcing money on me? I have more than you. And what can I do with it? There's nothing to buy but vodka."

"I'm going abroad. I can bring you something."

"Really? I'd love some comfortable shoes. My feet get sore from standing all day on the shop's concrete floor. Where are you going?"

"Germany."

"Aren't you scared?"

"Scared? Why?"

"Well, Fascists, after all . . . And you . . . aren't Russian . . ."

"Oh, that's what you mean. No, Stepanida, they aren't killing Jews there anymore."

"Don't think . . . I like Jews."

"I like Russians," I said. "Particularly women."

"Jews are hardworking."

"Russian women have a special soul."

"Jews don't drink."

"I like having a drink."

"That doesn't mean *drinking*."

"And I do like working."

"We can see how hard you work. That's why they didn't 'register' you."

"What do you mean? I went to the police station. Everything's in order there."

"I don't mean that. *Our* people didn't 'register' you."

"I don't understand."

"There's nothing to understand. New people, especially non-Russian, always need a beating."

"Why didn't they touch me?"

"Herman saved you. He said he'd vouch for you, that if necessary they could beat him. He said that only you understood him."

"Do you know where he is now?"

"Somewhere far away. He never writes."

"And the family? Aren't they interested?"

"Are you kidding? Well, I'm going. I'll stop by again."

I went back to my "solitaire." To avoid a new argument, I put the all-Russian program as number one, but to Borodin I added the forbidden Shostakovich and to Tchaikovsky the cursed Stravinsky, so that even in this program there would be music of different styles. In all the others, I put two Western composers with a Russian in the middle. I showed the programs to the quartet, and Berlinsky said, "The first program is marvelous, if only they let it through."

"I like it, too," I said.

"Let's see what they say at Goskoncert."

At Goskoncert the program editor called me in immediately and amiably offered me a chair. Then he quickly read through the programs, looked at me in surprise, and said sourly, "You're new here. That explains everything. You see, out of all these programs I can accept only the first one, but not altogether. Stravinsky should be replaced, and Shostakovich . . . Wait a minute. I'll be right back."

He had, of course, run off to ask about Shostakovich. But whom did he ask? In all Goskoncert he was the only man with any musical education. On the other hand, it was not a musical but a political question: had the time come to rehabilitate Shostakovich? He had been banned in 1948, and it was now 1955, so for seven years he hadn't been performed. I wondered how the program editor would ask about Shostakovich. And, even more, what the answer would be . . .

After half an hour the program editor returned. "It's like this: Shostakovich we'll allow, but take out Stravinsky."

"They're three tiny pieces," I said humbly. "They last only seven minutes, and for the whole program . . ."

"That's not the point," he interrupted. "We don't perform Stravinsky at all."

I looked at him as naïvely as I could and he decided to enlighten me.

"Recently Stravinsky said in public that all Russian music died in the twenties. By this, he meant that our great composers Shostakovich and Prokofiev don't exist."

" 'Great composers'?" I said to myself excitedly. "That means they've been rehabilitated!"

The editor, satisfied with my silence, continued: "Our musicians abroad should play as much Soviet music as possible. At a minimum, half of each program should be Russo-Soviet."

"I understand," I said. "Let me correct it."

"With pleasure." He handed me my sheet of paper. "You may sit at that desk." He saw that I was crossing out all the programs and smiled. "That's right!"

I quickly wrote new ones. Everything was clear. Out of every three compositions—two Russian. For example: Borodin and Shostakovich in the first half and Beethoven in the second, not too bad. Or Prokofiev with Mozart and Tchaikovsky, also pretty good. Or even better: Prokofiev, Shostakovich, and then Brahms or Schubert. Beautiful!

I put together four programs and gave them to the editor.

He read them and nodded. "Splendid. Thank you."

"I thank you, too," I said sincerely. We shook hands.

I went outside and immediately phoned Berlinsky. "Everything is all right!" I said.

"Tell me!"

"Shosty and Prok are great Soviet composers."

"Really?"

"That's what the chief said."

"Fantastic!"

"There are two months before the trip. What we really need now is to play a little onstage."

"That's right."

"Factory, school, club, doesn't matter what! Just so it's a stage."

"By the way, the tails . . . Ours are impossible to play in."

"We also need shirts."

"And cummerbunds."

"I don't have patent-leather shoes."

"Or black socks and handkerchiefs."

"Yes," I said. "But don't forget what we do have."

"What's that?"

"Freedom."

"Shut up!" Berlinsky snapped.

There was a week left before our departure. We had so many errands to run that there was almost no time for music. Official invitations followed one after the other. At first the whole quartet was invited, then only Alexandrov and Berlinsky, the quartet's "better half." They even began acting a little self-important and pretending that they knew something that Shebalin and I were not supposed to know. It was all the same to me. As the quartet's artistic director, I had my own troubles to worry about. We still had to play our first real concerts and bring to live performances what we had achieved in rehearsals. I knew we would get it sooner or later, but we needed it now; we had already paid ten years of our lives for this first appearance in the musical world.

During our evening rehearsals, at exactly five minutes to eight, we tuned our instruments, then ceremoniously bowed to the imaginary audience and sat at our music stands as if at a real concert. I raised my violin and we began the program. We didn't look at the "audience," but we felt its presence so much that we couldn't stop to correct mistakes. In four evenings we played our four programs, and I wanted to go through them again, but my colleagues said that we could do the rest in the G.D.R. Now there were more important things to do.

"Such as?" I inquired.

"Tails!" answered Shebalin for everyone. "I know that the Philharmonia recently got a set of tails, but they're only for the State Orchestra."

"Who's in charge?"

"Ivan Kharitonov."

"What if we talked to him?" I said.

"It's dangerous."

"I can try," said Shebalin. "Only give me some money, before the café closes."

Shebalin disappeared and came back after half an hour. Lowering his voice, he said, "After work, when everyone goes home, we need to go down to the basement one by one. I'll bring two bottles of special cognac."

At closing time I went down to the basement. The rest of the quartet were already there. Shebalin put a bottle of cognac in each pocket so that the tops were visible and quietly tapped on the door. Ivan Kharitonov opened right away, glanced down the corridor, and let us in, locking the door behind him.

"There's no one upstairs," Shebalin told him, "only the watchman at the entrance."

"Who?"

"Nikita."

"That's bad," said Ivan.

Shebalin pulled out a bottle of cognac and put it on the table. It was obvious from the label that the cognac was expensive.

"Very bad," repeated Ivan.

Shebalin pulled out the second bottle and put it next to the first. Ivan looked at them. There was an awkward silence, and I ventured, "Here's an idea. Take out the cello, put everything in the case, and go out as if we had two instruments. As if we are trying out a new cello before we leave."

Ivan nodded, and we followed him into the next room, where tails hung along the wall. "From these," he said. "The others have already been assigned."

"I need a big one," said Shebalin.

"Hurry, boys. Someone might come in."

We tried on only the coats; there was no time for the trousers. We threw everything in the cello case, and I picked up the naked cello. Ivan looked out in the corridor and nodded to us. We went out and heard the lock click behind us.

We went upstairs and slowly passed the guard, Nikita.

"You're early today," he said. "Not coming back?"

"Not today," answered Shebalin. "We're tired."

"All right, get some rest."

"Have a quiet evening, Nikita."

At the Philharmonia entrance a small woman with a violin was looking at us. "Who's that?" asked Berlinsky.

"Never seen her before," said Alexandrov.

"We need a taxi," I told Shebalin.

He stepped into the street and waved to every passing car. Finally one stopped.

"Let's go! Quickly!" Shebalin shouted.

The three of them with the two cellos just managed to squeeze in. I was left behind and looked around. The woman with the violin was still standing in the door of the Philharmonia, staring at me. As I caught her gaze, she took a step toward me and stopped. I went over to her.

"A colleague?" I asked.

She smiled shyly. "Excuse me." She was very thin, and in her small face her eyes seemed disproportionately large.

"For what?"

"I don't know what to say."

"What's your name?"

"Olya. My name's Olya."

"Hello, Olya," I said, and held out my hand.

Shaking my hand, she blushed.

"Shall we walk a little?" I asked.

We went along Gorky Street. "I've wanted for a long time to talk to you," she said with difficulty, "but couldn't make up my mind. I used to walk by the Writers' House when someone had . . . excuse me . . . died. It was the only place where I could hear you."

"We haven't played funerals for a while."

"I know. Now I come here. I watch you come out of the Philharmonia, turn the corner, and go into the subway. But today I decided to come closer, and . . ."

A certain emotional rapport slowly grew between us. The initiative, however passive, came from her, and I felt somewhat like a woman being courted. I decided to switch the conversation to a more prosaic track.

"I thought I knew the face of every violinist in Moscow, yet I've never met you before."

"You wouldn't know me."

"Where did you study?"

"Here in Moscow, a long time ago. And I didn't finish the conservatory."

"You got married? A family, children . . ."

"Oh, no . . . Not that . . ."

"I probably shouldn't ask."

"I'd like to tell you, if I may . . ."

We strolled along Gorky Street, and I learned that she had been born in Canada, but to parents of Russian descent. Her father was a passionate Communist who suddenly decided that he should live in the land of his political ideals, so he emigrated to the Soviet Union with his wife and children. The Soviet government gave him a job and a small house near Moscow. The Soviet papers then were writing about the enormous attraction of socialism and how people were rushing to leave the capitalist world of violence and injustice. This Canadian served as a happy example, and he spoke at meetings all over Moscow about how he and his family felt now.

In 1937 the family were arrested as American spies and sent to camps in Siberia. All of them died, except Olya, whose life was saved by her violin. The camp administrators made her play Russian and Soviet songs at their nighttime drinking parties, and for that they fed her a little extra. She lived to see Stalin's death, after which they let her out, apologized for the mistake, and even let her return to the little house.

I was ashamed that life had been so simple for me.

"I didn't tell you this to make you feel sorry for me. Things happened that way and there's nothing to be done. But my dream is still with me. I want to play chamber music and I'd like to take lessons from you."

"Do you work somewhere?"

"No," she answered quickly, "and it would be hard for me to find work now. But they paid me some money . . ."

She blushed, talking about money. Many returning prisoners were paid money, a kind of compensation for their suffering.

"Money has nothing to do with it," I said, trying to smooth it over. "I just wanted to know what you're doing now."

"Living. Everything was calm at first, and then I heard you. That affected my life. I'd never thought before that quartet music can say more than any other kind. If only I could play in a quartet."

"Would you like to play for me?"

"That sounds like a fairy tale."

"I'm leaving in two days. Tomorrow's a difficult day, passports and so on. How about right now?"

"Right away?"

"Yes, why not?"

"I'm afraid."

"We can play together at first, some duets, and then it will be easier."

"I can't believe it."

"But where? Back at the Philharmonia?"

"We could go to my house," said Olya very softly.

"Is it in Silver Grove?"

"Yes. The trolley runs straight from here to my house."

"So what are we waiting for?"

In the trolley I let her sit by the window and sat down beside her. We were quiet for a long time. She looked out the window.

"It's the end of April," she said. "It's not the best time of year, but soon the leaves will appear. Their very first green color is never repeated. Summer's pretty, too; the trees live fully in their own way. But autumn is best of all, when the forest slowly dies. The trees put on their best clothes, they die beautifully."

"I've never lived among trees," I said.

"It's good with them," she said. "Trees purify people. It's so important now, when . . ."

She didn't finish, but it was clear enough why it was so important right now. I quickly calculated in my mind: "1955. She was arrested before the war, she spent seventeen or eighteen years in camp. Oh, Lord! If she was about twenty when she was arrested, then now she must be thirty-six or thirty-seven and has to start life all over, and this is her first spring . . ."

I took her hand, she closed her eyes. When she opened them again, there were tears in them.

"I'm very happy," she said. "Forgive me."

We rode out onto Khoroshovskoe highway. The trolley gradually emptied.

"From here it's not far," said Olya.

"I'm not in a hurry," I answered.

She leaned her shoulder very slightly against mine. "I'm afraid I won't be able to play for you now."

"We'll do it as soon as I come back."

"Are you going for long?"

"Three weeks."

"That's not long. Weeks aren't long. I'll wait."

We passed a few more stops. The last passengers got off and we were left alone.

"We get off at the next one," she whispered.

I saw how the trolley drove into the woods, made a semicircle, and stopped. The driver looked at us but didn't say anything and got out.

"We have to get out," she said, not moving.

"I like this route," I said. "I think I'll ride it often. Let's go, show me the way to your house."

We crossed the circle where the trolley turned and entered an alley of trees and identical wooden houses. "These are the summer dachas of professors," said Olya. "In the winter no one lives here."

"Marvelous," I said. "Good to practice."

"Oh yes, any time. Day and night."

"It suits me," I said.

Olya convulsively squeezed my hand. "Don't tease me."

We got as far as her gate, and I stopped. Olya was looking at me, waiting. Then she said, "Won't you come in?"

I opened the gate and stopped again. I suddenly felt myself trapped and didn't know how to get out.

Olya looked at her shabby house. "Is something wrong?" she asked ruefully.

My spirit broke as I said, "I think I better go now. I have a hard day tomorrow and I leave at six the next morning. I'll see you when I come back."

"Will you? I'll be waiting."

We went back to the stop without talking. I got on the trolley and sat in the last seat. From the window I watched Olya's little motionless figure until the trolley turned the corner.

East Germany
1955

THE MORNING of our departure abroad was noticeably different from all other mornings. At six o'clock, a black ministry limousine came to pick me up. The driver, checking his list, called me by name, took my suitcase, and opened the car door for me. He repeated this sequence three more times as we collected the quartet one by one. My colleagues were all dressed in white shirts, and each smelled noticeably of wine.

At the airport, we and our luggage were separated from the passengers on domestic flights. Soon we were joined by several others, each pretending to be important. It was written on all their faces that they were going abroad. A general appeared in parade uniform, accompanied by two officers. And finally, the head of the delegation arrived—Ushakov from the Moscow Council. Compared with everyone else, we looked like children; only our instruments made us appear at all respectable.

Our passports were collected, meaning we would avoid a passport check. Our baggage was loaded on a cart without a customs inspection. We rode through the field on a bus and pulled to a stop next to a small two-engine airplane.

"IL-12," explained the general. "American Douglas type."

Ushakov climbed the stairs first, and after letting everyone else pass, we came last. A man in civilian clothes returned our passports and wished us a good flight.

We were seated in the tail of the plane. At the cockpit door a stewardess stood motionless. Without smiling, she announced that we had a special flight to Berlin, with stops in Vilnius and Warsaw. "Lunch will be in Vilnius," she added.

Someone tried to joke: "What's for lunch?"

Not having been programmed for this kind of question, the stewardess didn't smile and didn't answer.

"A serious dame," remarked Alexandrov.

I watched out the window as the propellers started moving. First one turned, the blades speeding up and gradually blending into a misty circle; then the second started. The plane began to shake slightly and taxied toward the runway.

Not only was this my first trip abroad, it was my first flight ever, and with each bump my stomach turned over. I tried to breathe deeper.

Passing on the way to the lavatory, Ushakov looked at us and smiled. "Oh, we even have our own music!"

"We could play a concert," Shebalin said lightly. "We've never played in the air before."

There was no room for the whole quartet, but the idea of practicing pleased me and I unpacked my violin, hoping that it would distract me from nausea. The two lower strings drowned in the noise of the motors, the upper were barely audible, but I could move my fingers. If only I didn't get sick . . .

Again Ushakov passed, and seeing me with the violin, he smiled and sat down. "My compliments!" he said. "When is your first concert?"

"We don't know yet," Berlinsky answered.

"Don't you have an itinerary?"

Berlinsky shook his head.

"How can that be? Who's taking care of you?"

"Goskoncert."

"Strange . . . Remind me, I'll find out. But don't you worry, you'll receive a detailed schedule when you arrive. Our German comrades are punctual people."

"German comrades." My ear was not used to this phrase.

"Has the quartet ever been in the G.D.R.?" Ushakov asked.

"No. This is our first trip abroad."

Ushakov looked us over carefully. "I see, I see . . . Well, you're clever people. I wish you good luck."

He returned to his place but left us with a feeling of alarm.

"Did you get the message?" asked Berlinsky glumly, looking at me.

"No," I said, fighting down my nausea.

"The situation is serious," remarked Alexandrov. "There are two Germanies in Berlin and it's still not clear how it will turn out. The Germans . . ."

" 'Our German comrades,' " I said, repeating Ushakov's words.

Berlinsky exploded, "Shut up! And think before you speak! I don't want your stupidity to . . ."

"Quiet, quiet," said Alexandrov. "This can be worked out without shouting."

"We need order!" Berlinsky shouted again. "We have to choose a director of the quartet and give him all rights to maintain discipline."

"We're adults," said Shebalin carefully, "we understand."

"No, a director is needed," Alexandrov joined in. "It's a complex situation. I'm for it."

Berlinsky quickly agreed and turned to Shebalin. "And you?"

"Director or no director, it's all the same to me," muttered Shebalin.

"And you?"

"There's already a majority," I said.

"Splendid," announced Berlinsky. "It's decided by a majority. Now, the next question . . ."

"I suggest you," said Alexandrov gallantly to Berlinsky.

"And I suggest you," countered Berlinsky, returning the compliment.

"You have more experience."

"But your German is better."

"Well, if you insist—I agree," concluded Alexandrov unexpectedly.

Silence reigned despite the roar of the motors. Berlinsky saw he had lost and started to bite his nails. Alexandrov contentedly opened a newspaper, while Shebalin settled down to sleep. I began to play scales again.

I could hardly stand the landing in Vilnius. I almost fainted, and my hands and face got clammy. Once on the ground, to calm down, I let everyone pass and then stood up carefully. The plane rocked a little, but I could walk. In the airport we were separated from the other passengers and escorted through the restaurant to the banquet hall.

The waitress served us borscht, and everyone poured himself vodka. There were no women at our table, so despite the difference in ranks, a certain camaraderie developed among us over our common attention to the food. The general praised the borscht and asked for more, the others followed his example, and the second glass of vodka poured itself.

I, however, was afraid to eat. When the waitress brought the second course, I apologized for not having touched the borscht.

"Isn't it tasty?"

"Oh, no, no, just the airplane, you see . . . I don't feel like eating."

"You want to see a doctor? We have a good one here."

"Yes, I think I'd better," I said. "Thanks." I stood up.

"Where are you going?" Alexandrov asked immediately.

"To see the doctor."

"In the future tell me where you're going. That will be better for all of us." He looked at me sullenly and waited for my answer.

I nodded my head.

At the door stood someone in plain clothes.

"Where?"

"To the doctor."

"I'll come with you."

Thus under guard, I went to the doctor's office. When I started to explain my symptoms to the doctor, he interrupted me.

"Is this your first flight?"

"Yes."

"Everything's normal. Fly more and you'll get used to it."

"Should I eat or not?"

"Doesn't matter. Here, take these two pills twenty minutes before takeoff."

When I returned to the table, I noticed that it was noisy and the vodka bottles were empty.

"Will you eat something, perhaps?" the waitress asked me sympathetically.

"Please bring me a cup of tea."

"I'll bring it with lemon. It's good."

"So, how are you?" Alexandrov asked gruffly. "Better?"

He was quickly entering into the role of director and even sat differently, scanning the room like a boss. I tried not to notice Berlinsky. I knew that now, after vodka, he was taking his loss very hard. When we all finally got up from the table and walked back to our plane, Berlinsky edged toward me and slowed his pace until we were behind the crowd.

"You and I," he started, and I heard tears in his voice, "you and I are the founding members of the quartet. We went through its hardest time. Our colleagues came when things were easier."

I knew what he was talking about. "But why the hell did you start that discussion? Everything would have been natural, everyone in his own place. And now what can you do!"

He took out his handkerchief and blew his nose.

"On the next trip I'll suggest that you be director," I told him gently.

"If there is another trip."

"There will be. I think we'll make a lot of trips. The doctor said I have to get used to airplanes."

"Well, if the doctor says . . ."

Alexandrov looked back at us. Berlinsky walked faster, catching up with him, and they strolled on together.

The medicine paralyzed my stomach. My nose felt swollen and it was difficult to breathe, but at least there was no nausea.

The stewardess announced that we'd bypass Warsaw and fly directly to Berlin. The altimeter showed that we were flying at 4,000 meters. But suddenly the needle started moving backward as the plane dipped abruptly. My body felt weightless, and we seemed to be falling into an abyss.

In the cabin vodka-reddened faces turned pale. The imperturbable stewardess appeared and explained that we were passing a large thundercloud and suggested that we fasten our belts. We were rapidly losing altitude, but I didn't feel anything, I didn't have a stomach, and I blessed the doctor and his pills. But the people around me were in trouble. A young officer flew past us, like a meteor, to the lavatory, but didn't make it there in time. The general slid out of his chair and lay on the floor in his parade uniform.

Shebalin, though pale, kept his dignity and even joked. "Look, the general's in his coffin!"

"I rather like the feeling," Alexandrov said. "It's like swinging."

Berlinsky was leaning back, his eyes closed. I put my hand on his cold, wet forehead.

"Feeling bad?"

He didn't answer. His face was turning unpleasantly green.

"Lie on the floor, like the general . . ."

He crawled out of his chair, lay down on the floor, and was sick. I leaned over him. "You should feel better now."

He opened his eyes with difficulty and mumbled, "I'm fine. I think I already died."

"So what's it like?"

"It's dark."

I moved to the window, looked at the black cloud, and recalled a childhood sensation of fear from when I was learning to swim and couldn't find the bottom with my feet.

Out the window, in the darkness, there were flashes. It must have been the glow of the motors. And what if it was lightning? And what if . . . ? The end. The end of everything—of all our great expectations. Just when I had started to feel a sort of future for the quartet. A bit more time and we could have made our own interpretive mark in music. But now . . . Could it be that up there, in heaven, there were also different administrations, creating and destroying, and just as on earth, one didn't know what the other was doing? Or just the opposite: if our lives were written in heaven and an unusual fate was offered to us, didn't that mean that now there was no real danger, that nothing would happen, we'd arrive and our noble destinies would be fulfilled? "Then," I told myself, "relax, and don't even think about the future. There everything is already decided."

I glanced at my colleagues: Berlinsky was still lying on the floor with closed eyes; Alexandrov and Shebalin were sitting like fearless Russian soldiers before a battle, not even looking out the window. To keep from thinking, I said the first thing that came into my head.

"What if we flew right through the cloud?"

"It's possible," Shebalin answered philosophically, "but why? Better to be an hour late in Berlin than to get 'there' fifty years too early."

"You think there's a chance of getting 'there'?"

"One bolt of lightning and that's it!"

"And then what?"

"Nothing."

"What about some sort of life after death? Some soul, some spirit?"

"Obviously you didn't learn anything in school," said Alexandrov. "You've already forgotten that you don't have a soul?"

"So what do I have?"

"All kinds of shit. Your brain, for instance. It just thinks a little. Through it—all your connection with life. The brain dies—you lose your link. Life goes on, but not for you. For you—it's all over."

"That's dialectical materialism. But I don't believe in it. Too straight-forward. In nature things are more complicated. We just don't know that."

"Don't know what? Is there an afterlife?"

"At least!"

"There isn't. And even if there is, we can't know it. It's easy enough to get 'there,' but no one ever comes back from 'there.' "

"I'm just coming back from there," said Berlinsky unexpectedly, from the floor.

"You're still alive?" exclaimed Shebalin. "I hope there's no concert today."

"Look, it's getting lighter!"

Out the window it was really getting brighter. We gained altitude again and suddenly saw bright sun and blue sky. The plane stabilized.

It was hard to believe that five minutes ago we could have been talking seriously about life after death. Below we could now see the unfamiliar houses and roofs of East Germany. And shortly afterward, we landed at the airport, where we were met by a crowd of Germans.

Someone made a welcoming speech in German, someone else translated into broken Russian, and for the first time we heard the words *"ewige Freundschaft"* (eternal friendship). I tried not to think that some of these Germans recently might have been carrying out the systematic destruction of the Jews.

A photographer appeared and we smiled into his lens. After that we rode a long time in a bus until we reached Berlin. The city was not yet rebuilt. There were few houses, just many huge craters surrounded by fences. On the fences were portraits of the leaders of the G.D.R. and Soviet slogans which repeated the words LENIN and STALIN endlessly.

After we pulled to a stop at the Johanneshof Hotel, we were collected into a flock again in the lobby to hear another speech about "the eternal friendship of our nations."

We were given keys to our rooms and ten minutes to get ready. We went upstairs, came down again, and were led into the restaurant, where we all sat down at one long table. There were no more speeches, only a schedule for the rest of the day: after lunch, we were to attend a gala meeting in honor of the tenth anniversary of Hitler's defeat with a speech by Prime Minister Otto Grotewohl. After that, a glass of wine with President Wilhelm Pieck, and in the evening a dinner in the restaurant with some city officials. For the following days, we would find detailed plans in our hotel rooms.

I understood only a few words of Grotewohl's endless speech, but it didn't matter: we had become used to that sort of speech in Moscow. The subject was always the same: how bad it had been under capitalism, how much better it was under socialism, and how beautiful it would be under Communism. Everything was supported by statistics, so there could be no doubt about the historical inevitability of human society's development. "All roads lead to Communism, comrades!" Even without knowing the language, we could tell exactly when the "stormy applause" was scheduled, and we applauded with our "German comrades."

The concluding slogans of the speech were drowned in ovations,

cheers in honor of the G.D.R., and calls for new victories of all
Communist countries, with the great Soviet Union in the lead. Next,
according to Soviet canons, "the skies should open" with a thunderous
fanfare played by an enormous brass band. But instead, the opera
orchestra very quietly began the overture to Mozart's *Marriage of Fi-
garo*. It seemed that this had somehow survived from a time before
Stalin and before Hitler. The music received a standing ovation.

Our row, where the Soviet delegation sat, began to move. Out in
the foyer we gathered around a column and were openly counted.
When the numbers matched, we were led backstage, where several
glasses of wine stood on a table. Each of us took a glass and moved
slowly to the center, toward the waiting President Pieck.

I went first. Holding the glass in my outstretched hand, I approached
the old man. A dark jacket hung on him as if on a hanger and a smile
was frozen on his face. By some miracle a glass stayed in his withered
hand, and when I moved my own, he made a convulsive gesture,
trying to clink but missing. He looked in surprise at his glass, so I
stepped closer, to reach his glass, but then he moved his arm, and
this time I missed.

"Stop your stupid jokes," Alexandrov hissed in my ear.

I stepped to one side to watch the President clink glasses with the
rest of the quartet.

In Moscow we had been told that our bows "were destined to
strengthen the cooperation of the socialist countries." And instead I'd
already committed an "anti-state act" by failing to clink glasses with
the President himself. I stood like an idiot with my glass of wine in
my hand while my colleagues carried on a friendly conversation with
our "German comrades" and didn't even look in my direction.

I didn't notice at first that everyone had begun moving toward the
exit until Alexandrov called me. Once we were out on the street, he
told us, "After dinner I want to see the whole quartet in my room."

I had to give him credit: he carried the tone of director naturally,
more easily than Berlinsky, who couldn't command without shouting.
Alexandrov didn't have to shout; he simply put a metallic edge on his
voice.

After dinner we all marched up to his room. He waited for us to sit down, waited a bit longer for the sake of importance, and then began. "I didn't think it would be necessary to call a meeting of the quartet on our very first day abroad. Obviously, not everyone took this trip seriously enough. That's the only way to explain the unforgivable thoughtlessness which we witnessed today. You know what I'm talking about."

I laughed involuntarily.

"There's no point laughing," said Alexandrov dryly.

"Tell me," begged Shebalin. "What happened?"

"Nothing," I explained. "The old man missed with his glass, and when I tried to touch his, he moved his hand."

"But do you know how this 'nothing' may be interpreted in our embassy?" said Alexandrov. "As mockery of the government of the G.D.R.! I do not need to explain where that could lead."

Now I didn't feel like laughing. Of course, we all knew that one didn't joke with the Soviet authorities, but the fact that "Soviet power" had appeared within our quartet had a crushing effect on me.

Everyone remained silent until I said that it was late, but before I went to bed I promised to think about my "conduct unworthy of a Soviet artist." The last words displeased Alexandrov and he snarled that he hadn't asked to be director of the quartet, he had been elected, and he wouldn't tolerate jokes at his expense. "In order to avoid future misunderstandings, it's better to decide everything right now. With the power given to me by the people, that is, all of you, I am obliged to introduce martial law into the quartet," he finished.

"What does that mean?" I asked dully.

"The last few weeks in Moscow, there were more latecomers to rehearsals."

Shebalin, who had been late more often than anyone, fidgeted in his chair. "Well, you see," he said soothingly, "no one comes late on purpose, but when it occasionally happens, everyone's unhappy, the latecomer most of all."

"Occasionally happens?" Alexandrov turned to Berlinsky. "Do you remember my ever being late?"

"No," answered Berlinsky.

"So you see! Why should I lose time when other people are late? I suggest that lateness be punished with fines. One ostmark per minute."

"I'm against beginning rehearsals at the sound of a bell," I stated. "A quartet is creative work and needs freedom."

"Freedom to be late?"

"Freedom to achieve something during the rehearsal."

"Who's stopping you? Only be there on time. What do you think?" he asked Berlinsky.

Berlinsky stopped biting his nails and spoke slowly: "To strengthen discipline is necessary, of course, but on the other hand . . ."

Alexandrov looked at him reproachfully, and Berlinsky quickly added, "I'm for it!"

"Let's vote," said Alexandrov.

He and Berlinsky voted for, Shebalin and I against.

"As director I have two votes," Alexandrov declared.

"That's abuse of power," I remarked.

"You think so? I don't complain when you begin a quartet up-bow and also play up-bow, even if I don't like it."

"We always discuss the bowings."

"Yes, but if there's a tie vote, your vote counts more."

"That's natural. I carry more responsibility."

"I agree. You're the artistic director of the quartet and answer for the quality. And I answer for order and discipline. Any objections?"

No one answered.

Alexandrov then issued more orders: We were not to go into West Berlin, and we were to move very prudently around East Berlin. Since it was easy to get lost and accidentally enter the Western part, where there were all sorts of temptations, it was better not to walk alone, and to tell the hotel porter when we left and returned.

Shebalin tried to contradict, but Alexandrov looked at Berlinsky, who nodded his head.

I didn't listen very attentively. If we couldn't, then we couldn't. The details have no meaning if the main point is lost. Alexandrov had calculated cleverly: Berlinsky would support him in everything in the name of Party solidarity, and together the two would always have a formal majority. Just as in the Soviet state, the machinery to crush freedom would do its job and all restrictions approved by the "will of the majority" would become rigid, unyielding laws.

They say that if you keep fleas in a matchbox for a week and then set them free, they'll jump into their former prison. With the Soviet people it is the same way. Freedom frightens us because we don't know what to do with it. Freedom—it's unfamiliar, incomprehensible, uncomfortable. But in a prison everything is so simple: you can't, and that's it. No problems.

The meeting at last came to an end, and we parted without saying goodbye.

The next morning the telephone woke me.

"Still sleeping?" Berlinsky's voice said. "Sorry, old man, but we meet in ten minutes."

"Oh hell! I fell asleep very late . . ."

"I thought so . . . Me, too."

"Thanks for calling. On my way."

I did everything at once—wash, shave, dress—and, racing downstairs like crazy, entered the lobby as the clock on the wall showed 9:30.

Alexandrov, noticing me, looked at his watch and shook his head.

"Am I late?" I asked innocently.

"Fifteen seconds."

"How much will it be?"

"Twenty-five pfennigs."

We marched to the dining room, where Ushakov read the schedule for the day and then turned to our quartet. "Our German comrades have arranged several concerts for you right after the holidays. But before that, how about playing for the Soviet soldiers?"

"Yes," the general joined in. "They would appreciate good music very much."

Both he and Ushakov stared at us expectantly.

Alexandrov, our commander in chief, spoke first. "It's our duty to serve the Soviet Army."

"We are also soldiers in a certain sense," added Berlinsky.

"Bravo!" said the general.

"When should we be ready?" Alexandrov asked in a military way.

"Right now. The car is waiting."

"Yes, Comrade General!" Alexandrov said, and I thought he was about to salute.

Fine Arts
1955

W<small>E STOOD BEHIND</small> a tattered movie screen and peered through its holes into the hall. The soldiers, joking and laughing, were taking their places. They had come to celebrate May Day at a "Big Festive Concert," as the poster on the hall's door announced.

Tumultuous applause greeted us as one by one we appeared onstage. Alexandrov stepped forward.

"Dear comrades, on behalf of our quartet I congratulate you on the First of May and the Day of Victory."

Loud applause and cheers.

"We travel all over the world and perform for different audiences. But we are especially happy to meet our countrymen abroad."

Applause again.

While Alexandrov spoke, we set up our folding music stands. This intrigued the soldiers and someone from the hall shouted, "It's a circus! They are musical clowns!"

Looking back, to see that everything was in order, Alexandrov continued, "We begin our concert with the first movement from Quartet Number 4 by the great German composer Ludwig van Beethoven."

Someone automatically began to applaud, but stopped, confused, and everyone laughed. We waited for silence, but it did not come. Alexandrov nodded to me to start . . .

We played a couple of minutes, all the while feeling that the noise in the hall was growing.

We finished to scattered applause, and Alexandrov announced, "Nocturne by a great Russian composer, Alexander Borodin."

The same voice that had called us a circus now shouted, "You guys better show us your muscles!"

"We'll show you our muscles, brother," Alexandrov whispered, as we started to play again, this time hardly able to hear ourselves.

"There won't be any circus! This is philharmonia!" we heard from the hall, and several soldiers, stamping their boots, marched to the exit.

"What shall we do now?" I asked.

"Start the scherzo, but very fast."

I saw my fingers moving, but I didn't hear the music. The soldiers were leaving the hall.

"Don't run off!" Alexandrov shouted to us. "Bow first."

We bowed to the soldiers' backs and went behind the movie screen to see what would happen next. At long last, a soldier appeared and gave us an envelope. In it was the address of another military unit.

When our German driver, Helmut, drove us to our next stop, not only were we silent, we could not even move. We were terrified that in two hours we would arrive at the next unit, begin to play, and the mood of the soldiers would quickly change to open displeasure, then to angry disappointment and hostility. This would happen again to-morrow, and the day after, as we, fulfilling our "sacred duty," con-tinued to "help" the Soviet Army in its "difficult but noble" life.

When we arrived at the next army base, a group of circus performers was already there. We met them in the mess hall, and their pianist told us that while he had had trouble with pianos everywhere, the one here was absolutely unplayable. The concert had already been an-nounced, however, and he didn't know what to do.

I realized at once that the quartet could help them, and at the same time they could get us out of the hopeless position in which we had landed. Of course, for a quartet it would be hackwork, but no one would know that besides us.

"What time's the concert?" I asked.

"Eight o'clock!" they answered in unison.

"What sort of repertoire?"

"Russian folk songs."

"Gypsy songs."

"Rumanian dance . . ."

"Any music suits me; I'm a juggler."

"I do an acrobatic routine."

"There's no time," I said. "We'd have to arrange the music and rehearse."

All the women took a step forward and imploringly clasped their hands. "Please . . . We beg you . . . Help us!"

I looked at my colleagues. They understood the situation perfectly. For the quartet it was a profanation of our art, but by now it was the only way out.

"Show us the music," I said.

The pianist brought us a pile of crumpled pages. We spread them out on the table.

"Make some music paper," I said, "fast, and as much as you can."

The women of the troupe, who had taken us under their wing, brought us a snack, and then led my colleagues and Helmut into the men's barracks. I stayed in the mess hall and began to rearrange the piano part for a string quartet.

I worked until evening. There was no time left to rehearse with the soloists, but we told them they could do what they always did and we would count on our ears to follow them.

The whole unit came to the concert, although it was supposed to be for the officers only. Soldiers sat on the windowsills and in the aisles. The entrance door was wide open and a crowd stood in it.

The announcer straightened his worn tuxedo one last time, adjusted his bow tie, and looked us over.

"Are you ready? I'm going on."

He ran out on the stage, joyfully shouted holiday greetings, and had just assured the public that they would see the very best Moscow artists,

when a loudly weeping clown came out after him. The clown pulled
out a huge tablecloth-sized handkerchief with big holes in it, and,
sticking his hand through one hole, wiped his nose with his fingers.
The soldiers laughed.

"Billy, why are you crying so bitterly?" the MC asked the clown.

"How can I keep from crying? I just became a father!" the clown
answered through his tears.

"You're a strange one, Billy! It's a happy occasion, and you're
crying!"

The clown cried even louder, squeezed a hidden rubber balloon,
and from his eyes, nose, and ears poured streams of water.

"There, there, don't cry! Tell me how your wife's feeling."

"My wife? That's the problem—she still doesn't know anything
about the baby!" cried the clown.

From the hall came healthy male guffaws.

Shouting over the laughter, the MC announced, "Our wide-ranging
and various program opens with the favorite of the Moscow public,
Mikhail Rubakov. He will perform two Russian songs, 'I loved you'
and 'No, I don't love you.' "

The audience laughed again.

"We have here, in transit from London to Paris, the world-famous
Borodin instrumental quartet! Give them a hand!"

We were met with thunderous applause. While we were sitting
down, the MC managed to make one more joke: "Rubakov has a
baritone, in place of a piano we have a string quartet, and what do I
have? A mother-in-law! Ha-ha-ha!"

We began the song. The soft sound of the quartet flowed through
the hall; we carefully followed the singer's tasteless phrasing and unavoidable *ritenuti* on the high notes. He probably wanted to show us
his musicality. After the songs, he performed the fashionable jingle
"Rulate." During the repetitive refrain, he desperately gestured at the
hall to join in. Toward the end of the song he succeeded, and left the
stage triumphantly.

We remained onstage, and the MC was about to announce the next
number, when the clown ran by, tripped on his own foot and fell, got
up, tripped again, and started looking for something on the floor.

"What are you looking for, Billy?"

"Some money I dropped in the street."

"Why are you looking for it here?"

"It's dark out there!"

After that the juggler performed, and we played Borodin's scherzo in the style of a Viennese waltz, speeding up and slowing down to keep time with the flying balls, hats, and plates.

The nocturne from the same quartet perfectly suited the gymnast and her flowing acrobatic movements. She bent as if she had no bones, and with the Oriental coloring of Borodin's music, the scene resembled a tale from the *Arabian Nights*. Her breasts and hips were covered only by narrow strips of shiny silver material, and as she performed, hundreds of male eyes were glued to her bare legs and stomach. The hall was tensely silent, from time to time breaking into excited applause.

"Our concert has only begun!" shouted the MC. "Meet the Honored Artist of the Buriat-Mongolian republic, Violanta Fioletova. Two Tchaikovsky romances, 'At first I did not love you' and 'He loved me so.' "

Once the laughter ended, the self-satisfied MC continued, "Violanta sings about love, the same quartet accompanies her, and what have I got at home?"

"Mother-in-law!" everyone shouted.

The blond singer was nervous. She wanted to show us that she was a serious musician, but her voice failed her. To encourage her, we immediately increased our volume, playing the accompaniment as a quartet solo. Gaining confidence, she sang the second romance pretty well. She bowed to the hall and then, turning, to us. There were tears in her eyes.

"And more about love!" announced the MC. "This time for two! The duet from Kalman's operetta *Silva*—'Silva, you don't love me!' Performed by Violanta and Mikhail."

We played the beginning sweetly. In the arrangement I had added tasteless little phrases to the viola part, which Shebalin played now with exaggerated feeling. The whole troupe stood in the wings and watched us with delight.

That ended the first half of the concert. Trying to outshout the cheering audience, the MC screamed, "Fifteen-minute intermission per person!" and we all left the stage. The troupe immediately surrounded us.

"Oh, you are wonderful!"

"We've never had such success!"

"I was nervous," the blond singer said, "and you helped me so much! I'd like to kiss each of you!"

"Then start with the first violin," I said.

"I want to kiss you, too!" declared the gymnast. "I never worked so well."

"Kisses must wait till after the concert," Berlinsky said. "We still have work to do."

There were still the gypsy songs, the Rumanian dance, the magician . . . The poetry reader was the only one who needed no music. He began the second half, and while he spoke we studied the music with our eyes.

The Rumanian dance turned out to be easiest of all. We endlessly repeated the same half-Moldavian, half-Jewish tune, until the dancers came to the last hop and we rushed through the ending to finish with them.

For the magician we played Tchaikovsky's "Andante Cantabile" very quietly, so quietly that at the proper moments the music could halt, making his tricks even more effective.

The concert ended with the "highlight of the show"—gypsy songs. We left the stage, waited while the MC and the clown told their last jokes, and came out with the brunette singer. She had on a long velvet skirt, earrings, rings, everything gypsies are supposed to wear, but in our tails we were out of style. We should have been wearing red silk shirts and carrying guitars. But when the MC announced the first number, "Sing, ring, my guitar . . ." we put aside our bows and played pizzicato, imitating the sound of guitars. The singer had a low, sexy voice, and she sang in the style of "cruel romance," swaying her plump shoulders and occasionally showing her rounded leg. She was a stunning success. The soldiers called her back again and again.

* * *

Going back to our barracks, we were a single unit. The soldiers followed at a respectful distance, the officers came closer and shyly complimented the women. But the women, like the whole troupe, were drawn to our quartet. They kept telling us that it was their best concert ever, that it was their first experience of real art.

First Quartet
Recitals
1955

W E STUCK WITH the troupe for a whole week, working two, sometimes three concerts a day. We would sing along with Rubakov and echo the gypsy's "Black Eyes." The clown thought up a pantomime in which we did silly stunts with our instruments.

After the last concert the whole troupe saw us off; the men shook our hands warmly, and the women kissed us and wept. This was our reward for making people happy for a while, but we knew we had been slipping out of our concert form.

That night we crossed the whole country, from north to south. Aware that we had a serious concert the next day, we tried to sleep, but in vain. Shebalin swore and Alexandrov would respond immediately, "Exactly! I agree with you." The night was painfully long.

We drove into Erfurt early in the morning and asked directions to the concert hall. It was still locked, but two girls were sitting on the steps. One was very young, the other a bit older. Alexandrov rolled down the car window, and they stood up.

"*Das Borodin Quartett?*" the older one asked. When Alexandrov nodded, she began to speak fairly good Russian. "We're your translators. We didn't know where to look for you and came here."

"Do you know where we'll be staying?"

"Of course. Hotel Erfurt. There are already four reservations for you."

"And where are *you* staying?" Berlinsky asked hastily.

"We too stay there. We always translate for you. It's our practice for the Russian language."

"Let's go, then," Alexandrov said. "There's not much time."

The girls shyly got into the car and sat together.

"What's your name?" asked Berlinsky.

"I'm Ursula, and this is Rosy."

"Rosy still hasn't said a word, either in German or Russian."

"Russian? Yes, I study Russian, but only one year and one half," Rosy piped up.

"Ursula," I asked, "what are we playing tonight?"

"A moment, please! I have your schedule. Here!" She took a packet of papers out of her purse. "Today in Erfurt you perform Mozart, Prokofiev, Brahms, tomorrow in Weimar—Borodin, Shostakovich, Schubert, and later in Jena all Russian—Borodin, Shostakovich, Tchaikovsky."

Just what we needed! To start with Mozart, the most demanding, when we were feeling terrible!

"It looks bad," I said. "To play a concert, we need to rehearse, to rehearse we first have to practice individually; to practice we need sleep, and to sleep we need time . . . I suggest we meet in my room at five in our tails, and at six-thirty go to the hall and play through the first half before they open the doors."

"Everyone agreed?" asked Alexandrov.

In the hotel Ursula efficiently collected our passports and quickly checked us into four private rooms. I walked to the elevator with my suitcase, went up to my room, and went to bed.

The moment I picked up my violin that afternoon, I felt that things were bad. The week with the troupe—the lousy concerts for soldiers and the lack of practice—had left their mark. I had lost the good form with which I had left Moscow. My hands kept slipping out of control. There was nothing to do but start from the beginning. I went to the bathroom and soaked my hands in hot water. How stupid not to be ready for our first concert! We couldn't explain to the German audience that we had been entertaining troops, accompanying a magician, a juggler, and a gypsy singer instead of playing Mozart. You can't ever make excuses to an audience. The audience pay for their tickets, sit in their places, and you come onstage at eight o'clock and . . .

A slight shiver went up my spine. I opened the Mozart Quartet in D-minor, K. 421, and started to play it very slowly.

All afternoon, I didn't put down my violin; we met as agreed, then set off for the hall, and played onstage until the last minute before the audience was let in. Still, it felt as if we were playing a day too early.

Once we began the concert, it seemed the ensemble and the intonation were not too bad, but the music didn't breathe. Music never comes by itself. It has to be invited by painstaking daily work. Then, maybe, one day it will favor you.

We decided not to change anything in the program but to carry our cross to the end. I began the concert with a troubled heart and heavy hands. I felt like apologizing to the audience, "Excuse me, I can do better." After the Mozart, to save the situation, I began trying harder, and that was the worst thing I could have done. We "delivered" Prokofiev in the style of "socialist realism," not typical for us, fast, loud, and empty. In the second half I tried to play Brahms in broad phrasing, with "soul," but it didn't work; the music never came alive.

Good concerts come and go; bad ones stay with you forever. Perhaps this one was no tragedy, for the audience seemed pleased. However, when you play below your potential, even under extenuating circumstances, you feel inferior, and you need another concert right away to redeem yourself.

All this was weighing on my heart after the concert, when, still in our tails, the six of us, including Ursula and Rosy, sat in the hotel restaurant. Ursula, sensing that something was wrong, had ordered an expensive dinner with Moselle wine. Our tails and the wine evidently looked good to outsiders, because people turned to watch us, and the waiters, smelling money, bustled around us.

"Well," said Berlinsky finally. "Why such a glum table? After all, it was our first real concert and we should drink to that."

"You played very well," said Ursula.

"We can play better," I answered. "It will be better tomorrow."

"It was splendid!" she repeated.

"And what does Rosy think?" asked Berlinsky. "Did you like it?"

"I like it!" answered Rosy, laughing.

"You were in the hall," insisted Berlinsky. "What were people saying?"

"I don't know," said Rosy.

"Ursula, why didn't you sit in the audience?"

"I stay with you always," she answered simply.

I raised my wineglass. "Ursula! It's a pleasure to drink to you. In one day you've become a member of our quartet. You helped us very much."

"What did he say?" Rosy asked Ursula.

Ursula quickly translated into German.

"I also helped," said Rosy.

"Of course, of course," answered Berlinsky. "You too."

Alexandrov turned to Ursula. "You understand Russian excellently."

"And you, I heard, speak German very well?"

"Ein Wenig und sehr schlecht."

"Not bad," Ursula praised him. "You studied in school?"

"Yes, but I've forgotten a lot. If you would speak German with me . . ."

"Ursula needs Russian," interrupted Berlinsky.

"It's Rosy that needs Russian," countered Alexandrov. "Why don't you help her?"

"I'll try," said Berlinsky complacently.

I watched the girls. Rosy was holding a glass of wine, looking at Berlinsky and understanding nothing. Ursula was eating, keeping her eyes down, understanding everything.

The next morning when we got in the car, the girls no longer waited for our invitation. Ursula sat up front with Helmut, Rosy in back with Berlinsky, and we three in the middle. Alexandrov and Shebalin had begun to put on weight, and it was cramped for the three of us, but since it was now the women's fault, male solidarity forced us to tolerate the discomfort without complaint. The depressing feeling after yesterday's concert had softened overnight, and we could even discuss our performance. I said that I would like to repeat the same program in Weimar, especially the Mozart. I was sure that today everything would be better.

We drove on the Autobahn. In the back we could hear Rosy laughing, although she didn't understand what Berlinsky was saying.

Ursula spoke with Helmut in German, then turned to us. "We'll be passing Buchenwald now. It's kept as a museum. Would you like to see it? It's close."

"Can I stay in the car?" I asked.

Ursula translated and Helmut nodded understandingly.

"It might be interesting," remarked Alexandrov. "What do you think?" He turned to Berlinsky.

"What? I didn't hear. What are you talking about?"

"Don't bother him," I said. "Better drive straight to Weimar. Today we have to play well."

Helmut started telling Ursula something. She listened attentively, then turned to us. "He says that the Germans found out about those camps only after the war. It was so unexpected that at first people refused to believe it."

"And when did they appear, the camps?" Alexandrov asked.

Ursula translated and Helmut thought for a while. Then, when he started talking again, Ursula translated as he spoke. "Probably right after Hitler came to power, in 1933. At first they were only for political enemies—Communists and Social Democrats. But soon there appeared special camps, whole settlements just for Jews. When the war began, there were a lot of prisoners from other countries. They were used as laborers, and the camps spread across Europe like mushrooms after rain."

"There must have been millions of prisoners," Alexandrov mused. "An army like that has to be fed . . ."

"That was simple—they didn't feed them. Or just enough to keep them alive."

We fell silent. But Helmut felt like talking. Perhaps the subject was a sore point, or else he had a good audience and wanted to show us what the Germans themselves thought about their recent past.

"Worst of all," he continued, "there were special death camps. Scientists worked only on how to kill people faster and cleaner. Hitler chose Poland as the place for the 'solution' of the Jewish problem. The gas chambers in Auschwitz, Majdanek, Treblinka, and others worked day and night."

"And in Germany itself?"

"I only know about Buchenwald and Dachau. There they had 'purely scientific' experiments. They injected people with different diseases and tried out medicine on them. They practiced surgical techniques, of course without anesthetics, and all sorts of things, on living people."

"How many died in Buchenwald?"

"About 60,000."

"And in the others?"

"I don't know for sure . . . Many. Very many."

"And this is the country of Beethoven," Alexandrov murmured.

"*Nein, mein Herr!*" Helmut answered without waiting for a translation.

I thought he could have just as easily said, "And there, to the east, is the land of Tchaikovsky."

Concentration camps appeared in Germany in 1933, but they had arrived in the Soviet Union in 1918, fifteen years earlier. The Nazis' main victims were Jews and war prisoners, while the Communists fought against their own people: the terror of the first years of the Revolution; the millions of peasants driven off their land during collectivization in 1929–30; the political trials of 1935–36 and the mass arrests of 1937–38; the repression of the Baltic states, seized in 1939; and the liquidation of returning prisoners of war, liberated in 1945 and returned to the "motherland" by the Allies. Helmut mentioned 60,000 victims in Buchenwald. But how about the tens of millions of lives destroyed by the Soviet regime?

I felt myself getting worked up and was glad when we finally arrived in Weimar. Ursula said that Weimar was home to the famous Liszt museum, and if we wanted we could stop by.

"Maybe for half an hour?" I suggested. "You never know when we'll be in Weimar again."

"And when will we be in Buchenwald?" Alexandrov asked bitingly.

I answered him, very softly, "Soon . . ."

"Then let's visit Liszt first!" he said loudly.

Still under the effects of Helmut's story, we felt none of the usual reverent awe in Liszt's house. Everything was rather ordinary. Even though Liszt slept here, dined there . . .

We went up to see Liszt's piano, and Alexandrov, holding back a smile, said to Shebalin, "Now we just need to play 'Moscow Nights' and we can go."

"Don't be sacrilegious!" shouted Berlinsky.

To be polite, we stood for a while in silence and wrote a respectful note in the visitors' book.

Our second concert in Weimar went well. Everything seemed to fall into place, and finally, we had the necessary feeling of confidence before a concert. It's funny how we only need one normal day: to sleep horizontally in a private room, to practice calmly and have an ordinary rehearsal, to take a nap after lunch, and to warm up before the concert.

We even went onstage differently, more freely and cheerfully. When we sat down, we began playing at once, as if it were the most natural act in the world. We performed the Borodin Quartet No. 2 in D-major, with the unrestrained music-making it required. In Shostakovich's fourth quartet we didn't hold back our emotions. It was surprising that our conversation with Helmut had taken place today, because Shostakovich's music was about that very subject—the so-called right of some people to destroy others. With Helmut we had spoken about Hitler's Germany, but now we were playing a piece about Stalin's Russia. By allowing Shostakovich's music to be played, the Soviet authorities had significantly complicated their lives, because the truth about the Soviet regime, concealed so carefully, began to reach the hearts of people all over the world. Judging by the silent hall, it was clear that his tale about twentieth-century tyranny was heard and understood. We ended the concert with Schubert, who, after the Shostakovich, acquired a special philosophical depth: as if regimes and rulers may come and go but another life, pure and elevated, remains undamaged.

We met with immense success, the kind I would always wish to have. We felt that with our music we had told people something important about their lives and themselves.

We were called back again and again. The audience wouldn't leave.

"Shall we play an encore?" asked Berlinsky.

"Not necessary," I said. "It's fine now."

"I suggest we play."

"Let's go out without the instruments. If they call us one more time . . ."

We went out and stood there longer. The audience rose from their seats and stood applauding.

We went backstage. The applause finally faded.

"We should have played an encore," said Berlinsky.

I didn't answer. I didn't yet know that I was making an important discovery for myself: when the program contains its own development, an encore isn't necessary. A concert whose program consists of three different composers is a psychological drama in three acts. And if in a concert, as if in a play, you have said everything you could and even died at the end, what more can you do?

People began coming to our dressing room. They came up to each of us, thanked us emotionally, and asked us to sign their programs. This went on for quite a while, and I had started signing without looking at the people, when a familiar voice said, *"Und ein für mich, bitte . . ."*

I looked up. It was Helmut. I wanted to tell him that he had also taken part in today's concert and that, if it hadn't been for him, maybe . . . and I wrote on his program *"Für dieses Konzert danke ich Ihnen!"* Then the girls came up. Ursula was crying, Rosy was trying to look serious. They both kissed me at the same time, one on each cheek . . .

* * *

On the way to Jena, Rosy began to follow Berlinsky everywhere and kept trying to carry his suitcase. Finally he gave her a music stand, and said that she must guard it with her life. Rosy took this very seriously. She brought it to the concert and fussed with it for a long time, until I showed her how to set it up. Rosy looked sad. She waited until no one was around and took me by the hand.

"I want to go to Moscow," she said.

"Why?" I asked stupidly.

"I want to go to Moscow," she repeated. I could see she was about to cry.

"But how will you get there?"

"With you."

"How?"

"Somehow . . . With the suitcase."

I didn't understand. "You need a visa."

"With the suitcase," she said stubbornly.

"Do you mean 'in the suitcase'?"

Rosy nodded. "I go with the big suitcase. I'm small."

"We'll discuss this after the concert," I promised.

"Really?"

"Definitely."

Rosy kissed my hand.

Before the concert I took Berlinsky aside. "Listen, what's the matter with Rosy?"

"Don't ask me! She's torturing me. Wants to come with me to Moscow."

"And what did you tell her?"

"It's useless to talk to her. She doesn't want to listen."

"Tell her you're married."

"I did. She doesn't believe it."

"Poor little girl. She'll have a hard time."

"Could you . . . you know . . . distract her?"

"I'm afraid it's too late."

We played the last concert. The first half, Borodin and Shostakovich, went well, but without the heartbreaking revelations of the day before.

After these composers, Tchaikovsky was hard to play. We didn't have enough emotion. If Shostakovich's music, though deeply personal, still rises to dramatic generalization, then Tchaikovsky, with his painful longing, makes a person even more lonely. It seemed to me that these two composers shouldn't be in the same program, since one is the other's antithesis. Only by his suicide could Tchaikovsky find the eternal peace which eluded him during his lifetime, while for Shostakovich there was no comfort in death, but rather a protest.

On the drive back to Berlin, Berlinsky sat in back and Rosy immediately crawled in after him. The idea of spending the night squeezed as if in a vise, three in one seat, was not the most appealing, and Shebalin (the stoutest among us) asked Ursula if she wouldn't mind letting him sit in front with Helmut, while she . . .

He hadn't finished speaking when Ursula wedged in between Alexandrov and me. Helmut started the engine.

It was quiet in the car. Rosy didn't make a sound. Ursula sat motionless between us. Time passed. Shebalin fell asleep in the front seat. I looked back. With both arms around Berlinsky's neck, Rosy was sleeping like a baby. I caught his eloquent glance and smiled at him sympathetically. He shrugged. Ursula and Alexandrov were looking straight ahead. What were they waiting for? For me to fall asleep? That could be arranged. I leaned my head back and closed my eyes. When after a while I opened them again, Ursula's head was on Alexandrov's shoulder and he had his arm around her . . .

I woke up when something jabbed me. In the dim light of the passing streetlights Alexandrov was staring at me. Ursula was asleep, leaning on his shoulder.

"I've 'overplayed' my shoulder and arm," he whispered. "Could you continue the 'fugue'?"

"We need to retune the instrument," I answered. "The keys might not fit."

"I'll try to change my bow smoothly."

Very gently, he leaned her head against my shoulder.

It began to grow lighter. We drove into Berlin, through familiar streets, and stopped at the Johanneshof Hotel.

"We're here!" announced Alexandrov loudly.

His voice sounded sharp after the mysterious night silence. Everyone stirred.

We got out of the car, kissed the girls, and firmly shook Helmut's hand. "*Auf Wiedersehen, Helmut, vielen Dank für alles!*"

"Goodbye, Ursula. Thanks for everything!"

"Goodbye, Rosy!"

Ursula gazed for a long time at each of us. Rosy looked only at Berlinsky, and her lips silently repeated, "With the suitcase . . ."

The Soviet delegation was generously paid by the East German government. We accepted the money as Soviet people abroad always do: with ostentatious indifference but inward rejoicing. Of course, we remembered that in our country an overabundance was promised year after year. Still, it was wiser to buy everything necessary abroad, so that back home we could believe the promises more easily.

We spent our last day shopping. To begin with, I went through every floor of the big Kaufhaus, not daring to approach the counters. I met my colleagues several times, and they all looked just as perplexed as I was. Bringing German money back to Moscow was strictly forbidden; the thick envelope with the "governmental present" made a lump in my jacket. I shyly went up to the toy department and felt my heart beat faster. I saw a huge metal Erector set with plenty of wheels and even a little motor. I had dreamed of such a set my whole childhood, then naturally forgot, and suddenly, after twenty years, before I could think what I needed it for now, I bought it.

"Well, that's not so hard," I said to myself. "Let's look at the suits . . ."

The suits were followed by shirts, linen, shoes, ties . . . Once I had several large packages in each hand, I went out, took a taxi, put everything in my hotel room, and returned to the store. I grew bolder, the speed of my purchases increased, and, overloaded with things, I took another taxi to the hotel. I came back and started spending money in a kind of frenzy. As the store began to close, I still had some money left, and I found myself in the women's department. I suddenly remembered and, calling myself an idiot, I ran up to the salesgirl, who was already looking at her watch. I put all my remaining money in front of her and asked her, in my broken German, to choose things for a small girl.

"How old?" she asked.

How old must Olya be, judging by her figure? I remembered that she was very small. But I couldn't explain to the salesgirl that she was already a woman, that she had spent most of her life in a Soviet camp, that it was a wonder she was still alive, as small as a girl of about . . .

"About fifteen," I said.

I nodded to everything the salesgirl showed me, and when there was a mountain of clothes I asked her to add up my bill and to count my money.

"Something else?" she asked.

"No, thanks. That's all."

She wrapped a huge package. I took twenty marks for a taxi and offered her the rest. "That's for you."

"*Nein, nein*," she protested.

"*Bitte*," I asked softly, looking in her eyes.

She looked around and took the money. "Have a safe trip home."

I was packing for half the night and wound up with four suitcases and several packages. I went to see my colleagues. From each room I heard swearing and the rustle of paper. I knocked and glanced in. Sweating, half undressed, they all stood in more or less the same pensive pose in the middle of a room scattered with things.

"You want some help?" I would ask.

"Catastrophe!" they all answered.

In the morning, when our delegation gathered downstairs, we didn't recognize each other at first. Everyone was dressed in foreign clothes, even the general, who was returning to Moscow in civilian attire. Everyone was excited. You could tell that no one had slept. To avoid attracting unnecessary attention, our baggage was left in our rooms. Another bus would bring everything to the airport.

We crossed the airfield solemnly. Our "German comrades" saw us off. At the plane there was a brief farewell speech about friendship, wishes for a good trip, handshakes, and we climbed the stairs. The plane rolled onto the runway, took off, and headed east.

Olya
1955

O<small>LYA</small> had become thinner. Her face looked longer and her features sharper. She watched me as I carried my suitcases into the house and tried to help me. I hated to think that the suitcase, although it was not very heavy, might weigh more than she did. She led me into the biggest room. It probably had been the living room.

"I hope you'll be comfortable here," Olya said. "This room's the best in the house."

"May I look at the others?"

"There are two more besides mine, but they're so small . . ."

"Let's take a look."

We went into the adjoining room. "This is for me," I said. "I'm used to little rooms. It's easier to work in them: your thoughts don't run away."

Olya smiled, but it was better when she didn't; in her smile there was so much sadness that it became hard to bear.

"Let's go, I'll show you something," I said cheerfully, and I opened "her" suitcase. A dress lay on top. Here in Moscow it looked even better than in Berlin. I said, as lightly as I could, "Try it on! Anyway, this is all yours."

She didn't move.

"Please," I asked again. "I hope you like it."

She took the dress and went out. When she came back I didn't recognize her. She glanced at herself in the mirror and started crying.

"Forgive me!" she said. "It reminded me of my childhood in Canada, when I would get a new dress for my birthday."

I bent down and picked up the suitcase. "I'll put this in your room. You can look through it later."

She followed me. "I know that what I'm going to say is stupid, but . . . You mustn't feel that you owe me anything. You're absolutely free. When I invited you here I only wanted you to . . . that here . . . for you . . ."

I took her by the shoulders and shook her slightly. She stopped talking. "Tell me, Olya, do you still remember English?"

"What a question! Why?"

"Would you teach me, maybe?"

Her glance was more eloquent than words.

"Splendid! When's the first lesson?"

"Whenever you want."

A little later, when Olya and I were sitting at the table drinking tea, I noticed that she had already gone through her new clothes. The lifelessness in her eyes, which had scared me before, was gone. Instead, she listened to my story about the trip as if it were already a part of her new life. Her breathing came faster when I spoke about our nervousness before a concert and how our hands would suddenly stop obeying. When she noted that in chamber music the participation of the listeners was more important than in any other kind of music, I gasped at how perceptively it was expressed. "Because," Olya continued, "chamber music is not a show but an experience, and in the life of each person in the hall something will be found for sharing it." I understood that now I would have an ally in music and my own special listener.

During the days I spent with Olya, I would wake up late and wander around the house. Although I had never before done much housekeeping, now my hands itched to repair something.

Olya taught me English, and during these lessons she grew more lively. The first English words I learned were "hello" and "okay."

On my first day I could already say, "I am okay," and even ask, "Are you okay?" Olya said I should memorize new words every day, best of all before going to sleep. It was excellent advice. I learned ten new words every night and would proudly recite them to Olya the next morning.

I would pick up my violin late in the evening, when most people had usually gone to bed. Olya would be playing in her room, but very carefully, pausing every time I stopped. I told her she could have a week to herself, but after that she would have to play for me.

"You teach me English, and I'll teach you violin!" I threatened.

Although I put my violin away very late at night, Olya wouldn't go to bed; instead, she would read, waiting for me to finish practicing. Then we would sit down and drink tea and take a walk outside.

It was very quiet. Trying not to break the silence, we would walk slowly to the river, right to the very edge of the water. The river was dark, even darker than the street. It flowed quietly, but if you stood still and listened, you could hear it. Dampness rose from the water, and Olya, shivering a little, moved closer to me.

It was odd, but I didn't feel a "woman" in her. And then I would remember what kind of life she had had, and I felt her pain. Carefully, I put my arm around her shoulders . . .

After a week, when Olya felt a bit braver, we had our first violin lesson. She understood right away from my expression that something was wrong. I told her to close her eyes and remember the movement of her arm when I moved her bow up and down. "The arm," I said, "should follow the bow as its continuation."

I was carefully moving Olya's hand, holding her elbow and wrist, when suddenly I felt her arm shaking.

"Are you feeling ill?" I asked.

She didn't answer. I took away her violin and bow, and with difficulty led her to bed and made her lie down. She had begun trembling even more.

"Has this happened before?"

"N-no," she said, her teeth chattering.

"Are you cold?"

"N-n-no . . ."

"Should I call the doctor?"

"D-d-don't . . ."

I lay beside Olya and held her with both arms. I felt her trembling from head to foot. Then she whispered something. I could hardly make out the words: "I n-ne . . . I've never . . . Not yet . . ."

And I understood. "It will be painful," I said.

"Pain . . . It's not frightening," she whispered.

"I'm afraid of hurting you."

"Please don't be . . ."

She didn't make a sound, only clenched her teeth, trying to stop trembling. Later, when she had calmed down, she lay without moving for a long time and, finally, opened her eyes.

"Hello," I said in English.

She smiled. "Hello."

"Are you okay?"

"Yes, I am okay."

I went to my room, lay on my back, and looked at the ceiling. I thought about our return from Berlin. The status of government delegation had been maintained to the end; we went through customs without a check; Ushakov and the general were met by black limousines, and we were given a bus with a driver. Getting off the bus, people said goodbye loudly and fussed over their many suitcases. My colleagues got off one by one, and soon I was in the bus alone. The driver looked at me questioningly, and I was ashamed to tell him that we had to go back across the whole city to Silver Grove.

"Where were you before? I could have taken you right away on the way from Sheremetyevo."

"I'm sorry. I'm going to Silver Grove for the first time."

"Where did you live before?"

"On Taganka."

"Got married, or just an acquaintance?"

"How should I say . . . neither."

"I understand," the driver said.

I smiled to myself. "He understands . . . And I don't. Should I tell him? Then maybe I'll understand better. He's a stranger, we'll never meet again, and I don't even know Olya's last name, so the story won't really be hers."

And, strange as it may seem, as we drove along Gorky Street and then along the route of Olya's trolley, I told this stranger everything I knew about her. He listened sympathetically, without interrupting, and when I had finished said only, "Don't hurt her. She's suffered enough."

In Silver Grove, at the last trolley stop, I showed the driver the road to Olya's house and gave him a carton of German cigarettes—a fortune in Moscow. He helped me with my suitcases and drove away, and I knocked on the door. I heard hurried steps. Olya opened the door . . .

I came back to reality. "Olya! How is she?"

I got up and carefully peered into her room. Olya was still asleep. I was glad. Now, probably, she felt calm.

I decided to go out and phone the quartet, to tell them my new address. The season hadn't ended yet and we still might get some concerts.

I was dressing quietly, trying not to wake Olya, when a taxi drove up to the house, a door slammed, and there was a knock. I opened the door and didn't believe my eyes: it was Berlinsky.

" 'If Muhammad doesn't go to the mountain,' " he began solemnly.

" 'Then the mountain comes to Muhammad,' " I finished. "How did you find me?"

"The intelligence service works," he said, pleased.

"Sounds ominous . . . Come in!"

Olya came out of her room.

"Let me introduce you," I said.

Squeezing Olya's hand and looking into her eyes, Berlinsky said, "I remember you! That time at the Philharmonia . . ."

Olya blushed. "Please sit down," she said, confused.

"Unfortunately there's no time to sit down. We have to go . . . ."

"Where?" I asked.

"We are expected," he said importantly. "Put on your best suit."

"Something serious?"

"I'll tell you on the way."

"I don't like it when people leave," said Olya.

Berlinsky smiled at her gently. "Don't worry. He'll come back." Then he added in the pleasant voice he had when he talked to women, "This time he will."

Olya saw us to the gate. Berlinsky held out his hand. "Sorry to disturb your idyll. But . . . business, you understand."

"I'll be back soon," I said.

"I'll wait," answered Olya.

"A sweet woman," said Berlinsky once we were a little way from the house. "Is she . . . Recently?"

"Yes," I said.

"It shows . . . Poor little thing."

We got on the empty trolley. "Well, tell me," I said. "How did you find me?"

"Very simple. The driver gave us your address."

"Oh, that's it! Simple and brilliant. And where are we going?"

"To see Schepalin."

"Gleb? Is he still Kholodilin's assistant?"

"Higher! He's already Kholodilin. And will go even further."

Kholodilin was the alternate head of the Cultural Office. When the forbidden bourgeois word "ministry" was rehabilitated, he was transformed accordingly into the vice minister, and his new assistant was my former conservatory fellow Gleb Schepalin. He had been a violinist in the conservatory also. In my mind's eye, I could see him with his violin case, but I could never remember having heard him play. He even managed to finish the conservatory without playing his final diploma recital. In his case it was irrelevant, because soon after his inglorious graduation, he was invited to work in the Ministry of Culture. He made his way at once into Kholodilin's circle, and very soon became his assistant. Now, whenever we met on the street, he would give me two fingers to shake. This indicated a certain respect for me, because to the rest of his former conservatory colleagues he gave only one, if any.

Alexandrov and Shebalin were waiting for us on the street. Together we climbed up the already familiar staircase. Schepalin himself opened his office door and with a broad gesture invited us in, holding out all five fingers to be shaken. Schepalin had changed a lot; he was twice his former size, and a wide gray suit made his figure even more imposing. Who would have thought that out of the pale, thin conservatory student would develop such a solid vice minister! Schepalin waited a little, clearly thinking over his first words, while we were respectfully silent.

"I hear you had a successful trip to the G.D.R.," he began at last.

"Not too bad," said Berlinsky carefully.

"And what did you play?"

This was my department. I noticed Berlinsky's warning glance.

"We sent the Germans four programs, but they were mostly interested in Russian and Soviet music."

Schepalin nodded. "You see, that's what I'd like to talk about."

And listening to himself with pleasure, he told us about the Russian Music Festival in Moldavia, littering the words "important task" and "responsibility." The State Orchestra, he explained, was to go with leading soloists, while chamber music—he paused significantly—"chamber music we entrust to you."

"Thank you for your confidence in us," Berlinsky managed to say.

"Well, what do you have in the way of Soviet music?"

"Why, just about everything," I answered.

"Really!"

"And if something's missing," Berlinsky added, "we can prepare it."

"Very good." Schepalin nodded. "What can you suggest?"

"Shostakovich," I said.

In spite of his recent rehabilitation, in this room the composer's name still sounded anti-Soviet. Schepalin hesitated and then, as if deciding, said, "At the conservatory I played his first quartet. A charming piece—bright and joyful."

Somehow these words did not suit Shostakovich, though in the first quartet, written in C-major before the war, the carelessness of youth is still felt. That's exactly why no one ever took this quartet quite seriously.

"That's just the piece for the festival!" said Schepalin.

Over my dead body, I thought, but aloud I said, "We've just played his fourth in Germany."

"I don't know it," answered Schepalin. "Is it good?"

My colleagues answered all at once:

"Remarkable!"

"Very strong!"

"A great success!"

"Well . . . I have no objection," said Schepalin generously. "But we are also interested in the works of other composers."

"Sure, sure," said Berlinsky hurriedly, and he looked at me.

Following his eyes, Schepalin also stared at me.

"We have some interesting pieces by Soviet composers," I said, feeling disgusted with myself.

"Splendid . . . I suggest that you make up a few programs and show them to me."

"We will."

"Very good," said the vice minister, and he began to get up slowly from his chair. "It's been a pleasure to meet and talk to my colleagues."

"Colleagues," my foot! I thought. Between these "colleagues" is a gulf wide enough to accommodate the whole Soviet hierarchy.

"They'll greet you for your clothes, but see you off for your wits" —so goes the Russian proverb. I'm afraid that in Soviet times the second half of this proverb has lost some of its applicability, while the meaning of the first half has grown immensely.

We experienced it ourselves. Our foreign suits, which we began to wear, made an immediate impression. People openly examined them and even felt the material. Suddenly we had a lot of acquaintances. They not only started talking to us but even listened to us and, as we later learned, repeated what we said. It was the so-called foreign syndrome, a disease which afflicts Soviet society from top to bottom. When the word got out that in the autumn we would be going to two countries in a row, Czechoslovakia and Rumania, we were counted among the chosen. We began to be scheduled at home as well. We were booked for concerts in Moscow and Leningrad and tours around the country. They couldn't resist the aura of success abroad.

In Moscow, Olya came with me to all our concerts, and afterward, while we sat in the trolley for the long ride home, she would discuss music as I never could. Because I am a performer I cannot experience the direct influence of my own playing. If someone asks me after a concert how I played, I answer honestly, "I don't know." I know only too well how many notes I missed, but as to the impression the quartet's playing makes on the listener, I can only guess from the reactions of the audience or from what I'm told after the concert. And although I knew that relying on other people's opinions can be dangerous (since there are as many opinions as people), I felt that Olya's pronouncements deserved to be written down. She spoke of concerts as treasures, acquired by searching and labor. And since she never paid attention to the failures, but only to the depths and summits of our playing, I often looked forward to her critiques more than to the concerts themselves. Of course, praise is always pleasant, but I hoped that it was not just her subjective opinion but the truth.

So one night, when we got on the half-empty trolley, and I laid the violin across our knees, Olya, understanding what I was waiting for, began at once.

"You aren't afraid of the slow flow of the music. You yourself enter into its sound, and you make us do the same. As if you are thinking aloud on the stage and so make the music audible."

"More!" I begged.

"You also approach the performance in a new way. With you, the composition, even though it has been heard many times, becomes an artistic surprise."

I began to believe that it really was that way.

"Just listening to you is insufficient. One must listen and think of what you are talking about. Following every detail. From them arise images, from the images—generalization. The beginning of Borodin's second quartet, its unforeseen flexibility, is real sorcery."

"I wonder whether it would have pleased Borodin. Shostakovich, for one, doesn't like interpretation."

"Borodin would have liked it," said Olya assuredly.

Moldavia

1956

FESTIVALS of Russian music in the Soviet republics were meant to cover up the destruction in Soviet music caused by the Party and the government in 1948. The musical depression which ensued was passed off by obedient propagandists as the flowering of Soviet music. And Soviet composers, many of them with a Party card in their pocket, quickly responded to the Party's call to create "masterpieces," accessible to the people and reflecting their "heroic feat of labor in the building of Communism." From the concert stages onto the stupefied listener poured a flood of primitive and empty music, for which the government generously handed out Stalin Prizes. In the quartet's early years, we played works dedicated to the Young Pioneers, the Komsomol, heroes of the civil war and World War II, and toilers of the fields and factories. Usually all these *chefs d'oeuvre* were played "two times at once"—the very first and the very last—but sometimes, under pressure from above, some of that rubbish had to be repeated. So in our official concert in Moldavia we had to play what was recommended: something we didn't believe in ourselves and which could not give any pleasure to the listeners. As a reward, we were allowed to play Shostakovich's fourth quartet in the second half of the program.

In contrast to the toothless and anemic music, each note of Shostakovich spread through the hall like a voice crying out in the wilderness. The big concert hall, filled with the Moldavian Party elite, of course, was that very wilderness, but the first row was occupied by leading Moscow composers, with Shostakovich himself in the center.

Sitting in front, he probably thought no one could see him, and his face unwittingly reflected what he had wanted to say with his music. But I saw his face: the contorted mouth and the eyes of a pursued, wounded animal. His face was the strongest impression I remember of the whole festival, a sharp contrast to the officially lacquered lie with which the authorities covered their crimes.

Twice in his life—in 1936 and in 1948—Shostakovich had suffered a "civil execution." Stones flew through his windows, accompanied by shouts of "Formalist," "Traitor," "Trotskyite," and even "American spy." The natural end of this "ideological" campaign should have been physical execution, but by some miracle that didn't happen. The expectation of violent death, however, became the main theme in Shostakovich's music and was stamped forever on his face.

We played the fourth quartet with this subtext of life and death. We were in no danger: the music was officially permitted, and the notes, after all, were only innocent sounds, all sorts of F-sharps and B-flats. Even Mozart and Beethoven played with them! Notes are not words, not yet—even in the U.S.S.R.! But playing now to Shostakovich about Shostakovich, we felt we were not obedient Soviet court musicians but fearless unmaskers of evil and hypocrisy. It's easy to be brave when there's no menace, but what kind of courage must it take when you risk your life for the truth!

We had just finished playing. The final pianissimo, like a last sigh, flew off into the hall and returned to us as a barely audible echo. We tried to prolong the silence, but the audience interfered. Destroying the fragile world of brief truth, uncertain applause broke out in the hall. We rose slowly, bowed very low to Shostakovich, and left the stage. The applause died out without gaining strength.

"Well, to hell with all of you," swore Berlinsky softly.

"I agree," I answered. "To understand that music, they'd have to forget about their Party card for half an hour."

"No, no. I meant that Shostakovich heard us, and that is enough."

"We could have played to Shostakovich in Moscow, without dragging ourselves to Moldavia."

"It's an important political trip," said Alexandrov significantly. "Even more important than going abroad."

We were putting away our instruments when the composer Nikolai Peyko came backstage.

"Thank you for the music! Dmitri Dmitrievich was very moved by your playing."

"Did he say anything?"

"No, he didn't. He couldn't speak at all."

"Thank you for coming to see us!"

"No, I thank you! Listen, could we have dinner together?"

"With pleasure. And invite Shostakovich. What do you think? Will he refuse?"

"Shostakovich has never refused anything to anyone. Many people take advantage of that."

"Then maybe we shouldn't, for that reason."

"We'll see how he feels. I think he will be pleased. After such a performance . . ."

"The audience didn't have much of a reaction."

"What are you talking about? That's no audience. It's a . . . Anyway, I'll meet you in the restaurant."

We changed quickly and went downstairs. At the restaurant door stood Peyko.

"Too late! Shostakovich was already invited to dinner by the ministry. Schepalin himself. To compete, you understand, is impossible. But Dmitri Dmitrievich asked that the quartet be there. So they're waiting for you."

We went into the restaurant. Shostakovich quickly rose to greet us, nervously shook our four hands, and four times repeated something like "Thank you for playing me . . ."

Schepalin watched us paternally, clapped his hands as if applauding, and said, like a host, "Please be seated!"

About ten other composers were there. On the table stood vodka and a dozen bottles of the fashionable Moldavian wine Fetyaska. But no one looks at wine if there's vodka on the table. Everyone began busily pouring vodka for one another and passing hors d'oeuvres.

With a shot glass in his outstretched hand, Peyko rose from his chair. "I suggest a toast, to the Borodin Quartet!"

"Absolutely, to Borodin, of course, to the quartet," Shostakovich said rapidly, raising and splashing his vodka.

"I wish to add," said Schepalin evenly, "that for a long time we have been following the growth of our quartet, and we are grateful for the assistance it has given to Soviet music."

A hum of praise and congratulations broke out on all sides, and then, as if on command, everyone fell silent: they were drinking the vodka. I made a sign to my colleagues to wait and then, once they had put down their glasses, said, "Tune the instruments, and here we go . . . Up bow!"

We drank and simultaneously thumped our glasses on the table.

"Now I understand why the quartet has such an ensemble," said Schepalin loudly, and everyone at the table laughed. Hands reached for vodka bottles. Someone obligingly filled my glass, and I thanked him. From the attention the quartet was given, it was clear that we had passed our entrance examination into proper society.

After the second glass, everyone wanted to talk. Disconnected phrases came to me from all corners of the table. Shebalin got a good laugh by saying that he himself drank very little, never more than one glass of vodka, which was enough to make him feel like a new man, but then this new man would also want a drink, and that was the cause of all sorts of trouble.

Shostakovich calmed down. He began to tell (and everyone at the table stopped talking) about how he had traveled to America.

"On the day of my departure my visa still wasn't ready, but they assured me that once I got to Reykjavík everything would be in order. I had a bad flight and was feeling sick, when two American journalists came up to me. They had flown to Reykjavík especially to be the very first to interview me. I was about to give them a hint about the, so to speak, poor timing of this undertaking when suddenly one of them, a

big healthy guy, slapped me on the back and roared, 'Hello, Shosty!'
I flew into the restroom, where I finally took care of my airsickness . . ."

"What a wonderful start on the way to America!" someone pointed
out. "What happened next?"

"Next, you see, there was nothing. And no visa either, so after an
hour I flew back to Moscow."

Once everyone was done laughing, the composer Evgeny Golubev,
who was sitting on my left, turned to me. "Today I was reminded
again how important the performance is for a new composition. I had
listened to the fourth quartet before, but today, I have to admit, I
heard it for the first time."

I answered with the appropriate gratitude, and Golubev continued,
"I also have a quartet which has been waiting a long time for its
performers."

"It hasn't been performed?"

"Only on the piano, four hands."

"I'll call you once we get back to Moscow."

"I have the score here with me. If you agree . . ."

"I'll stop by after dinner," I said.

"Thank you! I hope you like it."

Outside the room there was a noise; then the door flew open and
we saw a large man in a leather jacket.

"What is the trouble?" asked Peyko, and went to the door, but several
waiters dragged the man out and closed the door. Peyko stopped next
to me and smiled. "I see your glass is empty! That's disorder. Allow
me to pour some for you." He reached for the vodka bottle.

"I'd better have wine," I said.

"Then a goblet. I want wine, too."

I felt uncomfortable with him standing behind me, and I got up.
With our goblets in our hands, we stepped away from the table and,
looking into each other's eyes, took a sip.

"Good wine," said Peyko. "Nothing like this in Moscow."

"They say it can't tolerate transportation."

"It tolerates it as far as Moscow, but just doesn't make it to the
shops. It's sent straight . . . where it's supposed to go."

"Oh, that's it! I can't ever get used to the simplest explanations."

We drank the rest. Transparent and light, it went down without the slightest effort.

"More?" asked Peyko.

"Why not?"

He neatly filled our glasses to the brim. "Tell me, are you acquainted with Boris Tchaikovsky?"

"To say hello to. Why?"

"He recently finished his second quartet. He played it for me on the piano. In my opinion, it's a splendid work."

"It would be interesting to hear it," I answered obediently.

We both looked at Tchaikovsky, who, noticing our gaze, got up and came toward us.

"What are you two gossiping about?"

"We are speaking about music," answered Peyko, "and about wine."

"Then we must drink," said Tchaikovsky, pouring wine for himself and turning to me. "You played Shostakovich remarkably today."

"Thank you!"

"After the concert Dmitri Dmitrievich couldn't even speak."

"Let's drink to Shostakovich."

We clinked our glasses.

"I often think," said Tchaikovsky emotionally, "that it's my greatest happiness to live at the same time as Shostakovich."

"We all feel that way," agreed Peyko.

"We're now about to begin his fifth quartet," I said.

"Have you played the second?"

"Not yet. We're waiting for the right audience. Especially for the second movement."

"Oh! The recitative!"

"I feel it as the 'Lament of Israel.' "

"Not only of Israel," said Peyko. "Well, let's drink!"

We all drank half a glass.

"I can let you in on a secret," said Tchaikovsky, glancing at me. "Nikolai Ivanovich has written a marvelous quartet. I recommend it highly!"

"Don't listen to him," said Peyko.

To refuse when we were drinking wine together—that would be unthinkable. "Give me the score," I said.

"On one condition: without any obligation. Only if it pleases you."

"It's a deal," I said.

We drank the rest of the wine and sat down at the table.

The door opened again, and the same leather-jacketed man entered the room. He came up to the table, looked everyone over, as if deciding whom to address, stopped at Shostakovich, and drawled, with a Ukrainian accent, "Russian people! Would you let me sit with you a little at the same table?"

The waiters looked into the room, ready to throw him out at the first sign from us.

"Of course, of course," said Shostakovich hurriedly. "Sit down with us at the same, so to speak, table."

The man was offered a chair and a glass of wine.

"Thank you for not scorning an ordinary man," he said, and raised his glass in the air. "To the Russian people!" he shouted, draining his glass in one breath and looking around triumphantly.

Conversation at the table had stopped. Our guest evidently felt that he had impressed the "Russian people," because he reached for the bottle, poured for himself, and suddenly, imitating a Jewish accent, began in an unpleasant voice, "Abram! What front did you fight on? The Tashkent line? And how much did your medals cost? And how much did you sell them for?"

"What filth!" Shostakovich shuddered. He reached for the vodka bottle. Seizing it and pouring with trembling hands, he spilled vodka on the tablecloth.

There was a heavy silence around the table. How often, in the presence of rudeness, cultured people are petrified!

Peyko, however, marched right up to the man, who stood up, sensing no good. Next to him, the skinny Peyko seemed like a little boy. Looking the intruder in the face, Peyko said very distinctly, "You, it turns out, are shit!"

The man gasped in surprise. "What?"

"Shit!" Peyko repeated firmly. "We welcomed you to the table as a man, and you . . . Get out!" he shouted.

The man started taking off his jacket, but the waiters, hearing the shout, rushed in and grabbed him. Two twisted his arms behind his back, a third grabbed his hair, two more took him by the belt, and all five dragged him out through the door.

I glanced around carefully. Not counting Berlinsky, I was probably the only Jew at the table! But around me were the kind of Russians who, at the least hint of anti-Semitism, are mortally offended, both for the Russian nation and for Russian culture.

Everything was quiet. People were trying not to look at one another. I felt there was a way to save the evening and, without thinking, I said, "What if we bring our instruments and play Dmitri Dmitrievich's quartet one more time?"

Everyone spoke together.

"Please do . . ."

"A wonderful idea!"

"What do you think, Dmitri Dmitrievich?"

"Well, why not. Go on, of course, very good . . . Let's play it once more . . ."

"I can't play," said Berlinsky. "I'm drunk."

"That doesn't matter," answered Shostakovich. "That's, you know, even better . . ."

"I'm drunk, too," said Shebalin. "But I'm a sportsman!"

"Bravo, bravo!"

"Nikolai Ivanovich," I said to Peyko, "while my colleagues have one more drink for courage, you and I can bring the instruments."

"Why trouble Nikolai Ivanovich," said Alexandrov, "I'll come with you."

We left the restaurant and headed for the elevator.

"Let's take the stairs," suggested Alexandrov. "I want to tell you something."

We climbed up one flight.

"Well, I could refuse to play now," he began uncertainly.

"What do you mean?"

"You don't have the right to propose a concert without the agreement of the whole quartet."

"You saw the situation, and Shostakovich's face, when that thug . . ."

"True. There was no time to discuss it, so you shouldn't have suggested anything."

"Everyone was so glad."

"That's their business. But I've warned you. Today I'll play, but it's the last time. Remember!"

"I will," I said.

We each took two instruments and two music stands and headed downstairs without speaking. Four chairs were already waiting for us in a corner of the room. I opened my case, got out the violin, checked the tuning . . . And suddenly I felt an unusual lightness and freedom in both hands. What was it? Surely not a glass or two of wine? If so, then such a creative path threatened to become extremely dangerous.

I looked at my colleagues. Alexandrov was tensely tuning his instrument and probably cursing me. Shebalin and Berlinsky had clearly drunk to excess, and it showed. The former wisely did not try to tune his instrument, but repeated that he was a "sportsman," while the latter's hands were visibly uncoordinated. He tried his solo from the second movement, and at one point his fingers turned up on one string while his bow was on another. He laughed and turned to Shostakovich.

"Dmitri Dmitrievich, forgive me if something is not just so . . ."

"Everything will be 'so,' don't worry, everything will be 'so' . . ."

We began to play. In the first movement there were problems. Someone was always late, and it proved impossible to lead the quartet; instead, it was led by whoever played the slowest. The second movement went better. A peculiar, drunkenly rhythmical balance, from which it was dangerous to diverge, had settled in the music. We played fairly successfully up to the recapitulation, where the initial melancholy melody reappeared. Several voices began to sing along with us . . .

It really means something if people sing Shostakovich's music!

They sang along again in the scherzo, which we played in the manner of a street gang's song. With the discordant voices there appeared a particular musical effect, which would be impossible to write into a quartet score. This seemed to please Shostakovich, because he also started singing . . .

This was unexpected and even frightening. I never heard Shosta-kovich sing before or after that evening.

Gradually the quartet got used to the drunkenness, and by the "Jewish" finale we were all playing confidently. After the incident with the man in the black leather jacket, it rang out in a somewhat different key.

There was neither applause nor praise, only the long silence that is so necessary after such music, until at last Peyko said, "We have to drink. And right away!"

Around the table people stirred; there was the sound of pouring liquid and the clink of glasses.

I put my violin in its case and furtively watched our vice minister. I saw his frozen stare and his forehead covered with sweat. It was clearer than ever, to him and to all of us, why this music had been banned, and not very understandable why they had suddenly permitted it. Schepalin rose decisively from the table. "Dmitri Dmitrievich," he said to Shostakovich, "it's already late, and tomorrow we have an important meeting early in the morning. I think it's time we got some rest."

"Yes, yes, it's already late and time to go, time to go," Shostakovich hurriedly repeated, also standing up. "My gratitude to the quartet. It's time for us . . . And the quartet . . . Thanks very much. You see, it's late already, and early tomorrow morning . . ."

Schepalin headed for the door, and Shostakovich hastened after him.

"We still have to drink," said Peyko, and in a sort of frenzy added, "To Shostakovich!"

Nothing better could be suggested now. We all raised our glasses and held them in the air, until the mystical link between Shostakovich and the wine became tangible . . .

Siberia

1957

ONE DAY, a week before the quartet was to leave for Siberia, Olya put on her best dress—the one I had bought in Berlin—and applied a little makeup to her face, but even so she didn't manage to hide the dark circles under her eyes. Together we walked slowly under the bright sun toward the Moskva River.

Not long before, a canal had been cut between two bends in the river, turning Silver Grove into an island around which one could walk in two hours. There were many aging scholars strolling with their plump wives. In our foreign clothes we attracted their attention; they looked us over and sometimes said hello.

When Olya got a little tired from walking, we headed straight home. We passed the police station and Olya said that while I had been away a local policeman had come by.

"We were already reported! What did he want?"

"He asked whether everything was in order, but looked around very attentively."

"It's because of me. Without a residence permit I can't live here."

"If he comes, we'll say you came just yesterday and are leaving tomorrow."

"It's almost true."

"When do you leave?"

"In a week."

"For the east?"

"Yes, to the Krasnoyarsk region!"

"For a long time?"

I nodded and we were both silent.

Olya usually ate very little, but at dinner that night she didn't eat anything. Later that evening, when we were lying by the open window, I asked how she felt.

"Fine," she said, turning away.

"You haven't eaten anything."

"I can't. If I force myself, I still can't hold down the food."

"You should see a doctor right away. We'll go tomorrow."

"I already went," said Olya softly.

"What did he say?"

Olya didn't answer, only squeezed closer to me.

"Tell me the truth."

"I'm going to die soon," she whispered.

"Don't be silly."

"It came to me while you were in Moldavia."

I was frightened, because I believed her. Like many musicians, I was superstitious.

"You have to go to a good doctor."

"I went to a good one."

"Doctors often make mistakes," I said, not quite believing it myself. "It's too bad that I'm going away again. I can't cancel the trip."

"You have to go. It's your life."

"We need a telephone, so I can call you."

"I'm on the waiting list. They promised me one in two years."

I was afraid that if I stopped speaking she would talk more about death. "Tell me about the camp," I asked.

"Well, I don't have much to tell."

"Did they beat you?"

"Only once, and not very hard. They accused me of helping Canadian spies. They wanted me to sign a confession. I tried to explain that nothing had happened or could have happened. They told me, 'Prove it!' How can you prove something that never happened? I held out five days or, rather, five nights. And then they told me that my innocence wasn't proven. That meant a trial and a sentence. What could I do? I was sixteen. But I still said that my guilt wasn't proven and that there was nothing to try me for. They told me I could say that at the trial, and that Soviet justice is fair."

"Soviet justice is fair!" I repeated.

"In the thirties there were only two terms—ten years in prison or the death penalty. They gave me ten years. But during the war there were new decrees: twenty years of hard labor and various terms of correctional labor camp, from fifteen to twenty-five years. So they gave me ten years more."

I ground my teeth with anger, but Olya grew calmer as she spoke.

"In the camp itself it wasn't all that bad," she continued quietly, "especially later on, when we started getting musicians. They let us form an orchestra and freed us from work before holidays. We rehearsed and even played dominoes."

"How humanitarian!"

"We had a funny rule: the one who lost had to tell his name, say, 'I don't know how to play dominoes,' and give up the seat to a new player. There was one Armenian there, Aram Idilyan. He was a virtuoso domino player. After a few moves he already knew exactly which pieces the others had. It was incredible! But once he lost. We wanted him to keep playing, but he stood up heavily and said, 'I, Aram Idilyan, a fool, came from Istanbul . . . Why, for God's sake? Yes, brothers . . . I don't know how to play dominoes.' "

I felt tears coming into my eyes, but fortunately it was dark. I hugged Olya and pulled her closer.

Outside the window the summer night hung motionless. The silence was broken only by an occasional waking bird or the faraway bark of a dog. I didn't want to ask Olya about her family, but she unexpectedly began talking about them herself.

"My parents were shot right away, as spies. What they did with my brother and sisters I don't know. But once, in a transit prison, there were so many women that the guards couldn't manage us. They shoved four hundred of us into a cell for fifty and kept us there a long time. And later, when they called me out, I suddenly heard a heartrending cry, 'Olya!' It was my sister Marcella . . . Just think, we were together in the same room and didn't know it! The guard grabbed me at once. That shout, 'Olya!' haunted me after that, especially at night."

I couldn't stand it anymore and gently put my finger to her lips. In the dark we were silent for a long time, then I heard her even breathing . . .

The next morning, on our way to the grocery store, we crossed the trolley circle by the switching box, and in its open window we saw a woman smiling at us.

"Let's go over," I said. "I'd like to speak with her."

We said hello, and the woman said that she had seen us together several times. I explained that I was leaving soon, but "this girl here," I said, pointing to Olya, "needs some help. She is still a child."

"I've got two children of my own, and a husband who's worse than a child," replied the woman good-naturedly.

"We'd be so grateful to you. We'll pay as much as you say."

"That doesn't matter," the woman answered, and looked at Olya's dress. "Pretty! Is it foreign or something?"

"I'm going abroad," I quickly fibbed. "I'll bring you whatever you want."

Olya looked at me without smiling.

"What's the address?" asked the woman.

"Along this street," I said. "Number 27."

"I'll stop by after work."

"What's your name?"

"Valentina. And yours?"

"Her name is Olya," I said.

The trolley turned into the circle. The driver got out and came toward the switching box. Olya and I walked away from the window.

"I'll come by in the evening," Valentina shouted after us.

* * *

At Bykovo Airport, where planes left for Siberia, I immediately felt as if I were already far from Moscow.

The airport was not merely crowded. It seemed that people weren't here just waiting for flights but were living with their households and children. From time to time, announcements were made from two cracked loudspeakers at different ends of the hall. One loudspeaker was almost a word behind: "Attention . . . tention! Citizen passengers . . . engers! Flight number (unintelligible) en route from Moscow to (unintelligible) has been delayed by non-arrival of the aircraft . . . craft!" A crowd clustered around the information window despite the CLOSED sign.

"We'd better go talk to an attendant," said Berlinsky.

"I'll watch the suitcases," I offered.

My colleagues left, and I pulled a small edition of *Eugene Onegin* out of my pocket. I planned to memorize one stanza each day and by that count off the days, as if by scratches on the wall of a prison cell.

My colleagues were gone for a long time, and when they appeared it was obvious that they hadn't succeeded in learning anything.

"The flight's delayed," Berlinsky told me.

"By non-arrival of the 'aircraft . . . craft'?"

"Exactly." Berlinsky sighed into my face, his breath smelling strongly of vodka. At least they had managed to get through to the bar.

We waited about five hours for the flight to Krasnoyarsk, and when they finally announced it and opened the narrow gate, a crowd flooded toward it. We were dragged along by the current, pushed out onto the airfield, and carried along to the airplane itself. A black hole gaped in its belly, and we threw our baggage into it, handing it upward into somebody's strong hands. Then we raced up the shaky gangway into the airplane and barely managed to find the last four unoccupied seats. There turned out to be more passengers than seats on the plane, and after explanations, negotiations, and general swearing, the excess passengers were escorted forcibly off the plane.

From Moscow to the east of Russia the country is endless! Our plane touched down in Kazan, Sverdlovsk, Chelyabinsk, Omsk, and Novosibirsk. At each stop, we got off the plane and went into the terminal.

Everywhere, in odd poses, on benches and right on the floor, people were sound asleep.

After having flown across four time zones and lost a day, we arrived in Krasnoyarsk.

"Someone should meet us," said Berlinsky confidently. "Roskoncert alerted Krasnoyarsk by telephone, and I also sent a telegram."

While the rest of the passengers scattered, we waited in the center of the room with our instruments and our luggage. No one met us. Berlinsky ran to the telephone and returned.

"It's Saturday, no one's answering."

"That's why they didn't meet us. Who wants to spend their day off . . ."

"Well, what now? Go to the hotel?"

"To which one?"

"And how?"

We went out to the square in front of the airport. It was empty. After half an hour, a truck drove up and people started unloading boxes of soda for the airport restaurant. Shebalin walked up to the driver and started a conversation. We saw the driver nod. No one paid any attention to us when, a little later, we climbed into the back of the truck and sat down on our suitcases. We held our instruments up in the air to protect them while riding over the uneven road.

The hotel, the only one in the city, bore the proud name The Central. A sign at the front desk read NO VACANCY.

"We should have a Philharmonia reservation for four rooms," said Berlinsky to the woman behind the table.

The woman didn't answer. Raising his voice, Berlinsky repeated himself and this time was favored with a reply.

"Last name?"

"The Borodin Quartet!" Berlinsky said, as grandly as possible.

The woman looked through a few sheets of paper, curtly said, "No," and turned away.

"That's impossible," shouted Berlinsky.

The woman didn't stir. Berlinsky stood there a little longer, then came back to us. "I don't know what to do," he muttered through his teeth in helpless anger.

"I'm certain that she has rooms," I said. "If someone official appeared now, everything would be different."

"That's true."

"I suggest we declare a war of nerves against her! We'll sit here on the stairs and wait until some rooms turn up."

We settled down on the stairs with our suitcases and instruments, blocking the way.

An hour went by before the woman noticed us. "There's one room!" she shouted at us. "For six people. Four beds are still free."

"We have come to play concerts for the public of Krasnoyarsk," Berlinsky answered, trying to control himself. "We need separate rooms to work."

"There's nothing else!"

"We'll sit a little," said Shebalin.

"Well, sit then . . ."

As we sat, we watched outside as people gathered on the street in front of the restaurant. Shortly before noon the line had grown a block long.

"Perhaps, before it's too late, we should find a table," suggested Shebalin. "We have to eat, too."

"It's better not to move," I answered. "Otherwise our sit-down strike will be broken."

"You think it'll do any good?"

"A strike is the people's only means of struggle with those in power."

Berlinsky and Alexandrov glanced at each other, but didn't say anything.

The fortunate possessors of keys stepped over our legs, looking curiously at our instruments and their owners, dressed in foreign suits and sitting on the dirty steps of the staircase.

At twelve o'clock the restaurant opened. Through the glass doors we saw the human avalanche rush in. People were fighting for tables.

Another hour passed.

"This power can't be budged by a strike!" I said. "But what if we go, as Lenin said, 'by another path'?"

"That is?"

"I have a foreign pen, two colors of ink. I'll sacrifice it for the good of the cause. Whatever else is handy, as long as it's foreign. When no one is near, we'll put everything on that witch's table."

"What if she gets offended and refuses?"

"That means Karl Marx was right."

"I have a gas cigarette lighter. A pity to lose it, of course, but . . ."

"And I have some women's tights. I was saving them for a different occasion . . ."

"Will chewing gum do?"

"And how! So what do you think? Should we try? Something of a sociopsychological experiment. Just out of curiosity."

"And who'll play this psychological cadenza?" asked Berlinsky.

"You, of course! Our director!"

"Director, my ass! Give me the loot!"

He stuck our gifts into various pockets and slowly moved toward the woman.

"Poor guy," I said. "Let's not watch."

Berlinsky returned after five minutes. "Okay," he whispered, "third floor!"

Seizing his suitcase and instrument, he headed up the staircase. We didn't need to be invited twice.

The woman on duty on the third floor had already received instructions from below. She led us along the corridor and opened four separate rooms with sinks, beds, and even fresh linen.

"This is the life!" I said.

Alexandrov laughed. "Now, after a preliminary bite to eat . . ."

"Forget it! You saw what's going on down there."

"No hope for food . . ."

"In general, there's no such thing as a hopeless situation," I said.

"What? More foreign presents? But to whom this time? The waiter or the cook?"

"Not necessarily presents," I said.

"You have an idea?"

"I think so. Look . . . the Soviet people lose consciousness at the mere sight of foreign goods. Right? Right. If some people want to be fooled, why not give them a chance?"

"What do you mean?"

I explained the plan to my colleagues and we went down to the restaurant. All of us, except Shebalin, had dressed in our noticeably foreign suits, with white shirts, exquisitely knotted ties, and a large, bright handkerchief in the front jacket pocket. We spoke among ourselves in Italian musical terms. The crowd moved aside for us, and our large Shebalin, with his open Russian face, loudly and authoritatively knocked on the restaurant door. Carelessly tossing over his shoulder, *"Fermato poco ma presto subito,"* which we could guess was supposed to mean "Wait for me here, I'll be right back," he advanced softly to the doorman and whispered in his ear, "I have foreign guests. I'm going to the director." The doorman didn't dare to stop him. The people looked us over as if we were rare birds in a zoo. Shebalin soon returned, accompanied by a small, round man who, seeing us, said, "Please come in, gentlemen!"

Shebalin "translated" at once: *"Signori, andante fugato e molto risoluto."*

A service table next to the door of the kitchen was quickly screened off, a clean cloth spread over it, and the little man, rubbing his hands, asked Shebalin whether we liked Krasnoyarsk. Shebalin responded wearily that we had already been in Khabarovsk and Irkutsk and that everything was fine there.

"It will be just as good here, too, don't worry. I'll send you our best waiter."

"I'll translate that to the gentlemen," said Shebalin, and turned to us. He had gotten so completely in character that he didn't even smile as he drawled in Italian, *"Signori, maestro direttore e dolce espressivo con profundo sempre un poco piu mosso animato e crescendo."*

We three nodded gratefully, and the director, muttering, "Long live friendship among nations," bowed to Shebalin, then to us, and went into the kitchen.

"Bandits," said Alexandrov softly. "And what if he finds out now from the administrator what sort of Italians we are?"

"Don't talk," said Shebalin, continuing loudly for the benefit of the waiter, who had just emerged from the kitchen with a tray, *"Mezzo voce con sordino legato còmodo non troppo scherzando."*

Everything went well. We ate a decent meal and went to our rooms to catch up on our night of lost sleep.

On Monday morning we set off for the Philharmonia. As they might say in the newspapers, our discussion with the director was "in the spirit of mutual understanding and a candid exchange of opinions." Translated into intelligible language, that means that the conversation didn't come off. The director rolled and unrolled the telegram of our arrival without looking at us, saying that he had only just received it and therefore had not met us. We knew this was a lie, since he had been phoned from Moscow. If he had decided to lie, however, there was nothing we could do about it. Carefully avoiding asking us where we had spent our last two nights, the director started explaining that there was only one hotel in the city and its rooms were reserved by the city Party committee. The Philharmonia got what was left, but performers kept coming and coming. He listed the names of soloists and ensembles, painting a picture resembling the invasion of the Tatar Mongols, only this time from west to east.

Seizing on a momentary pause in the director's monologue, Berlinsky managed to say that there was no need to worry about the hotel, and the director, cutting himself short, asked with interest, "But where are you staying?"

"At The Central," Berlinsky answered calmly.

"Everything's in order with the hotel," Shebalin supported him.

"You mean you're not complaining about anything?" the director asked in surprise.

"No. We don't complain."

A strange silence followed. The director was visibly making up his mind about something. Suddenly raising his voice, he began to complain himself. "And what do you suggest we do? Does Moscow ask us? They just send us people. The good public stopped trusting us and won't come to concerts anymore. But do we have to fill the cash box? We do! Do we have to give a financial report? We do! And so it turns out that instead of concerts we have Lilliputians, gypsies, and all sorts of guitars—'singing,' 'silver,' 'blue' . . ."

He stopped talking and looked us over. Had he said too much? More calmly, he asked, "Are you willing to travel in the region?"

"We can travel if we have to."

"Well, good. Here in Krasnoyarsk I have only a music school and a couple of institutes. You have to travel. I'll give you a manager who knows the region. By yourselves with your Beethoven you'd be done for. You have the wrong genre . . ."

Behind this crude frankness there was life and truth. We were even grateful to him for not having to pretend. If we'd come to Siberia for money, then we might as well forget about high art, and the sooner we worked off the time, the better.

We got up to leave, and while shaking the director's hand, Shebalin said that his father had come from Siberia and had received his musical education in Omsk, where in the twenties they had had a musical society, and where his father had first heard the quartets of Ravel, Hindemith, and Bartók.

"In the twenties?" asked the director. "This is the fifties now. You're a little late."

"My father often talked about how they would get together on Thursdays and play piano arrangements of Wagner, Mahler, and Richard Strauss."

"And my father and his brothers," picked up Berlinsky, "had a quartet in Irkutsk. Except that they played on Wednesdays, not Thursdays."

"Yes," began the director, somewhat sadly, "in Siberia, after the Revolution, the local music-making went on for a good ten years . . . And what a public! The concert halls were always full."

"So what happened to it?" I asked foolishly.

The director only smiled. "Goodbye. I wish you success."

That night on the crowded train headed north, we slept in our clothes on wooden shelves built into the coach. During the night someone pushed me toward the wall, lay down beside me, and went right to sleep. Evidently this was typical on these trains, but I wasn't used to it. I slid off the shelf and took a walk down the corridor. Even in the darkness I could see that there were two people sleeping on each shelf. I went out onto the platform. The air was better there. Through the window I saw the darkness thin and the trees along the tracks gradually become distinguishable.

The first city where we disembarked bore the joyless name of Stupin. Our manager, good old Nikolai Bestuzhev, ran off at once to the city Party committee, returning an hour later in a half-collapsed bus. Bestuzhev announced that we were lucky, that today was the opening of the city library and we could play a concert there. Shebalin growled that a concert is, of course, wonderful, spiritual nourishment, so to speak, elevated and noble, but that one also needs to sleep and eat.

"Don't blab more than necessary," Berlinsky told him.

"I haven't slept and haven't eaten," snapped Shebalin.

"All the same, don't blab. Nikolai Andreevich knows what we should do."

I also hoped that Nikolai Andreevich knew, because whatever sort of concert it was, it was still an appearance onstage, and before that it would be good to eat and sleep a little.

"We have a hotel," said Bestuzhev happily, "thank God for that! And as far as food . . . Well, there should be a buffet there."

The hotel turned out to be a long corridor with narrow iron beds standing in a row along the walls, like horse stalls in a stable. At the very end of the corridor was a buffet with port and cognac, but the food, besides the tea and bread, did not inspire confidence.

A library really was opening in the city that day, but it was a children's library, and our audience consisted of preschoolers. In the reading room a woman was valiantly entertaining the children with riddles, and when we came out with our instruments she shouted, "And who loves music?"

"I do! I do! I do!" shouted the children on all sides.

"And how do we listen to music? Quietly, or do we talk?"

"Quietly! Quietly!"

"Right, children, you're clever! Quietly-quietly!"

We started playing.

The children weren't able yet to sit quietly without moving. For them it was punishment. They held out exactly one minute, and then all at once began moving their arms, legs, and tongues. The boys pushed the girls, who squealed with pleasure, and soon our music drowned in the noise. The little woman lifted her hand, held her finger to her lips, but nothing helped. We stopped playing.

"Try your riddles again," I said to the woman.

"I'm afraid it's too late. They're too distracted."

"Maybe they'd like to sing some songs?"

"Oh, that's an idea! Children! Children!" She clapped her hands. "Pay attention for a minute! How many of you know how to sing?"

"I do! I do!" the children shouted again.

I stood up and took a step forward. "Whoever recognizes this tune, raise your hand." I played the "Internationale." No one answered.

"And this?" Now I played the "Hymn of the Soviet Union."

The children were silent. Realizing that if none of these *Wunderkinder* recognized the melody, it could be considered a flaw in the political education of the children, I kept on playing, hoping that someone would finally raise a hand. I heard Berlinsky whisper, "Idiot!" behind my back, and quickly I switched to the soccer march which was played on the radio before every soccer game.

"Soccer! Soccer!" the children shouted joyfully, throwing up their hands.

"Good!" The woman clapped her hands, and I returned to my place, awaiting my punishment. It followed, of course, but only later, in the evening, when my colleagues went out to eat without me. I lay down on my bed, consoling myself with the thought that sleeping on an empty stomach is good for one's health.

The next day, Bestuzhev drove us to a factory, and we played in the factory workshop for the workers during their lunch break. By what means they had forced the workers to listen to music instead of eating could only be guessed from the grim, unsmiling faces. On the cement floor around us stood fifty people. It was unnaturally quiet. Neither the workers, the so-called ruling class, nor we "bearers of culture to the people" understood what was going on. Of all the possible forms of contact between performers and listeners in the mysterious process of music-making, what could be worse for a musician than mutual mistrust and misunderstanding?

Although it went on for only half an hour, the concert seemed to last an eternity. Finally, someone approached us and pointed to his watch. We stopped playing, and the workers soundlessly scattered. The ever-cheerful Bestuzhev slyly winked at us, disappeared, and, when he returned, triumphantly showed us the gratuity from the factory committee chairman for the "splendid concert, very appreciated by the workers."

"That's for our report in Krasnoyarsk," he said.

We quickly changed the conversation to a different theme: food or, rather, the lack of it. Bestuzhev said that we had only our own inexperience to blame; all performers who travel from Moscow to the east always bring along a sack of food—say, some sausage, cheese, all sorts of canned goods, evaporated milk, and so on. Our heavy Shebalin, who suffered more than the rest of us from not eating, shouted that Bestuzhev should stop tormenting him. The old man, fortunately, did not take offense but said that he had some bread and onions with him, and as soon as we got back to the hotel . . .

"Let's go right away," Shebalin interrupted him.

With a slight burning sensation in our stomachs from the bread with onions, we headed for the grocery store to test our luck. There were no sausages, cheese, or canned goods, but the jars of fruit compote marked MADE IN CHINA looked tempting, all the more so since articles about the harmful effects of meat had started to appear in the Soviet papers. In general I can get along without food for a fairly long time —it's not like cold or sleepless nights—but even so, after the appearance of the Chinese compote, I crowed an old Stalinist slogan: "Life has gotten better, comrades, life has gotten happier." We could only rely on Sino-Soviet friendship, hoping that it would in fact be "eternal," as the newspapers ceaselessly trumpeted, and that Chinese compote would be available at least until the end of our Siberian tour.

Our tour gradually gained speed. We traveled through cities and towns in the Krasnoyarsk region and played two and even three concerts a day. We played in factories, in train depots, in rural clubs, in movie theaters before film showings, in dormitories, and once even on a train, in a special car for passengers wishing to hear music.

We moved toward the north and, in the end, got to Norilsk, where our performances were to end. It was now the end of August. The short northern summer was surrendering to winter. A strong north wind suddenly started to blow off the Arctic Ocean, and the temperature fell to freezing, so hastily that we didn't even have a chance to buy gloves. On the way to our concert I kept my hands deep in my pockets, but even that didn't help—they wouldn't warm up. The club where we were playing wasn't heated, and furthermore, the wall on one side of the stage was unfinished, allowing an icy current to blow in on us. In the center of the club, huddling in a group, sat some twenty people in coats and hats. Berlinsky announced that because of the cold the concert would be shorter and that we would begin it with the first movement of Beethoven's fourth quartet. He had long ago given up saying "the great German composer" and said simply Beethoven.

I started playing with unbending fingers, and in the very beginning of the movement I couldn't manage a simple passage. Shebalin giggled. My second phrase came out even funnier, and Shebalin, trying to hide his face from the audience, struggled desperately to keep from laughing. I was playing, in fact, with only two fingers, and when, at the end of the first page, instead of a cadenza I produced one long slide, Alexandrov laughed out loud. His bow jumped from the laughter, and tears ran down Shebalin's cheeks. Then, when during the cello's beautiful solo, there came only a complaining squeak, I couldn't hold back either. I quit playing in mid-phrase and ran off the stage. The quartet followed me, and backstage we became hysterical with laughter. The director of the club appeared and started swearing and trying to push us back onstage. Having no strength to speak, I showed him my blue fingers, but he shouted that this was hooliganism and that he would definitely inform Moscow. It ended when he himself went onstage and, without any explanation, canceled the concert.

We still had a few days to finish up the required forty concerts. We had made heaps of money at the cost of the daily professional humiliation we felt playing for the handful of people who accidentally happened into our concerts. Although some performances were canceled because no one showed up, nevertheless we were paid as if they had been full concerts. At first the Party members in the quartet demanded that no one ever say a word about this, but later, I think, even they realized that their fears were groundless.

The closer we got to Moscow, the more strongly I was seized by anxiety. Olya! How was she? During the whole trip I had tried not to think of her, as if time had stopped and in Moscow my life would pick up from the day that I flew to Krasnoyarsk.

At Bykovo Airport I immediately took a taxi, and as we drove into Moscow I suddenly had the sharp sensation that time had not stopped here; a whole month had gone by and Olya had spent it alone. It was unforgivably thoughtless to go away for so long! Thank God it was over. Now that I had money we could repair the house and find Olya some sort of work to fit her skills, so she'd feel more sure of herself.

The taxi drove into Silver Grove. I showed the driver the street, and we stopped at Olya's house. I was already reaching into my pocket for money when I suddenly saw that two crossed boards had been nailed over the door. I jumped out of the car, hammered on the door with my fists, and only then understood that there was no use knocking. The taxi driver got out behind me, looked at the door, and pointed out what I hadn't noticed: from the door handle hung a lead seal . . .

I stepped weakly off the porch. The seal overwhelmed me more than the boards over the door. That meant the authorities had been here, had taken Olya, and had sealed the house. Could they have arrested her again? In that case, there was still hope.

"Let's go!" I said to the driver. "To the circle, to the trolley switching box. Valentina should be there."

Valentina was not at work, but they gave us her home address. "I'll take you there," said the taxi driver, and turned off his meter. I nodded to him at this sign of sympathy, but said that I would pay for the whole trip.

"No, that's not necessary," he said.

We drove to Valentina's house without talking.

"Should I come with you?" asked the driver, not out of curiosity but offering his help.

"Yes," I said.

Valentina opened the door herself, saw me, and started crying.

Clinging to my last hope, I asked, "Did they arrest her?"

"No," sobbed Valentina. "Come in. Sit down."

All three of us sat at the table. Crying, Valentina said, "I was only there twice. I cleaned up a little, made some food. She was so quiet . . . Only drank tea, and even that made her feel sick. Later on I came again, knocked at the door, but no one answered. The window was open. I looked in, and she was lying on the bed . . . awfully pale . . . not moving at all, eyes closed, only her lips . . . Are you called Rostislav?"

I nodded.

"Kept repeating your name while we were taking her to the hospital . . . Are you all right? Should I give you some water?"

I pulled out my handkerchief and wiped my eyes. "Where . . . ?" I couldn't finish.

"Where did they bury her? They took her to the crematorium . . . Straight from the hospital. We were there when she died."

Valentina stopped crying. "I wanted to send you a telegram, but I only knew Krasnoyarsk, nothing else . . ."

I tried to thank her, but my throat was cramped as if with a spasm. I pulled a hundred rubles out of my pocket and put them on the table.

Valentina waved her hands. "What are you doing! So much money! I won't take it!"

I hid the money under the tablecloth and got up. "Thank you," I managed to say.

The taxi driver and I went outside. We stood awhile beside the car.

"Where now?" he asked.

"I don't know."

"Do you have a place to go or . . ."

I didn't answer.

"Listen. I'll take you to my place . . ."

Let's Walk
1958

9:05 A.M.

The Central Committee Party building on Dzerzhinsky Square. Department of Travel.

"So, comrades, you are going to the West . . ."

"Rather, to the north."

"Sweden and Finland?"

"Yes."

"That means to the West . . . For the first time?"

"We've already been in East Germany, Czechoslovakia, and Rumania."

"So, for the first time. Bear in mind, comrades, the West is . . ."

"We're bearing it in mind."

"More caution with conversations."

"Of course."

"Contacts with foreigners . . ."

"We understand."

"So, everything clear?"

"Absolutely."

"Well, good luck . . ."

9:22 A.M. On the street by the entrance.

140

"Get a cab!"

"Hopeless!"

"Stop a car! Anything . . ."

"Let's walk. It's not far from here."

"Everyone has his passport?"

"I seem to have forgotten . . ."

"We were warned."

"Check all your pockets."

"I'm looking . . . Here it is!"

"But mine's expired . . ."

"We'll turn all four in at once. Maybe they won't notice."

9:47 A.M. The Ministry of Culture on Kuibyshev Street. Passport department.

"Good morning!"

"What do you want?"

"We've come for the passports."

"Quartet or something?"

"That's us."

"Sweden and Finland? Visas aren't ready yet."

"So when should we come back?"

"Later."

"About when?"

"Later."

9:58 A.M. On the street by the entrance.

"Get a cab!"

"Hopeless!"

"Stop a car! Anything . . ."

"Let's walk. It's not far."

10:27 A.M. Goskoncert on Neglinnaya Street. The desk of the secretary for Sweden.

"You've all four come together! Well, hello!"

"We need the contract for Sweden."

"You don't get a contract."

"What do we get?"

"Financial terms."

"That's for the impresario?"

"By no means! Only for you. How much you take for yourselves and how much you give to Goskoncert."

"And what if something unforeseen happens?"

"For example?"

"Well, say, the radio wants to record a concert . . ."

"No recordings, it's forbidden . . ."

"And if they set up the microphone themselves?"

"Before the concert, move the microphone aside."

"And if they hang it up?"

"Get a stepladder and take it down."

"And if . . ."

"Now really, are you children or something? Goodbye. Have a good trip."

10:41 A.M. The same place. The desk of the secretary for Finland.

"Please, what are we playing in Finland?"

"One moment . . . Borodin Quartet . . . You play in Turku and two concerts in Helsinki."

"But what?"

"Doesn't say."

"How can we find out?"

"The chief program editor has all the programs."

10:50 A.M. At the door of the editor's office.

"May we come in? We need to see Comrade Editor."

"He's at a meeting with the director."

"So when . . ."

"Later."

11:04 A.M. In the corridor by the stairs.

"Just a minute . . . I need a cigarette."

"What else do we need?"

"Baggage overweight authorization."

"Let's ask for forty kilograms for the four of us."

"They'll give us twenty."

"That's only five per head."

"Better than nothing."

"Let's ask for sixty."

"And what if they agreed? We'd have to come up with it somehow."

"Ten bottles of mineral water."

"They'd catch us at customs."

"So what? With my digestion, I can drink only that water."

"We all have bad digestion?"

"Can we take books?"

"Dangerous."

"I have the complete Lenin. It'd be enough for several trips."

"We still need to check the instruments."

"And a travel certificate for customs."

"That's back on Kuibyshev Street."

"Let's go."

11:15 A.M. At the door of Goskoncert.

"Get a cab!"

"Let's walk!"

11:36 A.M. The Ministry of Culture, the office.

"Hello. We're the Borodin Quartet. Tomorrow we fly to Sweden and Finland. We need a travel certificate, permission for four instruments, and baggage authorization."

"Passports with you?"

"No. They're in the next room. Still no visas."

"And your tickets?"

"Not yet."

"Come back with the tickets or passports."

11:42 A.M. At the door of the ministry.

"Get a cab!"

"Let's walk!"

12:08 P.M. At the ticket agent's.

"Hello! Are you responsible for tickets?"

"Yes."

"Four tickets for the quartet . . . Moscow—Stockholm—Helsinki —Moscow."

"I don't have any tickets like that."

"We're supposed to leave tomorrow."

"They didn't tell me."

"We have a concert tomorrow."

"I don't know anything about it."

"So who does know?"

"Go see the secretary."

"We were there already."

"Okay, wait here. I'll phone right now."

12:14 P.M.

"Hello . . . Yes, I have the quartet here . . ."

" . . ."

"I don't have anything for them."

" . . ."

"And how was I supposed to know?"

" . . ."

"Two weeks, at least."

" . . ."

"It's not my fault! You screwed up yourselves, and now . . ."

" . . ."

"I can't promise anything."

12:23 P.M. The same place.

"Well?"

"How do you like it! They mess everything up there, and I'm guilty . . Now I have to go back to the central bureau."

"But when . . ."

"Can't promise anything . . . Come by toward the end of the day."

12:55 P.M. In the corridor by the stairs.

"What time is it?"

"In five minutes, a lunch break."

"Let's go to the café."

"We'll smell of liquor."

"We can drink tea."

"*You* can drink tea!"

2:01 P.M. On the street by the entrance to Goskoncert.

"Get a cab!"

"Let's walk!"

Luba
1959–1963

THE TRIP to Siberia taught us something. We had come into contact not with the false country shown in the newspapers but with unembellished reality. But our strongest impressions of the trip were not indigestion or the lack of elementary sanitary facilities. Complaining about the discomforts of life in the Soviet Union only makes people laugh and say that "temporary difficulties are a constant factor in our lives." We came away from the trip having learned something entirely different. Without knowing the Bible, we had discovered for ourselves that "man does not live by bread alone." What the quartet had striven for from the very beginning—serious concerts in full halls—remained a dream, only even more distant. Even my Party colleagues fell silent. We had seen only the Krasnoyarsk region, but it seemed simpler to assume that the whole, enormous country resembled it rather than to hope for a better picture in other places. It's true that tours abroad lay ahead of us, but they not only failed to solve the problem, they made it even worse: the comparison was far from flattering to our motherland.

Anyway, we climbed aboard the plane to Stockholm as Soviet people flying to a capitalist country are supposed to: indifferently and scornfully. This was not a pose but a necessity; shortly before our departure a young man came up to us and announced that he was flying with us as our interpreter. He was imaginatively dressed: brown shoes, wide blue trousers, a black jacket, and a pink tie. In his hands he held a greenish oilskin briefcase and a canvas suitcase with big yellow buttons.

"Unpretentious but tasteful," said Shebalin under his breath.

A fifth person in the quartet meant that from now on we'd have our own personal spy, who could change our future with a single word. We'd have to weigh each utterance carefully or, even better, keep quiet, as we did now, uncomfortably shifting our feet. When the silence grew too long, I risked saying the most innocent sentence I could think of: "The Swedish language, probably, is very distinctive . . ."

"I wouldn't know," answered our Fifth. "I speak English."

Thanks to Olya, I could already chatter a little in English, but to advertise one's foreign languages could also prove dangerous, and we were silent again for a while.

In Stockholm, right after our first concert in a packed hall, for which we received a standing ovation and an honorarium, we took our Fifth to a large and fairly expensive store and dressed him in foreign clothes. And to "wet" the new suit so it would wear better (according to Russian custom), we fed him a dinner with vodka. The Fifth got sentimental and on the road to the hotel began to cry.

"You're good people," he said. "Sincere. I only beg you, be careful in front of me . . . Put yourselves in my position. I have to write a report on each of you. What you say and who you meet. Do what you want, but don't say a word in front of me. Understand?"

"What do you mean?" said Shebalin, putting one arm around his shoulders. "We're just being friendly. We don't have any of those sorts of conversations."

"Just so that in front of me . . . They'll ask me for material."

"Don't worry, old man! We won't get you in any trouble."

The Fifth turned out to be an honorable person, and before we left for home he showed us our dossiers, in which there wasn't a single "but."

This obviously made a good impression in Moscow, because before long we were offered trips to Italy and West Germany. Lev Kapalet, a nice-looking man from the Soviet-Italian Friendship Society, who spoke Italian fluently, traveled to Italy with us as the Fifth. He didn't pay much attention to us, however, and would vanish for days at a

time. Once, on our day off, he took us to Modena, where the influence
of the Italian Communist Party was very strong. At his request we
played a free concert there for the workers. We were reminded vaguely
of our tour through Siberia, but after the concert we drank new wine
along with the workers. They sang songs for us, not Italian songs, but
translated Soviet ones, which they all somehow knew a little too well.
Kapalet and Berlinsky sang along with the workers, each trying to
outshout the other, and kept looking at me, but I said that I was
embarrassed to sing in front of Italians. Berlinsky immediately swore
at me, saying that I would surely sing with Italian capitalists, and I
left the table to avoid scandal. Scandal still broke out, but not among
us; in the newspaper *Paesa Sera* there appeared a large article entitled
"Kapalet the Soviet Spy," and he was obliged to leave abruptly for
Moscow. We were provided with someone from the Soviet embassy
for the remainder of the trip.

The unexpected appearance in Western Europe of the unknown
Borodin Quartet from Moscow shocked the Western impresarios. From
a country in whose cities polar bears had recently roamed came a string
quartet whose mastery was no less than that of the best Western ensembles! Correspondents from various countries hastened to write stories about us for their newspapers, and Moscow Goskoncert was
showered with invitations for the quartet from all over Europe and
even from America. Word immediately spread around Moscow, and
more than before, people's attitude toward us turned into a complicated
chemistry of envy, ingratiating flattery, and barely concealed hostility.
Reports reached us of the "deep preoccupation" of a certain musician
with our success abroad, and once I was even summoned to the travel
department of the Party Central Committee.

It's always bad when you are "invited" to the PCC, but I had nothing
to conceal. I went up to the third floor to Comrade Duzhev, who got
right to business.

"I received this unsigned letter. They write that in school you were
expelled from the Komsomol for anti-Soviet statements and recommend that you be restricted from traveling abroad."

I said slowly, "I could not have been expelled from the Komsomol,
because I never joined the Komsomol."

"You were never in the Komsomol?"

Now I felt guilty before Soviet authority, but at the same time it was my salvation. "You see, my parents wanted me to play the violin, and so it happened that from childhood on I spent all my time . . ."

"That's not the point!" Duzhev interrupted. "You mean you were never expelled from the Komsomol?"

"No," I said.

I wanted very much to explain to him that the violin was not the only reason I had not been a member of the Komsomol but, fortunately, he no longer wanted to talk with me.

"At present we're not reacting to anonymous letters. Give me your pass, I'll sign it."

Having escaped from danger with unexpected ease, I slowly crossed Dzerzhinsky Square, walked past the KGB building, and even glanced fearlessly at the sentry by the main entrance. Damn it, I had been extremely lucky! I started thinking of all the musicians I knew. I didn't have many obvious enemies, but envy, alas, gnaws at friends as well. Besides, Soviet logic makes it clear that it's not enough for your own affairs to be in order. It's also essential, for complete happiness, that your neighbor's affairs should be bad, and then everything's just fine!

I took a long detour walking home, but from time to time you need to walk without any purpose and examine your thoughts, in order to see and understand anything at all. Ahead, no matter how much you look, nothing is visible. The present drowns in itself, and only the past stretches out in logical sequence, like a scale in one key. When you're walking, the thought itself slips into the rhythm of your steps. You have to go and go, the long way to your harbor, if only you have one.

I quickened my pace. My thoughts also started running faster.

I recalled how Sviatoslav Richter had become interested in our quartet. At just that time, our own audience had started to take shape. If the Beethoven Quartet's audience was slightly anti-Semitic, then ours was slightly anti-Soviet. Our style of performance was moving further and further from socialist realism. For instance, in Tchaikovsky's quartets we abandoned altogether the typical imperial cliché and tried to show most of all the tragic fate of the composer. Even more out of line was our manner of emphasizing the dark side of Shostakovich's music, for which, according to Soviet standards, we should have been brought to trial for anti-Soviet propaganda.

Fortunately for us, performing artists were still not under the constant surveillance of the Party, only composers. Contemporary music was forbidden, and the names Schönberg, Berg, and Webern were unmentionable words. Even "our friends, the Poles," Lutoslawski and Penderecki, not to mention the Italian Communist, the attractive Luigi Nono, who was married, by the way, to Schönberg's pretty daughter, all made Khrennikov foam at the mouth.

In Stockholm, the young Swedish composer Lars Werle had brought us his first opus, the enchanting "Pentagram," five miniatures for quartet. When we tried to slip it into the program of a Moscow concert, we were questioned about the political credo of the composer. We said that he had recently turned eighteen, and so far had written only this "Pentagram." We were "advised" to wait for this boy to grow up and show his political colors.

Only rarely did events turn out otherwise. At the first International Tchaikovsky Competition in 1958, the charming giant from Texas, Van Cliburn, had enchanted the Moscow public in the first round. After the second round, all Moscow wanted to talk of nothing besides Cliburn. He did, in fact, play remarkably. Even two members of the jury, Genrikh Neigaus and Sviatoslav Richter, applauded for the American in defiance of the rules. (That was their first and last participation in the jury of the Tchaikovsky Competition.) After the third round and Cliburn's unforgettable performance of Rachmaninoff's third concerto, the hall exploded. The audience, standing, chanted ceaselessly, "First prize! First prize!" There were political motives in this demonstration as well; the jury had decided in advance to choose a Soviet pianist as winner of the competition. Their victim was to be Lev Vlasenko, and posters had already been printed with his name and the words "first prize" in parentheses. The Moscow audience was in no condition to tolerate this. The public in the hall was repeatedly asked to settle down; the chairman of the jury, Emil Gilels, got up from his seat and raised his hand—but nothing helped. The audience raged . . .

Late that night the jury, conscious of the danger, was still deliberating, while the crowd on the street besieged the Conservatory's Bolshoi Hall and had no intention of leaving. It was two o'clock in the morning.

"I'll be right back," said Gilels, "I'm going to phone . . ."

He got through to Khrushchev's secretary, apologized for the late telephone call, and asked to speak with "himself."

"You know what time it is?" asked the secretary.

"Yes, I know. It's a very serious situation."

After a minute Khrushchev's sleepy voice spoke into the receiver. Gilels explained the problem. Khrushchev asked, "And is this American really that good?"

"Remarkable," answered Gilels.

"Then what's the trouble? Give him first prize and let me go back to sleep."

The competition ended, Cliburn went home to the United States, but the people of Moscow still celebrated the victory and considered, not without reason, that, thanks to them, justice had triumphed, if only once.

Not long after the competition, when we were rehearsing Brahms's Piano Quintet in F-minor, Richter said that he would probably have to change apartments, because the moment he began practicing his upstairs neighbor immediately played the recording of Cliburn at the competition at full volume; as if to say, "Don't forget what sort of pianist there is in the world! Remember! . . ."

Our alliance with Richter had already gone on for quite a while. We often played the quintets of Brahms, Schumann, and Shostakovich, both in the Soviet Union and abroad. Once we played Max Reger's quintet, which no one liked except Richter himself, and we were getting ready to play Dvořák and Franck.

Richter loved to have "the people" attend our rehearsals for inspiration. Among his fans was often an attractive young woman, who turned pages for him. Of course, she came to all our concerts. We always saw her backstage. She would thank us for the music and go back to Richter, and we would watch her go. She was very lovely.

Once, after a successful concert in the conservatory concert hall, where Richter had stunningly played Schumann's quintet with us, we

all went out together. There was a ring of people around Richter, and
it happened that this woman and I were left a bit behind. I took a
chance: "Don't you have to get back to the sultan's retinue?"

She smiled. "Not necessarily."

"Then may I see you home?"

"If you want. I live near here, in Karetny Ryad."

I was walking very close to her, and that made me nervous. Everything I said seemed dull to me. And I couldn't stop thinking that soon
we'd reach her house and she'd disappear. Cursing myself and my
stupidity, I asked her once again what she had thought of our concert.

"You played well," she answered.

"How was the quintet?"

"Brilliant, of course. The audience was delighted."

I sensed a "but."

"And you?"

"Me too, but not as much as before."

"That's interesting. Tell me why."

"You see, Richter forces the quartet to accompany his piano. But
sometimes you want his piano to play more with the quartet."

I was surprised. "You mean you don't entirely worship the genius?"

"He's a great pianist," she answered, and stopped. "Well, here we
are. This is my house and my entrance. Thank you for seeing me
home."

She held out her hand. I tried to keep her hand in mine, but she
freed it and turned to the door.

"Will I see you again?" I asked her back.

"Of course."

"Our next concert's not for a while."

She turned to me and smiled. "I know."

"What should I do?"

She made a gesture which could have meant anything.

That night I couldn't get to sleep.

The next day I bribed someone from the Bolshoi Theater Orchestra,
and he got me two tickets to Prokofiev's ballet *Romeo and Juliet*. I
called her immediately, and when she agreed to join me, my heart
started racing. We met in front of the Bolshoi Theater and pushed

our way to the entrance through the dense crowd. For a moment we were squeezed together, and she didn't hurry to move away.

Oh! Quite a different story! I thought.

Ulanova and Gabovich were dancing, and as Mercutio—the inimitable Koren. The orchestra sounded intoxicating, and the music, which we were both hearing for the first time, overwhelmed us. We sat with our shoulders touching. Once, I took her hand and she didn't move it away.

During the intermission, as is the custom in theaters all over the world, we strolled around the lobby with the crowd and suddenly saw Rostropovich. He joined us at once and gave my companion a long, appraising look. She accepted it gracefully, but I felt uncomfortable and asked him, like a provincial fan, "Well, how do you like Ulanova?"

Unwillingly, he turned to me. "Not bad. She doesn't spoil the music . . . Are you going to introduce me or not?"

"Oh, sorry. This is . . ."

"I am Slava," he said, offering his hand. "And you?"

"Luba. Luba Edlina."

Holding Luba's hand and looking into her eyes, Rostropovich leaned toward me and whispered, "Good job, old man. My compliments," before running away.

As Luba and I moved with the crowd, we found ourselves in front of a big mirror in a gilded frame. I saw us together for the first time and stopped to gaze at our reflection, until we heard the bell for the second act.

Although my prospects were looking more favorable, the situation between us was still uncertain. In anticipation of beginning a "theatrical campaign," I checked several theaters, but besides the Puppet Theater there was nothing interesting. I still didn't know whether Luba liked movies. That would have provided all sorts of possibilities . . .

After a few days, however, she helped me out by asking me to perform sonatas with her in the music school where she taught piano. Needless to say, I agreed.

Luba played amazingly well. I had never felt such unity with any pianist. She could play with different timbres, so that the sounds of the violin and piano, different in nature, blended in similar colors.

We performed four sonatas—Schumann, Beethoven, Debussy, and Brahms. That decided my fate for good, and as it turned out later, Luba's, too. After the concert we walked for a long time toward her building in Karetny Ryad and stood even longer in front of the entrance . . .

And now, a year later, I ran into that same entrance and, since the elevator, as usual, was stuck somewhere, rushed up the stairs two at a time to the eighth floor. Luba, now my wife, opened the door.

"Why so long? I was worried."

"Everything's all right," I said, and kissed her on both cheeks. "They're not reacting to anonymous letters right now. Everything's all right!"

We went into the kitchen. I told her the details of my conversation with Duzhev, and she said carefully, "I'm afraid that your trip to Austria might not take place."

I stared at her without speaking. In our lives we can expect surprises at any moment and from any direction.

"Okay, go ahead, tell me everything you know."

"I don't know anything. Only, Alexandrov is complaining about his finger. Berlinsky already called several times."

I dialed his number. "Well, what?" I asked as soon as he picked up the receiver.

"First, what's with you?"

"A false alarm."

"And what was it?"

Not trusting the telephone, I said in our jargon, "Someone doesn't like our bowings in Beethoven quartets, but I said that we play from the Ur-text. For now they believed me."

"Thank goodness. And our Alexandrov is deluded."

"Yes, I heard. Which finger?"

"Index finger on the left hand."

"Still three weeks before the trip."

"The doctor advised him not to play for a month."

"And if it gets better sooner?"

"Don't you know Alexandrov? A month means thirty days."

"Today's April 10."

"He'll call us on May 10 to tell us that he can start working."

"Our trip's from the third to the tenth."

"Exactly."

"So? Wait or warn Peter in Vienna right away?"

"Why wait? The sooner the better. Let him find a replacement."

"I'll try to get Vienna."

"Then call me right back. I'll be at home."

I got through to Peter Weiser, our manager in Vienna, after only two hours.

"Peter?" I asked. "This is Dubinsky from the Borodin Quartet."

"Oh, hi, how are you?"

"Peter, we have a problem." And I told him about Alexandrov.

"Listen, the tour is sold out. I can't cancel it."

"Maybe another group before it's too late?"

"Out of the question. People are waiting for you. What can you suggest?"

"Let me think . . . A piano quartet, maybe?"

"Not bad. And the program?"

"We have already played Mozart, Shostakovich, and Brahms."

"Excellent. Who is the pianist?"

"The best—my wife."

"Are you sure?"

"Positive."

"Well, I'll agree, then."

"Peter . . ."

"Yes?"

"She is my wife."

"You told me already."

"And I'm her husband."

"So what?"

"And we have no children . . ."

"Oh, I see . . . I'll talk to Goskoncert."

We said goodbye and I hung up the receiver. Luba, who had listened to the whole conversation, looked at me thoughtfully.

"Who knows?" I said. "What if they really let us go abroad together?"

*   *   *

Yura Markov, the assistant program editor at Goskoncert, called me the next day. I often brought him foreign postage stamps, and talking with him was always easy.

"Listen," said Yura, "Peter called us from Vienna . . . We've decided that a piano quartet should be sent to him. I urgently need a program."

"I have one. But, Yura, this time I'm going with my wife . . ."

"Don't worry. Permission has been given. Your first concert is on the fourth in Salzburg."

"Thanks, Yura. I'll bring the program tomorrow."

At our first rehearsal I felt the change right away. A beautiful woman was with us, and for that reason my colleagues had shaved painstakingly, put on cologne, and dressed with taste. They smiled and spoke pleasantly. Furthermore, without Alexandrov, Berlinsky seemed like a different person. There was now a non-Party majority in our piano quartet, and it was possible to relax for a while. This was especially noticeable when we rehearsed the Shostakovich Trio in E-minor. Berlinsky said that the officially accepted program of the work did not correspond exactly to reality.

My wife and I only glanced at each other.

The trio was written during the war, right after the Seventh or "Leningrad" Symphony. Soviet musicologists explained the complete absence of optimism in these works as the result of the treacherous attack of the Germans on the peace-loving Soviet Union and the ensuing war, unequaled in its brutality. They conveniently forgot that the first movement of the Seventh Symphony already existed a year before the war, back when Stalin was still Hitler's faithful friend. And really, how could one openly say that Shostakovich's music depicts the destruction of Russian thought and culture, their gradual ruin, which Stalin began and Hitler only wanted to complete?

To translate the sounds into words is an ungrateful task, all the more so because every listener interprets music in his own way. But if, after the performance of the trio, the whole audience is depressingly silent and doesn't hurry to applaud, does it not suggest that the bitter tale of the much-abused composer has been heard and understood?

And yet, if one wants to express the music of the trio in words, its very beginning sounds like an anxious premonition of misfortune. It overwhelms the listener without mercy, and eventually, in the second movement, in the scherzo, there bursts forth a fiendish, destructive dance of death. In the third movement, the passacaglia, one hears blood-curdling piano chords. Is it not the sound of a hammer on a railway track which tells the prisoners of the concentration camp that "one more day in the life of Ivan Denisovich" has started? While this evil sound reverberates across the hall, the violin and cello weep and pray for the people who perished.

The finale increases in tension, achieving in chamber music the rarely attained dynamic *fff*. When it seems that all means of expression are exhausted, the violin and cello unexpectedly become mute. As if in deathly agony, a wail escapes from a throat strangled by an iron hand. The trio ends with the initial Jewish motif, disappearing into nothingness, like a question mark about the fate of the whole nation. It was the courageous act of an artist who dares to tell the truth and who, for this, in four years' time would be condemned to silence.

I was afraid that Shostakovich's trio might affect our performance of Mozart and Brahms. It could be dangerous if in Vienna our Mozart suddenly turned out to be a gloomy pessimist. I felt that the so-called Mozart smile, if it appeared in our playing, did so only through tears. But I wanted to bring just that feeling to Europe from Russia.

We worked without looking at our watches and didn't hurry to leave after rehearsals. We began again, as before, to meet without the instruments, to go to concerts together, and to sit in the kitchen in the evening over a bottle of wine.

Then, five days before we were supposed to go, Yura called me late at night when we were already asleep.

"Did I wake you? I decided it was better to tell you right away— you're not going. Not because you're husband and wife, but because of the holidays."

"I don't get it."

"Listen . . . I went outside especially to call you from a pay phone. But I didn't call you and didn't say anything . . . Agreed?"

"Agreed."

"There's a rule that all telephone conversations three days before a trip abroad and three days after are recorded. Before departure the tape is carefully checked and if everything's 'clean' you go; if not, you don't. But now, because of the May Day holidays, everything will be closed and there'll be no one to listen to the tape."

"Yura, it's stupid. You know I will come back."

"The law is the law."

"That's final?"

"Unfortunately. Maybe there will be another chance."

"Then it won't be the holidays but something else."

"Well, you shouldn't say that . . . So long!"

I found the cradle in the darkness and put the receiver back. My wife moved closer to me and put her head on my chest.

"Don't get upset," she said.

"Damned authorities, eavesdropping on telephone conversations."

"Don't get upset. We'll go some other time."

"The hell we will!"

Oh, America!

1964

FOR THE typical Russian, the idea of traveling to the countries of
Western Europe calls up a whole gamut of feelings: Finland and
Sweden—an affectionate smile; the Benelux countries—reverence;
England and West Germany—deep excitement; France, Italy, and
Spain—utter delight. Japan and Australia sound like science fiction,
something like an interplanetary voyage, and the word "America" acts
like an electric shock.

Soviet performers who are leaving for America are subjected to this
shock twice: once at the official notification by the Ministry of Culture,
and then upon receiving the foreign passport. The ordinary Russian
passport is small, gray, and, as a rule, crumpled, because it must be
with you at all times. This passport is for internal use only, and it is
forbidden to travel abroad with it. It lists the bearer's first and last
names, and the date and place of birth, followed by the so-called fifth
point—nationality. (A logical absurdity, since the passport itself es-
tablishes the nationality of its owner.) The police can demand to see
it without the least explanation. Too many times I saw their eyes stop
at the fifth point and their curious expressions, as if they were wondering, What are you doing in the Soviet Union?

The foreign passport, however, was another story altogether. Larger,
and printed on the highest quality paper, it had no fifth point but,

rather, declared proudly that its owner was a citizen of the Soviet Union. It had to be exchanged for the ordinary passport as soon as the bearer returned home. But if I arrived late on a Friday, the Ministry of Culture would be closed for the weekend and for those two days the foreign passport would work wonders at home. With it I could get a ticket to the movies or the theater without standing in line, get a room in a Moscow hotel, and even make it into a restaurant in the evening. But, more important, with this passport I felt like a full citizen of the Soviet Union.

In the United States I was to speak about this many times with American Jews, but now, in 1964, when I was flying there for the first time, my thoughts were busy only with our first concert in New York's Carnegie Hall.

Our flight to America was a long one, with stops in Vilnius, Warsaw, and Copenhagen, and then a three-hour wait for the plane to New York. When we finally reached the Wellington Hotel exactly twenty-four hours later, it was nightfall, but in Moscow it was already morning. My body, accustomed to waking up at this time, refused to fall asleep again. After tossing in bed until 4 A.M., I went out in the hall to walk around a bit. The whole quartet was there, standing by the elevator, smoking and talking. An empty vodka bottle stood on the floor.

"Even a bottle, I see, didn't help you."

"One bottle can't help right away."

"What can we do?" I said. "Next time we'll be smarter and arrive two days before the concert."

"No way!" Shebalin assured me. "The Ministry of Culture has to place a request with the government for each extra day abroad."

"What if we explained to them that because of the time change it's essential for the success of the concert?"

"They don't care! We're allowed to go abroad for sixty days out of the year, and they want to squeeze sixty concerts out of us."

"Let them go to hell!"

"And us, too!"

After agreeing to meet downstairs two hours before the concert, we went back to our rooms.

Lying on my back, I tried to relax, using a yoga technique. In my thoughts I cut off my legs at the knees and imagined that there was nothing below them. Then I moved up to the hips, higher and higher, until only my head remained. According to the laws of yoga I now should have fallen asleep. Just when I was about to slip into some sort of non-being, I jumped as if I had been struck by a hammer. My pulse started racing and didn't calm down for a long time.

"Let's leave these psychological experiments for the yogis," I said aloud, went into the bathroom, and stood under the shower. The warm water was soothing. "Well, now for a much better cure for all sickness and misfortune: take the violin and play scales." To keep from disturbing my neighbors, I put on the heavy mute and had a good practice. I felt more confident and peaceful. This "yoga" is the best remedy for a musician before a concert.

Three hours passed unnoticeably, until my stomach reminded me that in Moscow it was already 5 P.M. I went downstairs to a little coffee shop. At the counter, a huge black man was working with fantastic speed, and as I got up on a high stool between two American women, he wiped the counter and glanced at me.

"Ham and eggs, please," I said.

"Sure thing. Why-or-whee?"

"Excuse me?"

"Why-or-whee?"

"I am sorry," I said, confused.

The lady to my right turned to me. "Do you want white or wheat bread?" she explained.

"Oh, thank you very much. White, please," I said to the black man.

He smiled broadly, showing a set of very white teeth. "Where are you from?"

"Moscow, Russia," I said.

"No kidding! You're a Russian, then?"

"I sure am," I answered without hesitation. I really did feel Russian. Yet in Russia I never would have been able to say that.

"You're the first Russian I've ever seen!"

"Well, now," I said. "The same two legs, two arms, and one silly head, right?"

"You bet!" the black man said, and everyone around us laughed.

"First time in New York?" he asked.

"Yes. I play a concert tonight."

"Really! A gig in the Big Apple! Where?"

"Around the corner, in Carnegie Hall."

"No kidding!" the black man exclaimed. "You must be very good, then. I hear they send only their best from Russia . . . Here's your ham and eggs, sir. Enjoy your meal."

"Thank you!"

As soon as the black man walked away, the lady to my right pulled a pair of tickets out of her purse and showed them to me. "I'm coming to your concert tonight. I'm looking forward to it very much!"

"I hope you'll like it!"

"Oh, I'm sure I will! I just love your recording of Shostakovich!"

"Thank you."

Immediately a man farther down the counter asked loudly, "I've read about Soviet Russia. Do you mind telling me if it's true that Russians have their wives in common?"

"Excuse me?"

"I mean, do you share wives?"

I laughed. "You see, sometimes we do, but their husbands usually don't know about it."

"Oh, I see! Like everywhere else in the world."

Now everyone in the coffee shop was laughing.

I felt the confusion and awkwardness which typically never abandon Soviet people abroad disappearing without a trace. It was as if I could talk openly about anything with these people, these Americans that I had met by chance.

Someone else asked, "The watch you're wearing, does it belong to you or to the government?"

"It belongs to me, as does everything else you see on me."

"The things you read in the papers!"

"But you yourself, who do you belong to?"

This was a serious question, and the Americans waited for my answer. I slowly said, "If you belong to your country, you have to accept its laws, even if they are not quite right."

As I was saying that pretty sentence, I felt that I was lying. In the first place, it wasn't mine; I had read it somewhere and now passed it off as my own. Furthermore, it gave a false impression of the Soviet people, as if they were able to admit that there could be imperfect laws in the idyllic state of the "workers and peasants." It would have been more honest to say that my watch and suit really did belong to me, but that I myself—my violin, my conversations, and even my thoughts—belonged entirely to the government. "And I, ladies and gentlemen, just like my colleagues in the quartet, like all my friends and acquaintances in the U.S.S.R., am no longer a person but a product!"

I knew that someday I would tell all that, but not now. Nonetheless, my answer sounded profound, and everyone nodded their heads approvingly.

I finished my ham and eggs and left a dollar tip on the counter.

"Thank you," said the black man. I shook his hand, and my hand was lost in his. He smiled broadly and said, "Good luck tonight."

When the alarm clock woke me later that afternoon, I didn't know where I was. Consciousness was slow in coming back. "Oh yes, New York, and soon the concert!" I tore my head away from the pillow and staggered into the shower on half-bent legs. The cool water made me feel better. I started getting dressed for the concert. At six we all met downstairs and set off for Carnegie Hall. When we passed the coffee shop, the door was open and I saw the black counterman. He waved at me and shouted, "Break a leg, boy!"

"Did you understand what he said?" asked Shebalin.

"He wished us luck."

"How would he know?"

"He's from the KGB."

Carnegie Hall seemed enormous, especially when we sat alone onstage. Berlinsky started to worry. "You think they'll hear anything?"

"You all play, I'll go out there and listen," I said.

From the hall the quartet looked like an island lost in the ocean, but the sound carried beautifully.

"Wonderful! Everything resounds!"

At seven-thirty the manager appeared and asked us to go backstage.

"Another five minutes, please?"

"Sorry," he said. "People are waiting."

At eight exactly, the manager opened the stage door for us. "Gentlemen, I wish you a good concert."

I took one look at the crowd and my first impulse was to go back. I turned around. Behind me, with pale faces, stood the quartet.

"Well, then. Shall we go?"

"Go to hell!" Shebalin said.

"God bless me!" I said, and took the first step. I could hear the manager behind me continue, "And everybody, amen!" and then everything was drowned out by the applause. It seemed to take an eternity for us to reach our chairs and take our places. I looked at the others and lifted the violin . . .

As a compliment to the Americans, we began the concert with Samuel Barber's only quartet, Opus 11. We had already played this quartet in the Soviet Union, and it had pleased everyone with its remarkable adagio in the second movement. It became so popular that it was even played at funerals, an honor twentieth-century music doesn't often earn. But I love the whole quartet, especially the second theme in the first movement. It's one of those melodies which can't be played rhythmically. For a long time I didn't know what to do with it, until after a concert in Riga an old Jewish man came to see us backstage. With tears in his eyes, he said that he had prayed along with us to the Hebrew God during the Barber. But of course! Why hadn't I caught on before! We changed the character of the music right away and started playing it like a prayer; Russian or Jewish Orthodox, it didn't matter.

The Barber was very successful. We had to bow several times. Then we sat down again and continued the concert with Borodin's second quartet. This was also a gesture, but this time to our own country, so that it would be clear to everyone where we came from. Our initial nervousness had subsided, and we allowed ourselves full interpretive freedom. When we finished, many in the audience rose from their seats and applauded. We heard shouts of "Bravo!" and in Beethoven's late quartet, Opus 131, we felt that our playing had taken off, carrying us into the realm of pure spirituality.

The audience gave us a long standing ovation.

The night after our first concert was even longer than the one before. There couldn't be any question of sleep. As I lay in the darkness with my eyes open, I heard my colleagues' voices in the corridor, the sound of pouring liquid, Berlinsky's shouts of "Pour more, don't be stingy!" Shebalin's deep bass, and general laughter. I didn't know whether I should go out or not, and lay without moving.

When I came out of my hotel room the next morning, violin in one hand and suitcase in the other, I saw two newspapers outside my door, each opened to the Arts page. I took them along. The others were already downstairs, holding copies of the same two newspapers.

Berlinsky waved the papers. "Well, what does the bourgeois press say? Have you read it?"

"Not yet."

"And don't right now," said Alexandrov. "When we get on the airplane you can translate everything in detail."

We had an early flight to Cincinnati, followed in the evening by a concert with a different program. We all sat in the same row on the plane, and when it took off I got out the newspapers. Both stories were headed RUSSIANS IN CARNEGIE HALL. *The New York Times* said that the Russians had crossed the ocean especially to show the Americans how Barber should be played, that Borodin himself could not have dreamed of a better performance of his music, and that in the Beethoven "the guests' " playing recalled the famous Budapest Quartet in its best years. "An altogether unforgettable evening."

"Look at that," remarked Berlinsky, "even the prostituted Western press occasionally tells the truth. Who signed it?"

"Some Harold Schonberg."

"A good guy! We should send him a bottle of vodka. Read the second one!"

It was the *New York Post*. The critic wrote that, as expected, the Russians had completely misunderstood Barber and shouldn't even have gone to the trouble of including him in the program; that Borodin's music, after the recent Broadway musical *Kismet*, simply couldn't be tolerated any longer; and that he had walked out during the Beethoven, because the Borodin Quartet had immediately shown its utter helplessness. "A forgettable quartet and a wasted evening!"

We looked at each other without speaking. Finally, Berlinsky burst out: "A typical anti-Soviet sally!"

"It's their democracy," said Alexandrov, "everyone says what he wants. He should come to the Soviet Union! They'd teach him what's what pretty fast."

"But what the hell does he mean?" I said desperately. "His first duty is to describe honestly what happened in the hall and the audience's reaction. And after that, damn it, let him write what he wants. But this way, what do you get? We didn't just dream up the standing ovation and the shouts of 'Bravo,' the crowd of people backstage, many of them with tears in their eyes; but none of that means anything to him, and the whole country will read his stinking opinion and start quoting it as their own . . ."

"I spit on the grave of his donkey's master!" Shebalin swore with Oriental color.

"It's better in the Soviet Union," said Berlinsky dreamily. "There's no criticism at all."

"That's true," agreed Alexandrov. "So? Send him a bottle of vodka, too?"

"He can go to hell!" said Berlinsky. "If I ever meet him . . ." He began frantically biting his nails and turned toward the window.

"Shostakovich once said something very good about criticism," remarked Shebalin.

"I don't know it," I answered, although I'd already heard this story several times.

"Well!" Shebalin livened up. "It's his favorite story. He comes into a restaurant and orders a steak. The waiter takes his order and goes to the kitchen. The cook makes that very steak, the waiter brings it, Shostakovich eats it . . . Everyone is happy, it seems that everything is fine! But not at all! Some critic comes over and goes on and on about what is none of his business."

"What a drone!" said Berlinsky.

"You try for them," sighed Alexandrov. "You don't sleep nights, you work your fingers to the bone!"

"Let them all go to hell!" said Shebalin, so loudly that the whole plane could hear. "Call the stewardess and order me some vodka."

"And me!" said Berlinsky.

"A double for me!" added Alexandrov, showing me two fingers.

I waved to the pretty stewardess and asked her for four double vodkas.

The Americans sitting behind us laughed loudly. "Are you Russians?"

"Yes," I said, "we are."

"Do you like it here?"

"Oh yes! Fantastic country."

The stewardess brought the vodka and made a sign to fasten our belts. The plane was coming in for a landing.

I got off the plane first. I usually did so when we were in English-speaking countries. If I hadn't moved toward the exit, my colleagues would just have stayed on the plane. It was easier for them in Europe, since they all spoke a little German, but here when we were met at the airport, for those first minutes of polite handshakes and tense smiles, they felt uncomfortable not speaking the language.

At the gate a crowd met us.

An elderly man with a sad face held out his hand to me and smiled gently. "Are you Mr. Dubinsky?"

"I am indeed."

"I am Mr. Schwartz. Welcome to Cincinnati!"

"Thank you."

He shook hands with each of us. Then he introduced everyone meeting us, and everyone shook our hands and smiled.

"How long have you been on tour already?" Mr. Schwartz asked.

"Yesterday we played our first concert in the United States."

"How many more to go?"

"Another twenty-nine."

"Oh my! Are you the leader of the quartet?"

"Let us say I am the only one in the group who speaks English."

He smiled politely. "And you translate for the others?"

"It depends. You see, they have already learned how to say 'One hamburger and two beers,' and as long as they have that and a quiet room to sleep in, they don't care much."

Mr. Schwartz nodded his head. "That probably will make my life a bit easier," he said thoughtfully.

"Easier? What do you mean?"

But he did not answer. "This way, please. We'll pick up your baggage first. You must have a lot for such a long trip."

"Not really, only four suitcases. We know how boring it is to pack and unpack every day."

"I understand," he said sympathetically. "But we didn't know that, and we came with four cars."

"One would do."

"I see . . . Listen, would your friends be kind enough to share the other cars while you come with me?"

"I'll ask them. Excuse us for speaking Russian."

"But of course, of course . . ."

"What do they want?" Berlinsky asked.

"They suggest that we each take a car so no one will feel slighted."

"The hell with them! I don't speak English."

"Me neither," echoed Alexandrov.

"You don't have to. Just sit there peacefully and . . ."

"And smile," Alexandrov continued for me.

"Like dummies," concluded Shebalin.

"We shouldn't offend them," I said. "Their host is a nice guy and happens to be Jewish."

"I don't speak Yiddish either," Berlinsky said.

"Any trouble?" Mr. Schwartz asked.

"Oh no," I said. "We were just discussing what time to meet before the concert."

"The hall is free the whole day, and you are welcome any time." I turned to the others.

"Well, so what? Should we make trouble or give in immediately?"

"Oh, the hell with them!" Alexandrov said. "They want it that way, we'll do it that way. The sooner we get to the hotel and get some sleep, the better."

"Okay," I said to Mr. Schwartz. "Let's go."

As we left the airport in his car, Mr. Schwartz said, "I'm afraid we're going to have some trouble tonight."

I waited.

"Looks pretty serious, unfortunately. There will be protesters. They have caused some unpleasantness with Soviet performers here before. Shouting and noise outside. Sometimes even worse: tomatoes and apples thrown at the musicians from the audience. Last time we had to stop the concert."

"What do they want?"

"They want to attract attention to the situation of Jews in your country."

"I know the situation in my country," I said. "And quite well. Better than they do."

Mr. Schwartz patted my shoulder. "Don't I know! Don't I know!"

And after a while he asked, "Are there any other Jews in the quartet?"

"No," I said. "They're Russians. They're good Russians."

"Mr. Berlinsky, too? He looks Jewish."

"Yes, he does."

"Would you talk to the others? Just to be ready in case anything happens."

"Let me think, Mr. Schwartz, let me think. There are two Party members in our quartet, and their reaction will be different from mine. When they're together, they think the same way. They have no choice, I'm afraid. But we'll see. Maybe I can talk to them separately."

Mr. Schwartz put his hand on my shoulder again. "Sorry, my friend, and . . . thank you."

When we gathered together again in the lobby of the hotel, I could tell right away that talking to them would be useless. They were all angry and wanted only the keys to their rooms. If I were to tell them now, they would immediately call the Soviet embassy to get instructions.

"We are soldiers!" Berlinsky would say. "If we are told to play—we'll play; if we're told to cancel the concert—we'll cancel the concert."

I looked at Mr. Schwartz and shook my head slightly. He nodded to me in return and said, "Is it all right if we pick you up at six-thirty, then?"

"Yes, please."

We went to our rooms. Without bothering to unpack, I undressed and went to bed. Suddenly the phone rang, jolting me awake. I picked up the receiver.

"Mr. Dubinsky?" came Mr. Schwartz's voice. "I hope I didn't wake you."

"It's all right," I said in a choked voice.

"It looks as if they're going to give you a very hot reception."

"What do you mean?"

"They know that you're coming to warm up before the concert and they want to meet you at the entrance. You know, with the slogans and shouts and who knows what else. The only way to avoid them is to come to the hall before they get there. Say at five o'clock."

"Okay, Mr. Schwartz. We'll be in the lobby at five."

"Good. Thank you. And please excuse me."

He hung up the phone. I suddenly felt lousy.

The relations within our quartet had changed in America. At home everything was normal. I was the coach of the quartet; I edited the scores, ran the rehearsals, and got the quartet ready for concerts. This arrangement suited my colleagues. As long as the work went well and the quartet was successful, everything was fine, and if ideological friction with the authorities developed for any reason, there was always me to blame. But it was another matter in the United States, where, with my English skills, the whole organizational side of the quartet's life was dumped on me. By default I was the captain of our team, something like a commissar, but a "White" one. That was the whole trouble! You have to be born a commander; you can choose your color later. I wasn't a born leader, and my "color," from the point of view of my Soviet comrades, was not right. They couldn't support me, because of their Party loyalty, even if they wanted to, and as a result a wall began to grow up between us. The longer we were abroad, the higher the wall grew. Were my colleagues simply more attentive than

I in reading *Rules of Conduct for Soviet Citizens in Capitalist Countries*—a book that stated that all foreigners are potential enemies of the Soviet Union, that personal contact with them was forbidden, that one should expect provocation from them at every step? Or was it the lack of language that created a barrier?

Of course, now I couldn't get back to sleep.

I didn't mind playing concerts every evening, even with the daily trips, suitcases, and hotels. When you play often, a certain inertia is created, making coming out onstage almost a habit, and the personal cost isn't so great. But you really need to sleep, and preferably at night. If that doesn't work out, then your only hope is sleeping in the daytime. And if that fails, too, the whole rhythm of concert life is ruined. In that case, people can't expect deep musical revelations from performers. You drag yourself offstage and thank God. Reluctantly, at four o'clock I phoned the other members of the quartet one by one. I knew they were all sleeping, but there was no other choice. I apologized each time and repeated, "I hate to wake you up, but we have to leave at five."

They answered me with curses.

We met downstairs and everyone asked why the hurry all of a sudden. There was no point trying to explain the situation now. I'd be to blame for everything.

"Who knows?" I said, like a coward. "They say there's heavy traffic, and it's a long way."

"And where were they before, damn them?" said Shebalin. "I can't play without sleeping."

"I can't either," echoed Alexandrov.

"No one can," I said.

"*You* can," said Berlinsky. "You and your 'Do you speak English?' " By the way, what did you talk about in the car with that Jew?"

"What do Jews usually talk about?" I asked him back.

"Watch it, you'll get yourself into trouble! And us along with you. Here he comes, your Jew!"

Mr. Schwartz appeared in the doorway. I went to meet him and, before the others caught up, managed to whisper, "They don't know yet . . ."

We all crowded into the car. Berlinsky lit a cigarette right away and smoked without stopping until we reached the concert hall. It was a quarter after five; we had never come to a concert so early.

"So where's the traffic?" asked Berlinsky angrily. "Ask him why we came three hours before the concert."

"They're afraid the concert will be picketed, so they've brought us before the crowd could gather."

"Why didn't we know anything?" he demanded.

"You were sleeping, and I didn't want to wake you up."

"We have to phone the embassy right away," he said.

"Everything's still quiet. There'll be plenty of time to phone."

"Then ask him to bring some coffee, and strong. I have no strength to play."

"What is he saying?" Mr. Schwartz asked.

"They want coffee."

"Oh, sure. I have coffee and tea with me."

I sighed with relief. So far everything had gone off without bloodshed.

We were gradually warming up onstage when from outside the hall came a noise that drowned out the music. It was repeated a minute later, over and over. We stopped playing. Mr. Schwartz came onstage. His face seemed paler than usual.

"Is that it?" I asked.

He nodded. The noise was coming more frequently, finally melting into a constant roar.

"I advise that you leave the stage," said Mr. Schwartz. "You never know!"

We could hear the roar from backstage. Berlinsky and Alexandrov whispered to each other about something, while Shebalin sat down heavily in an armchair and closed his eyes. I went over to Mr. Schwartz. "What if I try to talk to them?"

"Are you serious?"

"Yes, why not?"

"It might be dangerous."

"It's pretty bad now."

"Wait here, I'll come back." He went out.

"What did you say?" asked Berlinsky.

"I want to go out and talk to them."

"You're crazy! We're supposed to ignore them. Talking with them means we recognize them. What do you think?" He turned to Alexandrov.

Alexandrov nodded.

"There, you see! Under no circumstances," said Berlinsky, raising his voice.

"What should we do, then?"

"Nothing. It's not our concern. Let them get themselves out of this position."

Mr. Schwartz came back. "If you haven't changed your mind, it can be arranged."

"Translation!" shouted Berlinsky.

I translated. He and Mr. Schwartz waited to see what I would say.

"Okay, Mr. Schwartz, let me try."

He ran out of the dressing room.

"You trying to be Napoleon?" yelled Berlinsky. "You don't have any right! No one granted you that authority. Remember, we're all against it!" He coughed and nervously grabbed his cigarette.

Mr. Schwartz reappeared and took me through an underground corridor and up a spiral staircase. Then he opened a door for me, and I found myself on the street, face to face with a huge crowd of people. I stood in front of them clumsily in my tails, like a creature from another world, and it became very quiet. Hundreds of eyes looked at me from all sides. A lot of people were holding up posters that read, "Communism is Fascism." A woman stepped out of the crowd and came up to me. Thick black hair fell to her shoulders, and her deep-set eyes looked piercingly into mine.

"You wanted to talk with me?"

"Yes."

"I'm listening."

She stood in front of the crowd, the way generals have stood in front of their armies since the dawn of civilization. Behind her was her army, her people, for whose sake she was ready to fight to the death. And what was behind me? My colleagues, who were cursing me at that moment? My homeland, which would punish me severely, regardless of whether I won or lost the battle?

"Yes, I wanted to talk with you. I came here from Russia to play for Americans. When I play, I try to say everything in my music that I know and feel about Russia. I'm sure that there will be people in the hall who'll understand that. Maybe there'll be only a few, but they'll hear a living word from another world. During a concert, music brings people together and destroys the artificially created barriers between them."

While I spoke, her eyes drilled into mine. I could see her breathing. . . .

". . . I understand why you've come here. More than that, if it happened that I lived in this city, I think that I would be here with you."

Tears came to her eyes, and quickly leaning toward me, she kissed me on the forehead. Then she turned back to her own people and made a sweeping gesture away from the hall.

I went back to the door. Mr. Schwartz opened it from the inside and held out his arms to me.

"I heard everything," he said. "Everything!"

I went back to the dressing room and got my violin. My head was buzzing, my heart beating loudly, and my hands shaking. "It'll pass," I told myself, "just wait a little." From the hall I could hear the usual noise before a concert, but outside it was quiet.

A beaming Mr. Schwartz came to meet me. "There's no one outside! They all left!"

"Tomorrow all this will be in the papers," I said, "and they'll call us back to Moscow right away."

"Newspapers?" asked Mr. Schwartz. "Don't worry. I know a few people. I'll call right now. Don't worry!" He ran away again.

There was half an hour left until the concert. We all stood in separate corners and warmed up. At five to eight I went up to each of my colleagues in turn and checked the tuning as usual. Not a word was said.

Mr. Schwartz glanced in the doorway and smiled at me. "Everything's all right, don't worry. Play beautifully."

During the intermission people tried to come into the dressing room to thank us, but Mr. Schwartz wouldn't let anyone in and only repeated, "After the concert, please." And after the concert people flooded back to us. We signed at least a hundred programs and listened to many excited compliments. Mr. Schwartz was beaming, as if it were his birthday, but I could hardly stand up. The sleepless night and the nervous strain of the evening were having their effects. When the crowd had finally left, he said, "I know you're tired, but it would be my pleasure if you'd come to my house for dinner."

"Mr. Schwartz is inviting us to his house for dinner," I translated. My colleagues were silent.

"We have to say something," I said in Russian, but to no avail.

I turned to Mr. Schwartz. "My friends are tired."

"I understand. What about you? You must be exhausted!"

"What if I don't change clothes, and only for half an hour?"

"Oh, that's fine. We'll take your friends to the hotel in another car."

My colleagues had already put away their instruments and were waiting by the door.

"They'll drive you home now," I said.

"And you?" asked Berlinsky.

"I'll go visit the Jews," I said.

As Mr. Schwartz was driving me to his house, he reached out in the darkness and shook my hand.

"I appreciate what you have done for us. And don't worry, nothing will be in the papers. They promised me."

"Let's hope," I said.

"Oh yes, they understood. Your coming out to them before the concert disarmed them completely. They were ready for anything except that. They were prepared to walk across the stage with placards in their hands . . ."

"Thank God, it's over now."

"I wanted to ask you, Mr. Dubinsky . . . You talk so freely. We recently had several other Soviet musicians, and they wouldn't say a word."

"I know. They never do."

"My wife and some of our friends are looking forward so much to meeting you."

He stopped in front of his house.

"Mr. Schwartz?" I said.

"Yes, my friend?"

"I'm sorry. I'm afraid I can't talk anymore today."

"So don't. Just come in, relax, and have something to eat."

"I'm afraid I can't even eat right now."

"Come in and say hello. Then I'll take you back to the hotel."

"Please excuse me. Could you do that right away?"

Mr. Schwartz stared at me for a moment, then started the engine.

"I'm sorry," I said.

"I understand."

He drove me back to the hotel. We sat a while longer in the car.

"Where are you going from here?"

"Waco, Texas."

"A long way. You don't play tomorrow, do you?"

"No, not tomorrow."

"That's good. You need a rest. Sleep well."

"Yes, I certainly could use it."

"Thank you so much for the beautiful concert and for everything."

"Thank you, too."

He shook my hand firmly. "Goodbye, Mr. Dubinsky."

"Goodbye, Mr. Schwartz."

He lifted his hand and looked at me sadly. I waved and stood there until he drove away, then went into the hotel.

The clerk gave me the key to my room and asked, "How was the concert?"

"Good, thank you."

"There's someone waiting for you. A lady." He gave me a wink and pointed to a woman sitting in an armchair with her back to us. I saw dark hair hanging down to her shoulders . . .

"Hi," I said, walking up to her.

She was sitting with her legs crossed, smoking. The lovely lines of her full legs were clearly visible under her long skirt. "I wanted to talk to you," she said.

I sat down.

"You must be exhausted," she continued.

"Not any longer," I said. Strangely, it was true. I really did feel better now, and I was looking at her legs. Or should I say that I was looking at her legs and felt better? She noticed my stare and straightened up in the chair. Her hair fell across her face, covering her left eye.

"Look," I said. "Why don't we go up to my room and talk there?"

"No. We won't talk there."

"It's all right if we don't."

She was silent for a time, shook her head, and pushed her hair back. "No, I came to talk. I came here because you made a deep impression on all of us tonight. People keep talking about you. Why aren't you scared, like all your countrymen?"

"I am," I said.

"No, you aren't! The way you talked to me, the mere fact that you wanted to meet us . . . No Soviet would ever dare do that."

"I know. They have very strict orders from Moscow."

"Haven't you?"

I nodded. "Me too."

"So why, then? Why did you come out to us?"

"I told you already. I felt I could have been with you tonight."

"Oh, my God! That phrase again! It killed me when you said it the first time. Everyone's repeating it!"

I said nothing. Everything that had already happened this evening was receding into the past, and it seemed to me that this conversation was not really about me but about somebody else, and I was merely observing everything from the side.

"Where do you go from here?"

I held out our itinerary. She read it attentively, ashes from her cigarette falling on the paper. "Waco, Laguna Beach, San Diego, Los Angeles, Cleveland, Pittsburgh . . . Do you mind if I write down a couple of these telephone numbers?"

"Go ahead."

She returned the itinerary to me. "It's possible that in some places your concerts will be picketed again."

"Oh no. Not again. I can't do it twice. Let my friends handle it next time."

"I wanted to know about that. How did your friends react to all this?"

"Badly. Very badly. They've stopped talking to me."

She nodded. "It must be very hard for you."

"It is."

"What are you going to do?"

"Go to my room and get some sleep."

She smiled and looked at me with her dark eyes. "Are you going back to Russia?"

"I am."

"Why?"

This was the first time anyone had asked me that. I don't think I had even asked myself the question so directly.

"My wife," I said.

"Is that the only reason?"

"If I don't return, her life in Moscow will be a disaster. And I'd never see her again."

She put her hand on mine, drew closer to me, and whispered intensely, "You shouldn't go back. You're here and you belong here. Stay, and we'll start an enormous campaign to get your wife out. They listen to us in the Kremlin. I can't tell you any more, but believe me, I know what I'm talking about. We can get your wife out of there."

She was squeezing my hand firmly, her cheeks were flushed, she looked me in the eye without glancing away. I tried to look straight back, but I couldn't.

"Well," I said at last, "I only know that this time I'm going back."

She let go of my hand and looked away. "You're tired. I'd better go now."

She got up from the armchair and held out her hand. Then she bent over and, as she had earlier, kissed me on the forehead and said, "God bless you." I watched her walk to the exit, open the door, and go out to the street without looking back.

*   *   *

In the morning I came downstairs and bought the local newspapers. Mr. Schwartz evidently knew what he was talking about, for there wasn't a word about yesterday's incident, or even about the concert itself. So much the better. All that was yesterday and it seemed to have nothing to do with today.

I checked us out of the hotel. Although everything was paid for by our manager, I had to sign the bills. Walking into the coffee shop for breakfast, I met the rest of the quartet there. They politely said hello and continued their conversation. I sat down at a separate table.

At the airport, while my colleagues drank beer at the bar, I checked in four tickets to Waco, Texas. Fortunately, it turned out that there were not many passengers on the flight, so when I gave the stewardess my boarding pass she smiled and said, "Any place, sir." I went to the back of the plane, where there was no one around me. I fastened the seat belt and watched as the plane steered onto the runway and, without stopping, picked up speed. It rose straight into the clouds, the cabin became darker, and suddenly there was a bright sun and a white sea of clouds below us. The light was blinding, I closed my eyes and felt the warmth of the sunlight on my face . . .

When I opened them again, I saw Berlinsky in front of me with a glass of wine in each hand. He extended one glass to me and said, "This is for you from the quartet."

He sat down. A strong smell of alcohol emanated from him. He looked at me and raised his glass in a gesture of goodwill. We each took a sip, as if we were smoking a peace pipe. He asked thoughtfully, "What do you think, are there Jews in Waco?"

"Where don't you find them?" I replied.

"We'll get into trouble, then," he said gloomily. "If our people find out, that will be it! Finished! The quartet will be scattered to the devil's mother!"

"Can they find out in Moscow?"

"Easily. They have their people everywhere. Even among the Jews." I said nothing.

"Especially now," he continued cautiously, "that we have begun to travel without a Fifth . . ."

"No, that can't be! You think that there's a Fifth among us?"

"Anything is possible."

"How can we go on, then?"

"By keeping quiet," he said. "By playing and keeping quiet."

"That won't work. Everybody knows that I speak English."

"You can always give a reason: being tired, not having slept the night before . . . or, how do they say here, 'I'm sorry'?"

"Yes . . . 'I'm sorry.' "

"I'll breathe easier when this tour is over," he said unhappily.

"We'll return home and again be striving to go to the West."

"And if we're sent east for a long time, what then?"

"That's bad," I said.

"Exactly."

Above us the FASTEN SEAT BELTS sign went on. "I'm going back to my seat," he said, finishing his wine and leaving.

What was the meaning of this Fifth, I wondered. Did we really have our own informer among us? Or was Berlinsky's observation meant especially for me—to force me to keep my mouth shut? But if it was true, then who was he? Alexandrov, Shebalin—or Berlinsky himself?

Waco, Texas
1964

I n Waco we were met by a gray-haired man. "My name is Luin,"
he introduced himself. "Welcome to Waco."

"Thank you."

I turned to my colleagues and asked in Russian, "Should I translate?"

"No need," said Berlinsky. "I already know this part by heart."

"I translate for them," I explained to Mr. Luin.

"I see."

"Well, the luggage, and then to the hotel?"

"We've planned an interview for you on TV and then dinner afterward with us."

"Interview and dinner," I translated.

"What sort of goddamn interview?" Berlinsky asked.

"Careful. I'm translating every word."

"Find out what sort of interview."

"He asks about the interview," I said to Mr. Luin.

"It's for publicity, to attract more people to the concert. You're the
first Soviet musicians ever to come to Waco, and they're excited and
would like to talk with you."

I translated carefully. Berlinsky answered for everyone: "We came
here to play. Conversations aren't our business."

"What should I tell him?"

"No interviews. Just like that!"

Mr. Luin was watching us attentively.

"The interview was not mentioned in our schedule," I told him.

"Oh, don't worry, they understand. They'll ask you only about music."

I translated.

"Don't forget where we are!" Berlinsky snarled. "We talked about this back on the plane, right?" He turned to Alexandrov and Shebalin. They nodded. "So that's all. There's a decision by a majority of votes and nothing more to be said. No interviews. Without a phone call to the embassy I won't go."

"It's already evening in Washington, and no one's there."

"There's always someone. Let these society people talk with them and get hold of an official translator."

"Is there anyone here who speaks Russian?" I asked Mr. Luin.

"Why? Your English is excellent."

"Sometimes I wish I couldn't speak it."

Mr. Luin looked at me.

"They don't have an interpreter," I said in Russian.

"For now let's go to the hotel," said Alexandrov. "We'll decide on the way."

In the car, Berlinsky started getting angry. To distract Mr. Luin, I leaned toward him. "Excuse me, Mr. Luin, how do you spell your name?"

"L-u-i-n," he answered quickly. "Why?"

He squinted at me, smiled, and wanted to say something, but Berlinsky wouldn't let us talk. He raised his voice and said that back in Moscow we had been clearly told how to behave, but from the very beginning we had lost our vigilance, that we still didn't know how Cincinnati would turn out, and if in Moscow they found out . . .

I interrupted him. "What's happening at this moment wouldn't be approved in Moscow either."

"It would be!" he shouted. "This very moment would be!"

"American whiskey?" I said, especially for him (drinking abroad was a very serious crime). He couldn't think of anything to answer and nervously lit a cigarette.

In the hotel, once we had received the room keys, Mr. Luin asked, "So what should we do?"

"Give us fifteen minutes. I'll come down either way," I said.

"Okay."

I went into my room and the telephone rang immediately.

"Yes?"

"Cancel the interview right now!" yelled Berlinsky.

"Listen to me and don't shout. If we cancel it now, they'll have a wonderful excuse for being anti-Soviet. This Luin will talk about everything that happened: how we crapped in our pants with terror right away, how we wanted to phone the embassy to demand an official interpreter, and all the yelling in the car. Tomorrow all that will be in the papers, and we'll look great at the concert!"

This was the best way to talk with him, to frighten him even more. He quieted down.

"So what shall we do?"

"Not make Soviet poses in Waco. Here it's stupid."

He was silent.

"Luin is waiting downstairs. What should I tell him?"

"I don't know . . ."

"We'd better all go downstairs."

He didn't say anything and I hung up.

A barely noticeable smile was on Mr. Luin's lips when he saw the four of us downstairs. My colleagues, however, were acting like men condemned to be executed.

We were expected at the television station, and they took us straight to the studio. It was full of people. There were four armchairs in the center. We were pointed toward them and sat down in the order we used onstage. I looked at my comrades' anxious faces from the side. They were not a pretty sight.

"Relax," I said to them. "There's no tragedy. All this is for the good of the concert. A smile wouldn't do any harm."

"You go ahead and smile," Berlinsky replied.

A cheerful young man appeared and looked us over from head to toe. "Hi, my name is John." Turning toward me, he said, "I under-stand you will be translating for us."

"I'll try."

"Okay. I'll ask you where you're from, why your group is called," he glanced at the program, "the Borodin Quartet, where you have played already, and where you go from here. Is that all right with you?"

"It is," I said, and translated his words.

"Are you ready?"

"Yes, any time now."

A signal was given and he turned toward the camera. "Good evening, everyone. I have here with me the famous Russian group, the Borodin String Quartet. They have just arrived in Waco and were kind enough to come to the studio right away. Let me introduce our distinguished guests. Here is"—he turned to me—"but I'm afraid of mispronouncing your names. Would you say them yourself, please?"

"Sure," I said. "I know our names quite well. Just let me translate what you said to my friends."

"Of course. We'd like to listen to your language."

I translated and then introduced the whole quartet, mentioning our names and the instruments we played.

"Thank you. Would you tell us why your group is called Borodin?"

"In our country, string quartets traditionally bear the names of com-posers, most often Russian ones. There are and were quartets named for Beethoven, Glazunov, Tchaikovsky, and Prokofiev. And we go by the name of Borodin."

"I see here that you'll be playing an all-Russian program in Waco —Borodin, Shostakovich, and Tchaikovsky. By the way, Borodin is getting very popular now in the United States, because of the Broadway musical *Kismet*, which uses Borodin's music."

"Yes, unfortunately," I said.

"Why unfortunately?"

"Because two of the songs from *Kismet* are tunes from Borodin's second quartet. They even have titles in the show—'This Is My Be-loved,' and 'Bobbles, Bubbles, and . . . something else.' "

"You mean 'Baubles, Bangles and Beads'?"

"Yes. What are they?"

"Oh, just various kinds of jewelry usually worn by women."

"Well," I said, "we'll be playing this quartet here tomorrow, and quite frankly we don't want people to say afterward that we made the long trip from Russia to play 'This Is My Beloved,' and those 'Bottles, Brandies, and Beers.' "

There was a roar of laughter in the studio, but my quartet mates still looked gloomy. I quickly told them what was being said, but they didn't even smile. "Do you want to say anything?" I asked them. "I'll translate."

"Bring this farce to an end," Berlinsky said.

Oh boy! I thought to myself. How many times during these first few days in America had I found it difficult to communicate with my Soviet comrades. And at the same time, how easy it was talking with Americans.

John asked us whether we were married and had children.

I said, "We are all married and we have altogether seven children."

"You even consider your children in common?" John responded immediately. "How many do you have personally?"

I decided to amuse the audience. "You see, the founder of scientific Communism, Karl Marx, would probably answer your question like this: If I am poor and have nothing to eat, and my wealthy neighbor has a chicken for dinner, then one could say that each of us had eaten half a chicken. Personally, I don't have any children, but dividing our seven kids among the four of us according to Marx, it comes out that I have one whole child and three-quarters of another."

The people in the studio reacted with amusement and John giggled. "That's probably a strange way of looking at things—for us, anyway." Then, looking at his watch, he said, "Well, we have just enough time for the traditional last question. What is your musical credo? And maybe your friends would like to answer, too?"

"We're being asked," I said in Russian, "what our musical credo is. Will you answer?" I asked Alexandrov.

"Yes," he said. "My credo is: to have a good, long sleep."

I translated into English and everyone laughed loudly. "And yours?" I asked Shebalin.

He suddenly broke into a wide smile, looked around, and unexpectedly said in English, "One hamburger and two beers."

The laughter increased.

I turned to Berlinsky. "Say something to sustain the mood."

He was silent a while, then pointed his finger at me and ordered loudly, "Translation, please!"

Everyone immediately became quiet and watched him.

"I want to take this opportunity to say that all Soviet people condemn America for her dirty and secret war in Vietnam. As for my credo, that can be expressed in two words: Beethoven and Shostakovich."

He stopped speaking and everyone turned to me. Alexandrov shoved his elbow into my side, but I was on the alert anyway.

Okay, my dear friend, I thought to myself. I'll translate for you now, and how! Just watch me!

"My friend says that this is our first visit to the United States, and we are happy to play for such friendly Americans. As to his credo, it can be put in just two words: Beethoven and Shostakovich."

Loud cheers and applause ensued. John smiled happily, then waved his arms for silence and turned his face to the camera. "Yes, ladies and gentlemen, our time is up. We thank our guests very much for being with us, and wish them a very successful tour in our country."

The broadcast ended and young Americans surrounded us, introducing themselves and trying to shake our hands. "You're the first Russians we've ever seen. And you're so different from what we thought . . . Thank you, thank you . . . We're definitely coming to your concert tomorrow."

Alexandrov squeezed through to me and tugged my sleeve. "I hope you didn't translate that nonsense about Vietnam?"

I quickly shook my head.

"Thank God! You played that passage well."

Berlinsky, as gloomy as before, was biting his lips. When the car started he asked, "Can I out of curiosity ask what it was that you two were whispering about?"

"Nothing important," Alexandrov answered.

"Something about me and Vietnam?"

"Oh no, of course not!"

"I still would like to know."

"Well, if you insist . . ."

"Yes, I insist!"

"I said I won't be able to make it to dinner," concluded Alexandrov.

"Then I won't go either."

"And what should I tell the gentleman behind the wheel?" I asked.

"That's your problem. You're the translator!"

"He's a great translator," Alexandrov said approvingly, still trying to smooth over the situation.

"Well, thank you! I just serve—how do they say it?—I serve the Soviet Union?"

"It's still not clear whom you serve!" continued Berlinsky, taunting me.

"Why not? I serve—if we can leave the Soviet Union aside—Russian art."

"Oh yes, especially with the Jews in Cincinnati!"

I waited until I had stopped shaking with anger and then said, "I serve Russian art as a Jew. It's always been that way: civilizations would die; the Jews just moved from one to another. The Jewish contribution to every nation's culture has been immense. Just consider that I'm also helping Russians to create their own culture."

"Stop talking rot!" Berlinsky shouted. "You don't help anyone! You're a product of Russian culture yourself. You're a Russian!"

"Really? And what do the Soviet authorities think about that?"

"Back to your anti-Soviet remarks? Just wait, you'll get what you deserve! You'll forget not only about the Jews but what your name is!"

"But why? I don't understand."

"Oh, you don't understand? Then I'll explain it to you. Listen carefully. A thug comes up to this intellectual and punches him hard in the face. 'What's that for?' shouts the intellectual. The thug hits him again, harder. 'I'm being beaten!' shouts the intellectual, 'and I don't understand why!' 'Oh, you don't understand?' says the thug, hitting him as hard as he can. The intellectual falls down. The thug bends over him: 'So? You still don't understand?' 'Now I do,' says the intellectual."

"Now I do," I repeated.

We drove to the hotel in deathly silence. In the vestibule a man and a woman came up to Mr. Luin.

"The president of our musical society and his wife," explained Mr. Luin.

I shook hands with the woman and then with her husband. The handshaking procedure was repeated with the whole quartet, and as soon as it was over, Alexandrov said to me, so that everyone could hear, "Please translate . . . I, unfortunately, can't be at dinner. Think of something. Thank you very much!" he added in English, turned around quickly, and walked away.

"Wait, I'm coming with you!" Berlinsky shouted, and ran after him.

Shebalin watched them go, then smiled awkwardly. "I think I'll go, too. I don't speak English. Explain everything to them."

I remained alone with the Americans. "I'm sorry," I said. "They feel embarrassed because they don't speak English. They asked you to excuse them."

"How about you? Will you have dinner with us?"

I didn't have the strength to refuse. "Yes, with pleasure."

"Good," the president said. "What kind of food do you like? Have you tried Mexican?"

"No, never. I'd like to very much."

"Good! This restaurant is an excellent place for it."

We went into the restaurant and were ceremoniously led to a table.

The waiter appeared. "How are you folks today?"

"Fine. And yourself?"

The waiter quickly answered with something which was obviously funny, because everyone laughed.

It would be impossible to begin a meal that way in the Soviet Union. Russians are afraid of waiters and flatter them, while the waiters hardly pay any attention to the guests, serving them as if they were doing them a big favor, and without thanking them for tips. In the United States, even in expensive restaurants, there are always friendly relations with waiters, and a feeling of equality appears. Sometimes you even want to discuss your own business with them.

The president ordered exotic-sounding dishes which I had never heard of, and when the waiter left, he turned to me. "We watched your interview. It was very interesting, and you were brilliant."

"Thank you."

"We laughed when you talked about 'Baubles, Bangles and Beads.' Isn't it ridiculous to give a string quartet a name like that? And Mr. Berlinsky was so kind, saying such warm words about American audiences."

"Yes," I said. "It was good of him to say that."

The waiter brought us the food, hot and spicy, which we washed down with cold beer. Everyone seemed relaxed, and I told a few stories about the Soviet Union. The Americans listened with interest and reacted in the right way and at the proper places. Time passed quickly. I thanked the president for the dinner, for his tact and his ability to create a pleasant atmosphere at the table.

"No, I should thank *you* for being with us," the president replied, and we all stood up. I kissed his wife's hand and he shook mine firmly. Mr. Luin assured them that everything was taken care of for tomorrow. The president and his wife headed for the door, and Mr. Luin turned to me.

"How about a liqueur or a brandy?"

"A beer would be nice, thank you."

"I'd like a beer, too. We can sit in the lobby, and I'll ask them to bring the beers there."

We sat out in the lobby, and the waiter brought us the beers. I wanted to pay for them, but Mr. Luin wouldn't let me.

"You can do that when I come to Moscow," he explained.

"When are you going?"

"I don't know yet," he said uncertainly.

"Is anything the matter?"

"No, not really . . . But in the car when you asked me about my name, it's really spelled L-e-v-i-n."

I imagined writing the letters out and suddenly said in Russian, "Levin!"

He nodded.

"You're Russian?"

He nodded again.

"And you speak Russian?"

"Yes, I speak Russian," he said with a slight accent.

I felt I had been tricked and hoped the quartet had said nothing unkind about him in his presence.

"You're probably wondering why I didn't tell you right away?" he continued in Russian.

"I'm wondering why you told me now."

"Please don't think that I wanted to spy on you. You see, I left Russia in 1924. We had nothing to do with the Revolution. But one day they came to our house with three trucks and took everything away. Books, furniture, plates, clothing, even the curtains from the windows—everything! Our two German shepherds, Boda and Vesta, ran through the house howling like lunatics. My father couldn't stand it and hanged himself in the washroom; my mother lost the ability to speak. By some miracle she managed to hide an antique ring, and people helped us to get abroad in exchange for it. We made it to Europe first, and then here."

"What happened to the dogs?" I asked, shaken.

"Oh, later they took them away, too. Told us that it was for the needs of the Red Army. To defend the Revolution from its enemies."

"And were your curtains necessary for defending it from enemies, too?"

He smiled. "I knew I'd be able to talk with you. But at first I wasn't sure. Russia's not the same now as it used to be. It's a different country, with different people. I learned a lot today, spending time with all of you. And the way you acted in the car and the studio really impressed me. I just wanted very much to talk with you in Russian."

"What's your full name?"

"Pyotr Andreevich. Pyotr Andreevich Levin."

"What should we do tomorrow? I mean, with the rest of the quartet."

"Well, if you don't mind," he said, returning to English, "let's keep it the way it was."

We still hadn't touched our beers.

"Do you have anyone in Russia?" I asked.

"No, no one by now."

"Do you have a family here?"

"No, somehow it didn't work out."

I didn't know what to say.

"I probably shouldn't tell you about all this, but at the same time I wanted you to know."

We drank our beers in silence.

"Tomorrow," Mr. Luin said finally, "if you want, I can pick you up and show you our city. There are interesting places here."

"Thank you. Let's phone each other in the morning."

We got up. I walked with him as far as the door. We shook hands and he left, then turned around and waved.

I didn't see the quartet until the next evening. I had left everyone a message: "The concert at 8:30; downstairs at 7:00; Borodin, Shostakovich, and Tchaikovsky." This meant that everyone was free until the evening to do whatever he wanted. A rehearsal in the afternoon wouldn't have hurt, especially since everyone had drunk a lot the day before, but it was more important not to see each other for a while, so that the tension that had built up in the quartet could dissipate. It worked to a degree, and we played well.

During the intermission people started gathering backstage, looking at us the way one looks at sick people or little children and talking in quiet voices. Not until the concert ended and we went back to the dressing room did I see the evening newspaper unfolded on my violin case. On the front page was a picture of Khrushchev; the caption below mentioned a coup d'état in the Kremlin.

"Guys!" I called to the others, "Nikita's crashed!"

They all ran toward me. "Show us!"

Khrushchev's familiar face—sly yet boorish, funny and even likable in its crudeness—looked out at us. Meanwhile, the Americans watched us attentively through the doorway. Our reactions to the events in Moscow interested them more than the concert we had just played.

"Quiet," I said. "We're being watched. Keep calm!"

"I beg you," said Berlinsky, "no interviews and conferences today! And even better, I invite you all to my room. We'll sit a little and talk. There's plenty to talk about!"

The president, Mr. Luin, and a few other people came to invite us to dinner. But I told them that today it would probably be better for us to be alone. They nodded and said, "We understand." What it was they understood, I couldn't say. We ourselves didn't understand anything. If we didn't understand our own country, what could we expect from foreigners?

In the hotel we quickly changed clothes and met in Berlinsky's room.

"Excuse me, I have nothing to offer you. Here's everything there is," he said, getting out a bottle of vodka, with only a little left in the bottom.

"I'll go to the bar," I said. "I'll get something."

"You're crazy," Alexandrov protested. "Everything's three times as expensive at the bar."

"But we need it for such an occasion! It's Khrush's doing that we started going abroad."

I stood at the bar until the bartender noticed me.

"May I help you?"

"Yes," I said. "Do you have vodka?"

"Sure."

He was about to pour me a glass, but I said, "I'd like the whole bottle."

Several people turned and looked at me. I can only imagine what would have happened in a bar in Waco, Texas, if I had told them where I was from and why I required a bottle of vodka today of all days.

I paid for the vodka and returned to Berlinsky's room. I put the bottle on the table.

"I'll pour," said Shebalin. "They just showed Nikita on television, banging his shoe at the U.N." He poured a quarter of a glass for everyone.

We each took one, sat down, and looked at the television. A commercial was playing.

"Would you turn off that chatter!" shouted Shebalin. "Makes my head hurt, and besides, we have to drink."

Berlinsky turned off the set. "But maybe it's a fake?" he said.

"You don't often see a fake of this magnitude," remarked Alexandrov.

"I agree," I said. "Especially since the papers here, as a rule, don't lie."

"Why not go on and say that the papers lie only in the Soviet Union, and here it's all true!" Berlinsky reacted immediately.

"In the Soviet Union they print only what the government wants," I said, continuing the duel.

"Here they'll print anything if it's sensational enough," he shot back.

"I suppose. But then it'll turn out that it was a false alarm, and if that keeps happening, people stop buying that paper."

"Don't idealize the West."

"That's not the point. They have an open society, open! And in the Soviet Union we're used to everything being a lie, and we think it's like that everywhere."

"Listen, you're a good violinist," he summed up, "but you're anti-Soviet and you shouldn't be allowed to go abroad."

"And you're a splendid musician," I complimented him back, "but we're talking about the press, not about me. And I say that democracy's a thing that we're unable to understand."

"And I say that you're a counterrevolutionary!"

Shebalin interfered. "Gentlemen, Messieurs Performers, damn you both, stop your idiotic argument."

"Really, at a time like this! The vodka's getting old," said Alexandrov.

We drank it down in one gulp. I felt the vodka spreading warmth through my chest.

"And what if some commotion starts and we're delayed in the West?" said Alexandrov, partly anxious and partly hopeful. "It wouldn't be our fault if we got stuck abroad. We could live and play for a while like human beings."

Whenever Alexandrov expressed himself in this manner, Berlinsky was silent. A Party member was speaking, what could he say?

"Read us the details from the paper," asked Alexandrov.

I read it to myself and then said, "They say that Khrushchev was urgently summoned from the Crimea, where he was vacationing; that in Sheremetyevo he was met not by a cheering crowd but only by a chauffeur and car. He went right to the Kremlin to a meeting of the

Central Committee, and Suslov spent several hours chewing him out for the failures in agriculture and in China. At first Khrushchev defended himself, even shouted, but then shrugged and sat down tiredly."

"It really says that?" asked Berlinsky.

"No, I made it all up myself!" I joked.

"Let me look!"

"Here, read it yourself . . ."

"What's there to read!" said Shebalin, and poured more vodka for everyone.

"And what'll happen to him?" I asked. "They wouldn't shoot him, would they?"

"Anything's possible," said Alexandrov, stating what everyone else was thinking.

"Poor guy," said Berlinsky.

"Yeah, it's a pity. He didn't build Communism, it's true, but he did a lot of good."

"He promised," I said, "the highest standard of living in the world, an abundance of material and cultural benefits."

"They've all promised that, starting with Karl Marx."

"But Khrushchev even named a date. In twenty years. He said that people in our generation would live to see Communism."

"Don't talk nonsense," Alexandrov said calmly.

"Those are his words."

"It's all chatter. There's nothing to eat in the whole country."

"That's why they drink."

"Not only because of that."

"Do you remember, the very first time we drank together was a situation just like this—when Stalin kicked off in '53."

"Yes, on the stairway in the Hall of Columns."

"I wouldn't have believed it if someone had told me we'd drink to Khrush in America."

"But just between us, there's still something strange," I said. "We spent three days and three nights burying Stalin and they put him in the mausoleum with Lenin. And then at the Twentieth Party Congress . . . What year was that?"

"Nineteen fifty-six," said Alexandrov. "You should know that!"

"I just forgot the year, but I remember how, all over the country, they were reading Khrushchev's secret speech about Stalin's cult of personality. Then a year later Khrushchev turned around and declared that Stalin was a devoted Leninist and firm revolutionary and that the Soviet people loved him. And then, at the Twenty-second Congress, I remember this very well, in 1961, all the people talked about Stalin's bloody crimes, and it ended with some Pridurkina or Khazarkina . . ."

"Lazurkina," prompted Alexandrov.

"Suddenly there was a breath of mysticism and spiritualism at the congress," I continued. "This Lazurkina announced from the podium that the day before she had talked with Lenin himself and that he was very upset to be lying beside Stalin, who behaved so badly while he was alive, and that Stalin should be taken out of the mausoleum."

"Don't make things up!" said Berlinsky.

"I swear! I even remember that after those words the papers said, 'Stormy applause.' "

"Do you remember that?" Berlinsky asked Alexandrov.

"There was something like that, it seems."

"Well, it's just like a detective story," said Shebalin. "Lie some more; it's interesting."

"After that they took Stalin out and buried him a second time, in the Kremlin wall. And the whole country, as it had with Stalin, started worshipping Khrushchev."

"Maybe they'll let him live," said Berlinsky. "After all, he didn't shoot Molotov, Malenkov, and Kaganovich."

"But he shot Beria!"

"I'd still drink to him! He opened the iron curtain a little, and we started traveling."

"He let them give Cliburn the first prize at the Tchaikovsky Competition."

"He opened the avant-garde art exhibition, came to it himself, stood in front of Ernst Neizvestny's painting, and asked loudly, 'What is this shit?' "

"Well, good for him! An honest question."

"Yes, but they closed the exhibition right then."

"Even so, we can drink to him."

"Rest in peace, Nikita! May you reach heaven!" said Shebalin.

"Don't clown around. The next one, whoever he is, will be worse."

"That's true."

We drank.

"And how did we play today?"

"I've already forgotten. Seems it was okay."

"And in the audience everyone but us knew about Khrushchev. I wonder how we would've played if we'd known sooner?"

"It's good that we didn't know."

California

1964

I GRADUALLY started developing my "American" routine. Sleeping was as bad as before, and the early-morning flights forced us to get up around six o'clock. In the airport before boarding, I'd have a glass of milk and apple pie for breakfast. On the plane I'd find a seat in the very last row, in the corner by the window, and fasten the seat belt right away, so the stewardess wouldn't interrupt me and I could sleep until we landed. It was sound sleep, as a rule, in spite of the noise, and when I woke up from the jolt as we landed, I would feel refreshed. In the hotel after lunch I would practice for the concert. I also discovered that a fifteen-minute nap in a hot bath before the concert had a reviving effect, and I'd go to the concert feeling pretty calm.

After Waco and our farewell party for Khrushchev, the tension within the quartet had eased. The Jewish protesters didn't trouble us anymore, our manager canceled all other interviews, and the Soviet embassy was quiet. Having successfully played seventeen concerts in twenty days, we could envisage the end of the tour.

In San Diego we were met by several young people, two girls and two boys. The girls carried bread and salt: an old Russian custom that had disappeared after the Revolution. It meant "Welcome."

"We probably have to try it," said Alexandrov.

Shebalin took the bread and broke a piece off.

"Salt it!" advised Alexandrov, laughing.

We really didn't know how to act in such a situation. Shebalin tried the bread. "Real!" he said. "And tasty!"

The young Americans smiled. One girl said in Russian, "This bread we ourselves . . . for you."

"You speak Russian?" exclaimed Berlinsky.

"Yes, we . . . a little."

She was very attractive.

"What's your name?" asked Berlinsky.

"Cathy."

"Katya, that means. And how come you know Russian?"

"We have Russian Club. There we speak only Russian."

"That's very interesting," said Berlinsky sweetly.

"Tomorrow after concert . . . We did Russian borscht for you."

"We'll certainly come," answered Berlinsky immediately. "Are all your girls so pretty?"

"What do you say?"

"I say that we'll come for sure," repeated Berlinsky.

"Mrs. Voloshin will telephone you."

"Who is Mrs. Voloshin?"

"Oh, that's our Russian teacher."

When she spoke Russian, Cathy turned a little red from the strain, which made her even prettier. Berlinsky couldn't take his eyes off her.

"Tear yourself away," Alexandrov told him. "There's still time. Let's go to the hotel."

"A beautiful girl," said Berlinsky. "I'm in love already."

"She's still young. She looks about seventeen."

"You, my dear colleague, have dirty thoughts."

"Quiet," I said. "They catch everything."

I turned to Cathy. "Are you taking us to the hotel?"

"Yes. We have two cars."

"I'll ride with you," Berlinsky told her. "You don't mind?"

"Please," answered Cathy, and blushed.

In the hotel the porter gave us a message. Mrs. Voloshin had phoned and left her phone number with a request to call back.

She answered right away when I called.

"Mrs. Voloshin?" I asked.

"Yes, it's me," she answered in Russian. "We're expecting you this evening. The kids have been making borscht for you all morning. Please don't refuse, I beg you."

"We couldn't even think of refusing. You sent such lovely girls."

"Well, wonderful! We'll all be at the concert, and then at my house."

"Thank you. See you later."

Voloshina's house was about ten miles from the hotel. After the concert we stopped to change clothes while one of the boys who had met us in the morning waited in the car. Berlinsky had gone to the barber in the afternoon and now, when we met downstairs, his hair was carefully combed and he smelled strongly of cologne.

"The guy's in the stirrups!" Alexandrov whispered to me.

As we drove up to her house, Voloshina came out to meet us. She was younger than I had expected. For some reason I had thought that she must be an old lady who had left St. Petersburg long before the Revolution. She kissed us each three times in the Russian way, saying grandly, "Welcome, dear guests."

At the entrance hung a big poster, written in Russian: "Not a word of English past this threshold."

"For today I promise to speak no more English," said Berlinsky.

Voloshina took his arm, and we went into the dining room, where four tables were already set.

"Please be seated, gentlemen! Only at different tables, please."

She sat down herself and put Berlinsky next to her. We went to the other tables.

"What will you drink, gentlemen? Wine or vodka?"

"And beer," said Shebalin, laughing loudly at himself.

"Did you understand the joke?" Voloshina asked her children.

"Yes, yes," several voices said at once. "Beer. We know."

"We also have mulled wine. They prepared it themselves. Try some! Girls, see to the guests."

"With your permission, I'll have some vodka," said Berlinsky.

"Of course!"

They poured borscht into everyone's bowl.

"I hope you like our borscht."

When everything grew quiet for a second before the meal, Berlinsky banged his knife against his goblet and stood up. "If it's Russian, then it's Russian. We can't do without a toast. I would like to say that today, for the first time in our tour around America, I feel as if I'm at home. I thank you for your warmth and want to drink to the health of our dear hostess . . . Forgive me, I don't know your name."

"Ellen," Voloshina prompted.

"To the health of our enchanting Ellen!" Berlinsky repeated, and drained his glass.

The young Americans looked at him with respect.

"Well, if we've come to that," exclaimed Ellen, "then I'll have vodka, too."

"Now, that's Russian, that's our way," said Berlinsky, pouring her a shot glass full to the brim.

"I drink to the health of our dear guests!" she said.

"Don't mix toasts," observed Berlinsky severely. "It's not done. This glass is to you, and to the bottom!"

She drank it up and broke the glass on the floor.

"We don't do *that* anymore. That was long ago."

"Really? I didn't know."

"There aren't enough glasses!" Shebalin said loudly from another table.

"Quiet!" Berlinsky shouted at him. "Don't spoil the service!"

"Please sample the borscht," said Ellen, "and tell us honestly what you think of it."

Berlinsky took a taste, put his head back, closed his eyes, and moved his lips. Everyone watched him. "Interesting!" he said at last. "Very curious! But it's not borscht."

"So what is it?"

"It's . . . it's . . ."

"*Quasi una Fantasia*," I suggested.

"Correct. But very tasty."

At my table the young people ate quietly, embarrassed. I tried to tell some suitable story but sensed that they didn't understand. Cathy, who understood the language a little better than the rest, was at another table. She was sitting across from Berlinsky and I noticed that he didn't take his eyes off her. He was extremely cheerful. He made another toast, this time to women. "Once," he said, "they were called the weak or fair sex. In our time this sex has become less weak, but even more beautiful." As he said this he looked at Cathy.

"Bravo!" I said. "Wonderfully said."

"I'm afraid not everyone understood," said Berlinsky. "Translate."

"English isn't allowed here," I answered. "But it would be a pity if such a toast were lost. Repeat it once, but slower."

"It's still hard for them," said Ellen. "Let's sing instead. We know a lot of Russian folk songs." And she began singing in a high voice, *"I've heard many a song in my home countryside . . ."*

The students sang along and got through the whole first verse, pronouncing the Russian words amusingly, but then suddenly stopped.

"Why did you stop?" shouted Berlinsky. "Go on!"

They maintained an embarrassed silence.

"What's the matter?"

"Maybe because of the words? They don't want to offend us," I suggested.

"But what's in it? 'Russian *muzhik*'? Nonsense, you can't toss words out of a song! Well, come on," he shouted to everyone, and began singing himself: "Well, the Russian *muzhik*, if he has no strength to work, will just sing his favorite 'Dubina' . . ."

He had a pleasant voice, and the students sang along with him for one more verse. Someone tried to sing "Yo-heave-ho!" but didn't get much past the beginning, so they tried to think of other Russian songs. We ourselves never sang them at home; these old songs had long ago been crowded out by other, Soviet ones. Gradually people started leaving their tables. Shebalin sat down at the piano and started "Moscow Nights." Berlinsky began singing, went up to Cathy, and took her hand. "Sing!" he said.

She shook her head.

A young man came up to me. "I know that where you come from almost everyone plays chess."

"That's true."

"I love it. I have a set here, complete with a clock."

"Splendid," I said. "Let's play."

We sat on the floor. Several people sat down around us.

"How many minutes?" I asked.

"Five," he said. "Or if you want, only three."

That meant he knew the game well and played often. His first moves, quick and accurate, confirmed it. I lost the first game when I ran out of time, the effect of slowed reactions after the concert. I lost the second one, too, making a mistake at the end of the game.

Ellen came over and leaned down to us. "Well, how are you doing?"

"Steve's a fine fellow," I said, "he's already won two games."

"Steve, behave yourself and don't offend our guest."

Perhaps for the first time I was getting some pleasure from losing, and I liked Steve, too. I started playing the next game very quickly, hoping to win with time, but Steve also sped up and kept on playing slightly more accurately than I did. When our time expired, we had already exchanged the last pieces and each had only a lone king.

"Good!" said Steve.

I became more accustomed to his exact and active style and started to play more attentively myself. We finished several more games with varying results. I was losing myself in the contest until Alexandrov and Shebalin sat down on the floor next to me.

"How's it going?" asked Alexandrov loudly, and then whispered to me, "Stop that guy. He's putting the moves on the girl in front of everyone."

"Palm him off on our hostess."

"What do you mean! He's lost his senses. Take a look at him, but inconspicuously."

"Steve," I said, "play with my friend. I'm a little tired."

I went into the kitchen. Berlinsky was sitting on the floor at Cathy's feet, holding a goblet of wine in one hand and trying to put the other on her knees. She kept taking his hand off, embarrassed, but he would put it right back. The students around them were pretending not to notice. Ellen stood in the doorway. She was no longer smiling.

"Steve's a remarkable boy," I said.

"He's very clever," she answered dryly.

"I really enjoyed playing against him. They're great kids."

"Yes, they're very sweet. But they're still young," Ellen said, looking at Cathy and Berlinsky. "She's still a child."

"She should probably go home," I said. "And it's time for all of us. Two o'clock already."

"No, no, you should sit a little longer. I'm so anxious to talk with you. I'll send them away now."

She went into the living room and clapped her hands. "A moment of attention, please. Our dear guests thank you for this warm evening."

She spoke very slowly, one syllable at a time. I went into the kitchen, found a can of beer, and began to drink straight from the can. I felt guilty, as if I had chased everyone away and spoiled the best moment of the evening for Berlinsky.

But she was still too young . . .

I slowly drank the beer and waited while everyone left. When I returned to the living room, Ellen was saying goodbye to Cathy. Berlinsky stood next to her. Cathy went out and he went after her.

"Where are you going?" Ellen called after him. "We're going to sit a little longer."

"I'll be right back," he answered.

We remained alone—Ellen, Alexandrov, Shebalin, and I.

"Sit down, gentlemen! Please tell me about Russia. Are you all from Moscow?"

Shebalin was the first to answer. "Yes, we're all from Moscow."

"Well, how are things there? I've never been in Russia."

"You speak perfectly."

"My parents spoke only Russian, and here I teach Russian and literature. What are they printing in Russia now?"

I joined in the conversation. "Oh, the same stuff. The only good thing is Bulgakov's *The Master and Margarita*."

"I don't know it."

"Oh, you must read it. It's great literature. The first and last time the image of Christ has appeared in Soviet literature."

"I should make a note of it. And have they printed *Doctor Zhivago*?"

"Unfortunately, no," I said.

"What a book! It's about the fall of the Russian intelligentsia."

"I know. I've read it."

"Really? Well, what do you think? Did you like it?"

"A remarkable book."

Shebalin suddenly giggled. "Berlinsky says the best thing in it is Lara. He's in love with Lara. He's in love with all pretty women."

"By the way, where is he?" asked Ellen, suddenly alarmed.

"Still saying goodbye to Cathy?"

"I'll go see."

She went out, but returned right away. "No one! And Cathy's car is gone, too."

"He probably ran after the car to see her off." Shebalin laughed again.

"I think they drove away together," sighed Ellen. "He could have said goodbye first!"

Alexandrov stood up. "Ellen, it's probably time for us to go, too. Tomorrow we have to get up early again. It's a daily torture."

"I'll drive you to the hotel."

Ellen drove quickly. It was three o'clock at night and the road was deserted. Part of the road went along the ocean, and in the darkness we saw the pale band of the surf. At a turn Ellen put on the brakes and we saw several police cars; behind them was another car, on the side of the road, facing the oncoming traffic, its front crumpled.

"I hope it's not one of ours," said Ellen.

"Why, it couldn't be," said Shebalin to calm her.

At the hotel, the night porter gave us our keys. "Who is Mr. Dubinsky?" he asked.

"I am," I said.

He handed me a piece of paper. "Call this number."

"It doesn't say when."

"Now."

"So late?"

"Yes, right away. Use my phone."

Alexandrov and Shebalin stood by the elevator, waiting.

"Go on up," I said. "I have to make a phone call."

Alexandrov nodded understandingly. "I wish you luck! If she has a sister, don't forget about me. My door is open."

I dialed the number.

"Yes?" answered a woman's voice.

"I got a message to call this number."

"Are you Mr. Dubinsky?"

"Yes."

"Come to the hospital immediately. Take a taxi."

"What happened?"

"Please come as soon as you can." She hung up.

"I need a taxi," I said to the porter.

"I thought so. There's one waiting for you."

I tried not to think about what might be ahead of me. The nurse on duty led me down the corridor and into a room, where I recognized Berlinsky lying fully clothed on a table. He looked awful. My legs buckled, and if it hadn't been for the nurse I probably would have fallen.

A doctor was bending over Berlinsky, and without turning toward me, he said, "I asked you to come to translate. I have to be able to communicate with him, so I didn't put him to sleep. Ask him what he's feeling."

I stepped closer and shook inside. All the skin on Berlinsky's forehead had slid upward toward his hair, exposing the white skull beneath, flecked with spots of red. His eyes and his whole face were covered with blood. A crack opened in the lower part of this bloody mask, and Berlinsky asked, "Is that you?"

"What are you feeling?" I asked in a voice that wasn't my own. "The doctor has to know."

"Nothing," he said calmly. "One finger on my hand hurts a little."

I translated.

"He's in a state of shock," the doctor said. "Talk to him. Ask him what day it is."

"What's the date today?" I repeated.

"I have no idea. What is it?"

"And what day of the week?"

"How should I know!"

"What city are we in?"

"Laguna Beach."

I translated everything for the doctor.

"Keep talking. About anything."

He started pulling the skin back across Berlinsky's forehead. It seemed to me that there wouldn't be enough skin. I turned away.

"Keep talking," the doctor repeated, "and don't faint yourself."

"It's not hard for you to talk?" I asked Berlinsky.

"No, I don't feel anything."

"What happened to Katya?"

"I don't know."

"And what happened to you?"

"I don't remember."

"You followed her out of Ellen's."

"Ah . . . We set off together."

"We know that. And then?"

"I don't remember."

"We saw her car on the road. The front all smashed."

"I remember something hitting me in the face . . . Oh hell, my finger hurts."

"What's he saying?" the doctor asked.

"He doesn't remember much and complains about his finger."

"That's nothing. Tell him he's lucky. Just a little lower and he would have lost his eyes."

"Should I tell him?"

"Yes, to wake him up."

"The doctor says you're lucky. You could have lost your eyes."

"I can't see anything."

"That's from the bruise on your eyebrows. It'll swell up."

"Where am I?"

"In the hospital."

"How did I get here?"

"An ambulance."

"And why are you here?"

"How should I say it? Out of curiosity."

"Don't be funny! How did you find out?"

"They called the hotel."

"Who else knows?"

"No one yet."

The doctor was stitching together the skin above his eyebrows.

"What's he doing?" asked Berlinsky.

"Making you beautiful."

"Ask him where it hurts now," the doctor said.

"Where does it hurt?" I asked.

"My finger," Berlinsky said, and moved his left wrist.

"The finger," I said in English.

"That's later. Ask him about his neck."

"You feel anything in your neck?"

"Nothing."

"He doesn't feel anything there."

The doctor finished stitching Berlinsky's forehead together and wiped his patient's face. He moved Berlinsky's head slightly and nodded. "Tell him he was lucky twice. Right next to the carotid artery. A quarter inch closer and nothing in the world would have saved him."

"He says you lucked out twice."

"What?"

"You have a hole in your neck right next to the main artery."

"Yes, I'm lucky . . ."

The doctor gave him an injection right in the wound, put some stitches inside it, gave him another shot, and started stitching up the edges of the skin. The nurse wiped Berlinsky's face and eyes very carefully. He opened his left eye slightly. The right one had turned blue and would not open.

"Hi!" I said.

"Have I been here a long time?"

The clock on the wall said it was ten to four.

"About two hours."

"My damn finger hurts," he said.

There were spots of blood on his shirt and jacket. They had put him on the table just the way they had brought him, in shoes and suit. The doctor finished stitching up the wound and attentively looked over Berlinsky's face and neck.

"He won't die now," he said to me.

"Thank you, Doctor. What is your name?"

"Watters."

"I would rather call you Paganini."

He smiled. "Now let's see the rest of him." He gently prodded all of Berlinsky's body. Berlinsky moaned several times, but not too loudly.

"Okay, let's look at his finger now."

From the outside nothing looked suspicious.

"It's difficult to say. We'd better X-ray it."

Together we moved him to a cart and rolled him along the corridor to the X-ray room. Dr. Watters took two pictures from different angles. We waited while they developed, and then he put one into the viewing machine. I was afraid to look.

"Take a look," Dr. Watters said to me.

I saw the wrist and five slender bones. The bone of his ring finger was split at the end. "Oh, my God!" I said in horror.

"What?" asked Berlinsky. "Bad?"

"What should I tell him?" I asked Dr. Watters.

"The truth," he said.

"Well, what's there?" Berlinsky repeated impatiently.

"A small fracture," I said, "but no dislocation . . . It'll grow together. It's just a question of time."

"That means it's bad," said Berlinsky, and fell silent.

Dr. Watters turned to me. "There's not much I can do here. The best thing would be to find a specialist. Where do you live?"

"Moscow, in the U.S.S.R."

"They have good specialists there." He looked at his watch. It was a quarter to five. "Well," he said. "That's it. If he's in pain, give him these pills, one every four hours. Talk to the nurse now. She'll ask you some questions."

We sat at a table, and she filled out some sort of form and started explaining to me what sort of work Dr. Watters had done, but I told her not to bother explaining, because I would just sign everything anyway. Then she wrote out a bill for $1,250. I said that the bill would be paid, but I couldn't tell her how. We didn't have any money of our own, and we wouldn't have dared to pay with government money without Moscow's permission, and Moscow would never have allowed it. You could die, that was allowed, but God forbid that you waste even a kopeck of the government's foreign currency! I left the nurse the address of our hotel, plus the address and phone number of our American manager, and asked her to wait until morning. The nurse and I wheeled the table with Berlinsky right up to the exit. He said he wanted to try to get up. We held him on both sides. When he stood up he staggered.

"Maybe you should lie down? We'll roll you out."

"No, I can get into the car."

We carefully helped him in. I shook the nurse's hand and asked her to tell the driver to go slowly.

"He knows," the nurse said.

We pulled away from the curb.

"So, will you make it?" I asked Berlinsky. "If anything goes wrong, say something right away."

In the hotel the porter had already thought to give us two rooms next to each other with a connecting door. Together, we helped Berlinsky upstairs and laid him on the bed.

"He had an accident," I said to the porter.

"I know," he answered. "The police were here already."

"What did they ask?"

"Oh, names and everything. How is he?"

"It's a wonder that he's still alive."

We remained alone. Berlinsky refused to undress. I just took off his jacket and shoes and fluffed up his pillow.

"Can you sleep?"

"I'll try."

"Will you take a pill?"

"Maybe."

"I'll leave the door open. I'll hear if anything . . ."

"Thank you," said Berlinsky, starting to cry.

I brought a glass of water from the bathroom and stood it on his table, put the medicine next to it, and went to my room so he could calm himself. A little later I heard him quiet down. I hoped he would go to sleep, but he moaned, "Oh, God! What shall I do now?"

I went over to him. "Take some medicine, and when the pain lets up, try to sleep. It's the best thing."

"I'll try."

I also lay down without undressing and listened to the sounds in his room. For about ten minutes everything was quiet, then he groaned. I went to him.

"Hurts?"

"It does."

"Now you just need patience. It'll take time for all this to get better."

"And what about the concerts and . . . everything?"

"It's five in the morning. For three more hours we don't need to think about that."

"The trip is ruined. And how can we go home? If they find out in the embassy . . ."

"We'll have to think of something. We were all together in the car, you were sitting in front and caught the whole force of the crash, the rest weren't hurt, just slight bruises. One of us will limp to make it more convincing."

"And where were we after the concert? And who was at the wheel?"

"Don't worry. I'll talk to Ellen in the morning. You don't remember what happened with Katya?"

"Not at all. I remember the crash, and then the hospital right away."

"But she hadn't been drinking. Did you start pawing her in the car?"

"I kissed her one time."

"And then?"

"A crash, scraping, and something hitting my face . . ." He started crying again. "Listen," he said, his voice breaking, "I understand everything. I know that I'm just shit . . ."

"You just had some bad luck."

"I'm shit!" he repeated bitterly, and sobbed.

"You had an accident. It's just chance."

"Marxism teaches that nothing is by chance," he said through his tears.

"Pardon me, but you can fuck your Marxism."

"I think so, too," he said with obvious pleasure.

"In Moscow, when we get back, we have to know what to say. We all have to tell the same lies."

"Just so long as they don't make us sign an explanatory note."

"Anything but that."

"Or else there'll be . . . summons to the ministry . . ."

"And to the travel department of the Central Committee."

"They'll sit us all in a row and start brainwashing . . ."

"Tell us about the 'decadent influence of the West . . .' "

"About the 'lack of vigilance.' "

"Certainly about discipline in the quartet."

"And about how we need to study the classics of Marxism-Leninism better."

"They'll stick in a reprimand. And along the Party line."

"They won't let us abroad again, of course."

"No doubt about that."

"Not letting us abroad is the best punishment. They know that."

"Better say that it's punishment to keep us in the Soviet Union!"

He stopped crying. "But seriously, what should we do?"

"Right now I see only one way out: you'll get to Moscow and obtain a medical certificate."

"No problem."

"We'll all keep the deepest silence, not chat on the phone, not go anywhere, and let everyone think we're still abroad."

"We have to turn our passports in right away."

"We can do it quietly, through my friend Zinaida."

"The financial account?"

"That's the main thing. We'll have to bring foreign presents for everyone, and not be stingy. A couple of foreign goodies and everything will be fine."

"I hope to God!" he said.

"Are you feeling better?"

"Seems like it. Maybe I'll sleep a little."

I turned off the light in his room, went through to mine, leaving the door open, and sat in the armchair. "I hope to God," he had said. When a Communist says that, it's wonderful. But the poor fellow! Ah, what a poor fellow!

I heard his even breathing. I was glad that he had at last fallen asleep.

At eight o'clock I closed the door and phoned our American manager, Mariedi Anders, in San Francisco. She gasped and was silent for a long time, and then said that she would call me back. Then I called Ellen.

"You haven't left yet?"

"Not yet, but soon. Ellen, my dear, please phone Cathy."

"What happened?"

"Nothing. I just want to know how she is."

"Did something happen?"

"No, nothing. Will you phone?"

"All right."

"Thank you. I'll call you back."

Finally, I had to inform our colleagues. In half an hour we were supposed to meet downstairs. I called Alexandrov.

"Get Shebalin and come to my room."

"Something wrong?"

"Yes. Come by. I'm in a different room, on the second floor, I don't remember which number. I'll meet you at the elevator."

I carefully opened the door onto the corridor, but Berlinsky was still awake and groaned. I glanced in at him. His face looked even worse in the sunlight. The right eye had turned black and was swollen, the left one would only open halfway; above his brows was the red stripe of the wound, his neck was plastered with bandages, and his cheeks were a muddy color.

"Well, how do I look?" he asked.

"Lovely," I said. "I'll go to the drugstore and buy you some dark glasses."

"That bad?"

"The others are coming. Don't get worried."

I went out to the elevator. Alexandrov and Shebalin were already coming toward me.

"What's the matter?"

"Come here."

We went into Berlinsky's room and looked at him without speaking. After a pause, Alexandrov said, "That wrecked car we drove past yesterday?"

"Yes," I said, and told them everything I knew.

"*A man had no luck in love*," began Shebalin, reciting a popular Moscow song.

"Idiot!" said Berlinsky.

"How's the finger?" asked Alexandrov.

"I can't stand to touch it."

"We're going back home?"

"What else can we do?"

The telephone rang. It was Ellen. "I phoned Cathy. Her sister said she'd already left for school."

"Thank you, Ellen. We wish you all the best. Say hello to Steve." I hung up.

"Katya's fine," I told Berlinsky.

The phone rang again; it was our manager. She said she would fly out to see us right away. She appeared in our hotel room that afternoon and announced that she had already been to the hospital, the police, the insurance company, and the travel agency, and everything was in order. We would fly today to New York, from there to Amsterdam, and then by Aeroflot to Moscow. I helped Berlinsky clean up and change clothes and bought him some big dark glasses, which covered half his face. Next, I took a belt and made a sling for his left arm. We divided his baggage among the three of us. Berlinsky was able to walk slowly but fairly steadily. He said that the only thing that didn't hurt was his legs. The manager agreed not to hurry with the letter to Moscow and not to pass on any details.

On the way to L.A. we made up a list of all the people who would require presents. It turned out to be an imposing piece of paper. We pooled together all the money that was due to us and, while waiting for the plane in New York, bought all sorts of junk. We knew that in Moscow almost any item from America would make a big impression and help us to survive.

On the airplane, the stewardess gave us the whole last row, and we laid Berlinsky down across the seats. I asked for a bottle of vodka for him in the hope that along with his medicine it would put him to sleep. We had a long trip ahead of us.

Back Home
1964–1966

WE LAY LOW, but the news of our unexpected return to Moscow spread all the same. Though Berlinsky's finger and neck were bandaged, and his face and swollen eye looked sufficiently eloquent, our "truthful" account of the automobile accident ("It was so stupid, you know, he was sitting in front and wasn't buckled in, and a dog ran across the road. The driver unexpectedly braked, and Berlinsky was thrown against the windshield . . .") was hard for people to believe. Especially the part about the dog. Everyone wanted to hear that it was some sort of thrilling anti-Soviet attack against innocent Russian musicians, or the act of "typical American bandits," about which the Soviet papers wrote so much and so eagerly.

At Goskoncert everything was quiet. No one, as always, was interested in us personally. Our most important duty was to turn in the financial report, and to make sure that they would accept it. This time it meant they would have to excuse the $5,000-plus that we weren't giving to the government.

We phoned the Goskoncert financial inspector, Vasilyeva, and agreed to meet Friday evening, when everyone would be in a hurry to go home for the weekend. Vasilyeva, as we had expected, understood this to mean that we had brought her something from America and didn't want any witnesses. She wanted them even less than we did.

The quartet, as always, entrusted me with this delicate operation. I came a little late, so as not to meet anyone in the corridors. Vasilyeva was alone and expecting me. She immediately noticed the two bulging bags in my hands but carefully kept from looking at them.

"What happened?" she asked. "Why aren't you in America?"

"America can go to hell, we got bored . . ." I tried to speak carelessly.

"But seriously?"

"It was all that Berlinsky of ours. He's a fool! Went and broke his finger. Just a little fracture, but we had to cut short the tour."

"How did it happen?"

I told her about the dog.

"How many concerts were left to play?"

"Eight."

Vasilyeva picked up a pencil and started calculating something quickly on a sheet of paper. "$5,120. Rather a lot."

She paused to think. I waited patiently.

"Okay," she finally said. "You understand that I can't guarantee anything."

"I understand." I nodded.

"But we can try."

"Maybe wait to turn in the report until right before New Year's?" I suggested carefully.

"Don't try to teach me!" said Vasilyeva curtly, and started cleaning up her desk.

"You'll get to spend Saturday and Sunday at home, I hope?" I asked.

"Where else! But I don't know which is worse! The house is a mess. I have two little bandits growing up. Completely out of hand."

This was a convenient moment. I looked at the ceiling. "I have here a few children's things for the winter . . ."

"Oh, thank you! As it is, they aren't taken care of at all. Thank you!"

"And a little for you . . ." I dared.

"Listen, you better wait for me outside."

"I came in a cab," I said quickly. "I can give you a lift."

"Then drive a little away from the entrance. And that"—she nodded at the bags—"take them yourself, but be careful, the watchman's there . . ."

I went downstairs, walked past the watchman, and greeted him politely. He followed my bags with his eyes but didn't say a word.

A few days went by, then a few weeks. Nothing happened, except that all our foreign concerts for the next two years were canceled. This was the minimum punishment. We wisely kept from explaining anything, so that everything would be forgotten as quickly as possible. We couldn't play concerts now in any case, and how much time was needed before Berlinsky would be able to play again no doctor could say.

I tried to find some work teaching. At one time it had seemed that the Moscow Conservatory might be interested in me. Right before leaving for the United States I had helped a young group prepare for a quartet competition in Liège, Belgium. We worked together through the spring and summer; in the autumn they successfully auditioned in Moscow, and in October, when I was already in America, I received a brief but expressive telegram from them: FIRST PRIZE THANK YOU. I also received a letter signed by Minister of Culture Ekaterina Furtseva herself, thanking me for preparing the quartet. They heard about the letter in the conservatory, and at a faculty meeting my old chamber-music teacher Mark Milman suggested that I be invited to work there. Asatur Grigorian, the faculty chairman, agreed, saying that the conservatory needed teachers who also played concerts—it would be a great stimulus and a good example to the students. Everyone nodded, and Milman phoned me the same evening.

"No one objected," he said. "Can you imagine? Not even Grigorian, who runs the quartet class and for whom you're a dangerous competitor. I'm sure that everything will be fine."

"I'll buy you dinner at a restaurant."

"That's not necessary. I don't like restaurants."

"And what do you like?"

"I don't need your gratitude. I want you to be in the conservatory. We need a quartet specialist."

"Thank you, Mark Vladimirovich," I said with emotion. "I really value that."

He phoned me a few weeks later, on December 31. "Happy new year," he said to me dully.

"And the same to you!"

"I'll get right to business, okay? We had another faculty meeting last week. Discussed your candidacy again. I repeated everything that Grigorian said last time, about how you play concerts and how important that is for the students. For some reason, this time that didn't make much of an impression. Grigorian spoke right after me. He said that he had been your friend since childhood, loved you a lot, and valued you as a musician. 'But, comrades,' he added, 'do you understand what we're doing? The Borodin Quartet represents Soviet culture abroad. That's an important governmental task, and we'll have to limit their trips to thirty days a year. You understand what will happen? We'll be interfering with the spread of Soviet culture abroad! Frightening even to think about . . .' "

"Clever," I said. "Just virtuosic."

"He's very sly, that Grigorian. Found a strong argument."

"And what about the others?"

"This time they were all quiet."

"Does the conservatory actually limit Oistrakh, Gilels, and everyone else who travels to thirty days?"

"Don't be silly! They travel as much as they want. Or rather, as much as they can. It's not a question of the thirty days."

"Why don't I suit them?"

"Probably the same old reason."

"So why, in spite of that, do they still let me go abroad?"

"That's different. There are four of you in the quartet, and you're the only . . . I mean to say, the other three . . . Oh hell! Well, you understand . . . And the state needs the hard currency."

"Right now I could use some of the local money. Any work would do."

"You'd be very useful to the conservatory."

"Mark Vladimirovich, why is there such stupidity everywhere?" He didn't answer, and I continued, "Why are there so many lies around us? And why is that the way of things?"

He became frightened and hurriedly said, "Well, okay, take care. Happy new year!"

The lack of trips abroad quickly made itself felt. First we depleted our supplies of Colgate toothpaste and Lux soap. The switch to Soviet toothpaste turned out to be extremely painful; I felt sick at least twice a day—in the morning and in the evening—after brushing my teeth. Once we used up our last certificates (exchanged for foreign currency and for use in special shops), we even started having trouble with food. We had become spoiled by the hard-currency store and had forgotten how simple Soviet citizens ate. Returning to the old way even proved to be dangerous: my wife and I promptly poisoned ourselves with store-bought cottage cheese, and for a long time after that our stomachs hurt. We stopped trusting the stores and went to the free markets. Everything there was fresh, but very expensive. But who said there's no way out of a hopeless situation? That would be so primitive! There's always a way out. In order to find it, however, you have to collect exhaustive objective data about the country and its people, put it all in your brain, as if in a computer, go to sleep, and not wake until some decision pops up. And indeed, one morning one did pop up, simple and life-saving. During my travels abroad, we had collected a considerable pile of foreign goods. In the Soviet Union, you can easily sell anything foreign, from Agatha Christie in English to polyethylene bags, not to mention shoes or clothes. We carried one piece of junk after another to the secondhand store and lived for a while without feeling sick.

Meanwhile, Berlinsky was gradually getting better. After six months he even started playing, though sparing the sore finger. And after two more months we started playing a few concerts.

A year went by. Goskoncert was silent. Berlinsky said, "No water gathers under a lying stone," and insisted on my calling the chief of the Department of Capitalist Countries, Elena Zaharova, with whom I had earlier established warm and "mutually advantageous" relations.

"Good day," I said into the phone, feeling the shame of a person asking for charity.

"Who is speaking?" asked Elena.

"You used to know me by my voice . . ."

"Oh, it's you."

"I'm calling only to say hello. How are you?"

"Busy. You know that we now have a new director?"

"Yes, I'd heard . . ."

"So, there it is. Goodbye!"

There was a sharp click in the receiver. Berlinsky was standing next to me. When I recited our conversation to him word for word, he swore.

"We didn't bring enough from abroad," I said.

He didn't answer and lit a cigarette.

"It was dumb to phone and humiliate ourselves! Two years is two years! No help for it. We have to wait."

"Let's go by Tchaikovsky Hall and drink a glass of beer," he suggested.

"Good idea! Let's go."

There was no beer at the café, but there was cognac. We bought a bottle and went into a corner. At this early hour the room was empty. We silently had one drink, then a second . . .

Without trips abroad, our life had lost its main attraction. Inside the country, with Brezhnev's accession to the throne and the all-out creation of a new cult of personality, the stifling atmosphere had grown heavier. It was clearer than ever that no hopes, not even the humblest, for any sort of renewal of the country were fated to be fulfilled. Of all possible forms of the dictatorial regime, from the maniacal brutality of Stalin to the "liberal" clowning of Khrushchev, the dead calm of Brezhnev seemed the most suitable for a lifeless socialist society. Brezhnev correctly understood that the status quo could be maintained only by painstaking inaction. And most of all, by not depriving the Soviet ruling class of its unlimited privileges.

Berlinsky and I each drank a third, then a fourth . . .

You get drunk differently in different situations. When everything's okay, you quickly soften, or if something goes wrong, you can become furious. This time we sobered up.

There was nothing to do. We went outside and headed along Gorky

Street toward Red Square, by Lenin's mausoleum to the Moskva River. We leaned on the granite railing and looked into the murky water.

"Shit!" Berlinsky said.

I told him how I had been invited and then uninvited to work at the conservatory.

Berlinsky smiled crookedly. "Rostropovich tried to get me something there."

"And?"

"As you see."

"But why you? You're not a leper the way I am."

"They know about my wrong half," he said, falling silent as he looked into the water, and then added hopefully, "Maybe Sveshnikov will leave. He's already over seventy."

We were silent again.

"The Jews are stirring," I said.

"Yes, I heard . . . A special letter is being prepared."

" 'Secret,' we have to assume?"

"Sure! So that the whole country knows right away."

"Poor Jews! All over again from the very beginning."

"Well, what do we have for the coming season?"

"Only Chausson with Oistrakh, otherwise—just hackwork."

"Not much! Well, shall we go?"

We walked back to the Philharmonia without speaking. The bright summer sun shone over Moscow.

Schnittke

1966

THE GREATEST COMPOSERS of the past were also great innovators. Often without knowing it, they outstripped time and their contemporaries. The breathtaking flight of twentieth-century music is linked with the names of Bartók, Stravinsky, Ravel, Shostakovich. With his new twelve-tone system, Arnold Schönberg, even though he reduced all music to its "common denominator," opened not a road but a superhighway. And when he said his famous "Now any fool will be able to compose music," his prophecy proved to be correct to a certain extent.

Yet after the devastation the Soviet authorities inflicted on Russian music, it took decades for the new tendencies, which in the West had long ago become orthodox classics, to reach the Soviet Union. Slowly, there appeared new young composers, nonconformists. It was a strange group, possible only in a country as tightly closed as the Soviet Union, where everything is subject to censorship. The notoriety of these composers was immense, even scandalous, because their music was not openly performed. Their names did not and could not appear on concert posters. But when the word spread that something "like that" was being played nonetheless, the halls were always packed. Most probably this heightened interest in new music existed because of its official ban. Forbidden fruit, as everyone knows, has been sweet from the dawn of humanity.

I often wondered what would have happened if the authorities had suddenly permitted the performance of contemporary music. Would it have lost its admirers or not?

All the same, music was in a privileged position compared to painting, and especially to literature. This, of course, was understandable. Of all the arts, music is perhaps the most abstract, and the hardest of all in which to trace so-called anti-Soviet tendencies. Still, the Communist Party managed to put its mark on traditional Soviet music. Compositions in minor keys or ending in pianissimo were subjected to sharp criticism as examples of pessimism, distortion, and even slander of Soviet reality, or a lack of faith in "the triumph of Communism and its bright future." But the new twelve-tone or serial music infuriated the authorities even more, because it led to a quest for new paths in art, and by doing so threatened the holy of holies: the unquestioning acceptance of Soviet ideology.

Khrennikov fell upon the avant-gardists with all the malice appropriate to his role as the devoted jailer of Soviet music. Back in Stalin's time he had somehow failed, in spite of all his efforts, to destroy Shostakovich completely. So when the Soviet government declared Shostakovich the greatest composer of the twentieth century, Khrennikov transferred all his anger to the new music. The composer Alfred Schnittke was especially subjected to his attacks, since in the atonal music of the Soviet avant-garde, Schnittke played the same role as Shostakovich in traditional tonal music. Schnittke was not arrested simply because, after Stalin, cultural figures who did not suit the regime were no longer destroyed physically; they were only deprived of freedom.

Schnittke fought the regime by writing one remarkable composition after another. When a rumor reached Moscow that Schnittke had written a string quartet, I phoned him and asked right away, "Is it true what people are saying?"

"I don't know what people are saying, but if they're saying . . ."

"They say you've written a quartet. Could I have a look?"

"It's not ready yet."

"At least show me what there is already."

"Well, all right, come over."

We spent the whole evening going over the score. There were still empty pages in it, but the scheme of the quartet was evident. Schnittke said that at the very beginning he wanted to convey the process of creation. Even on the piano it sounded interesting; one could only imagine how much it would gain by being played by a quartet, when the different timbres would be added to it. Then came a cadenza for the quartet, in which all four instruments in turn play separately, creating the effect of a single string instrument with an immense range.

The climax of the quartet, called "Disintegration," was a complete contrast. After the scrupulous exactness and organization of all the music, everything suddenly fell apart. The analogy with Soviet society clearly suggested itself. The whole composition ended with a return to the initial series of twelve tones, like the results of a search.

The next day we had an important and nerve-racking concert. In the Bolshoi Hall of the Moscow Conservatory, for the first time in the U.S.S.R., Stravinsky's *The Soldier's Tale* was to be performed. Stravinsky himself had been in Moscow not long before, and it seemed he had been forgiven for not returning to Russia after the Revolution. A dinner was given in his honor at the Ministry of Culture, and the ban was removed from his music. Stravinsky was even shown on Moscow television, answering the standard selection of questions, the last of which had to do with what he thought of contemporary music. Stravinsky answered, in perfect Russian: "Oh, absolutely the same thing I said thirty years ago; my opinion has not changed in all these years."

"Very interesting. And what was that?"

"I'm sorry, I don't remember."

The Soldier's Tale was in the second half of the concert, and in the first we played Shostakovich's quintet with Richter. The quintet went well, and Richter, pleased, invited me to go with him to hear Stravinsky.

During the intermission, a bulky man approached the quartet and said that he wanted to talk with us. His accent gave him away as a foreigner, though he spoke Russian fluently.

"I'm Milović. From Yugoslavia. I need to see you about a contemporary music festival in Zagreb."

"I'd like to hear the Stravinsky," I said.

"Programs are your department," answered Berlinsky.

"I think you can handle it," I said. "Write down all the twentieth-century composers in our repertoire and put together something interesting. Mr. Milović will help you."

The Soldier's Tale came off poorly. The audience, raised on Tchaikovsky, didn't know what to expect from Stravinsky's music, and the performers, subconsciously broken by the lengthy ban on his compositions, were trying to speak a foreign language which they did not yet understand. The flash of Stravinsky's musical wit was dulled, and the soldier's story itself, filtered through the unavoidable Soviet censorship, lost all sense.

I dozed off and was awakened by applause. Richter and I returned to the dressing room and found Berlinsky standing at the entrance, smoking nervously.

"How's it going?" I asked him.

"We have to talk." He grimaced.

We went to the restaurant where Milović was sitting at a table between Shebalin and Alexandrov. Once we were seated, Berlinsky said that we needed a program for Zagreb.

"You still haven't agreed?" I asked in surprise.

"It just isn't working out."

"Why not?"

"Mr. Milović wants only Soviet music. Prokofiev and Shostakovich are fine, but we need one more piece."

I turned to Milović. "What else would you like?"

"I await your suggestions."

"And what have they already suggested to you?"

Berlinsky spoke up quickly and with irritation. "We suggested everything we have. And none of it will do."

"You see," said Milović patiently, "our festival is unusual. I came to Moscow especially for this. I spent three days with Mr. Khrennikov, who played various tapes for me. I listened to a great deal of music. Our festival . . ."

He didn't finish, but what he wanted to say was clear. He wanted Soviet avant-garde music.

The audience dispersed and soon we were alone in the restaurant. The waitress kept looking in our direction.

"We're holding her up," said Alexandrov. "We have to decide this question somehow."

"What do you think?" Berlinsky asked me.

"There's one composition," I said uncertainly.

"Which?" asked Milović quickly.

"I heard it played on the piano yesterday."

"What is it?"

"Schnittke's quartet."

"I'll take it!" Milović said firmly.

My colleagues were silent.

"A splendid composition," I continued. "Very original. About twenty minutes long."

"I agree," Milović repeated.

"But you see, usually we send our programs officially, through Goskoncert, and if . . ."

"I understand. Don't worry. Whatever program I receive, we'll play what we just agreed on. You can depend on me. I won't let you down. Okay?"

We said nothing and Milović rose from his chair. "Thank you. I'll see you in Zagreb next year."

We went outside without speaking and said goodbye to Milović.

"Have you really heard the quartet?" asked Berlinsky.

"Just yesterday evening."

"Well, how is it?"

"Marvelous!"

"Twelve-tone?"

"Of course."

"They're bound to find out at Goskoncert," said Alexandrov.

"Not necessarily," I said. "Milović will keep quiet, that's obvious. It won't even get to Goskoncert."

"It's dangerous," Alexandrov said again.

"We'll have to hope for disorder at Goskoncert. I think it'll go all right."

"God willing!" said Berlinsky.

Crack-up
1967

It was early June. Before the summer break, as always, we met at the Philharmonia without our instruments. Berlinsky would read out everything we had done during the season, listing our tours inside the country and abroad, the number of cities and concerts played, radio broadcasts and recordings, even funerals and the names of the deceased. He calculated how many kilometers we had covered by car, by train, and in the air, approximately how many people had heard our concerts, how much money we had earned during the year, and how much foreign currency we had given to the state.

The figures turned out to be very impressive. They piled up unnoticeably during the everyday life of the quartet, which despite its variety had gradually become monotonous.

We were already about to shake each other's hands and go our own ways, when Berlinsky said that our next season, likewise, promised to be very rich, and asked whether the artistic director of the Borodin Quartet would be so kind as to inform its members about all creative plans.

"Why repeat all that again?" I said. "Everything's clear as it is."

"Not everything!" said Berlinsky.

"Well, what then? All the trips are settled, and our season in the

Soviet Union, too. We discussed all the programs, and everyone has written them down."

"I would still like to hear it one more time." Something in his insistence was alien, as if someone else were forcing him to say it.

"What would you like to hear?"

"The programs to be played abroad."

"Oh, come on!" said Shebalin. "We've heard it all a hundred times."

"I'm waiting!" said Berlinsky stubbornly.

I shrugged. "Well, all right. I can repeat it. In October we have a trip to West Germany. Two programs: Borodin, Shostakovich, Beethoven, and Prokofiev, Stravinsky, Brahms. The season here . . ."

"We don't need to hear that!" interrupted Berlinsky. "Only abroad."

"Later, in February, we have Sweden with Wilhelm Stenhammar by request of Swedish radio, and in May the festival in Zagreb: Prokofiev, Schnittke, Shostakovich. In the summer, Australia and New Zealand. Four programs have been sent there, but there's still no answer. That's all. Is anything unclear?"

"Yes," said Berlinsky, not looking at me. "By what means did Schnittke's quartet get out of the U.S.S.R.?"

"Don't you remember Milović and our conversation in the Bolshoi Hall?"

"I remember."

"So why ask, then?"

"Why, in general, did Schnittke's quartet come up?"

"You'd probably do better to ask the composer about that," I said.

"Don't play the fool!" said Berlinsky seriously.

"Which one of us is playing the fool?"

Berlinsky turned to Alexandrov. "Why are you quiet? Tell us everything you think about this."

"Just like a conspiracy," I said. "May I ask what the problem is?"

"It is," Alexandrov said with emphasized calmness, "that you have dragged a forbidden composition outside our borders."

"It isn't forbidden yet."

"It will be forbidden, and you know it."

"So where the hell were you before? When we all agreed with Milović?"

He didn't answer.

"Have you forgotten how you three sat with Milović for a whole hour and couldn't agree on anything? He refused all your suggestions."

"And then you came and offered him Schnittke. He grabbed it, of course."

"It's just what he needs for the Zagreb festival. Music, and not the shit that Khrennikov was shoving at him."

"Watch your language," said Alexandrov maliciously. "We don't know Schnittke's quartet and don't want to know it!"

"And I know that it's a remarkable piece, and I suggested it so we could have an interesting concert in Zagreb."

"You're exploiting your position as artistic director and propagandizing anti-Soviet music."

"What! . . . Do you mean that seriously?"

"Absolutely! And we won't tolerate it."

I didn't know what to say. These were no longer my quartet mates. And who were they now? Musicians or Party officials?

I looked at Shebalin. He was sitting still, with his head down, looking at the floor. "Well, and what do you say?"

Without looking up, he shrugged.

Trying to calm the wild pounding of my heart, I said, "Well, all right, everything's clear. We'll just say that the artistic director has been dismissed for anti-Soviet activity. And for the future—if there is one—find yourselves another line of work."

I quickly walked out of the room. I was shaking. It seemed impossible that all this could be serious. "Anti-Soviet music," and Party principles. Principles, my ass! They just wanted to protect themselves. Now if there really was some sort of problem because of the Schnittke, they would be able to say that they had been opposed and had even held an "open Party meeting" in the quartet, at which (I could hear how it might be said) "the mistaken actions of the quartet's artistic director were decisively condemned with uncompromising Party directness." This would save them from punishment "along Party lines."

I couldn't imagine our next meeting. What could we talk about?

The weather? And rehearsals? How could they be carried on? Our group wasn't an orchestra, where you could refuse to talk with your neighbor but still play under the conductor. In a quartet, mutual understanding between partners is simply indispensable. The catastrophe seemed to me irreparable. The trip to Yugoslavia was not that important now, but how would we go on living?

The days of vacation passed quickly. Schnittke finished his quartet and sent me the music. Not wanting to tell him the state of our quartet, I only asked him to keep our Zagreb concert a secret. He understood this perfectly. At home, in his own country, there could be no hope of performance, and playing it abroad, without the approval of the Composers' Union and Comrade Khrennikov personally, was categorically forbidden.

Not knowing how events would unfold, I sat down to the score all the same. My worst fears were justified: it was a splendid composition, clear and very expressive. I found in it a whole series of performing devices, which contemporary music needs more than classical, and pointed them out to the composer. I said that they might be called anti-Soviet by some people, to which he answered that he could hardly wait to hear it in live performance.

"Me too," I said.

September 1 arrived, the start of a new quartet season. I didn't phone anyone, because I was no longer artistic director of our quartet, and no one phoned me, assuming, evidently, that I should be the first to admit my mistakes.

Three weeks passed. We had no concerts and the Philharmonia did not disturb us. On the twenty-second, nonetheless, one could get paid for the first half of the month. By the cashier's window I saw the rest of the quartet. They got their money and passed by me without saying a word, yet they stopped in the hall to wait for me to come out. I knew that a difficult conversation lay ahead, and I was ready for it in the sense that I had nothing to add to what I had said earlier. I went out into the hall. It was strange to be together again.

"Hi," I said. They didn't answer.

"What's going on?" asked Berlinsky. "Do we have a quartet or not?"

Now it was my turn not to answer.

"Why aren't we working?" Berlinsky went on. "If there's no longer a quartet, I'll look for other work. I have a family to feed."

"That's logical," I said, knowing ahead of time that he would soon lose his temper.

But Alexandrov said quickly, "Let's go to the studio. We can talk there."

We went into our studio and sat down, by some idiotic coincidence, in the same order in which we had been sitting the last time we had used the room. Berlinsky started shouting.

"I want to know what's going on!"

"Are you shouting at me?"

"At who else?"

"Maybe that's enough shouting?" I said, trying to control myself.

"It won't be enough until we find out why this season we didn't start working on time as usual. You answer for all the quartet's work. You're the artistic director, understand?"

"I was once," I said.

"What sort of reply is that? I want to know what's the matter!"

"As if you didn't know."

"No, I don't."

If, instead of all this nonsense, he had said that the meeting at the end of the last season had been a necessary show, to keep the quartet out of danger in case of scandal over the Schnittke, we probably would have gone right down to the restaurant and downed a bottle of cognac together. But he kept heaping all the blame on me in his insistence that the Party line in the quartet was correct, while I alone was spoiling everything.

I couldn't stand it any longer.

"If you don't know, then I don't know either," I said, and stood up. "If you need me, you know where to find me."

Berlinsky phoned me that evening. "We're rehearsing tomorrow at noon," he announced.

"Okay," I said.

"What will we rehearse?"

"Don't ask me. I no longer exist."

"Cut out the sabotage! We order you! Start fulfilling your duties, and fast."

"I have no duties. I'm no longer the artistic director."

"No one dismissed you. Your attention was simply drawn to your errors. You have to admit them and continue working."

"Forget it! From now on, we'll decide all artistic work with meetings. What the Party orders, we'll play."

He swore unpleasantly.

"Is that for me, or the Party?"

He swore again and hung up.

I went to rehearsal the way people go to be executed. I felt that I was not only incapable of running the rehearsal but even of saying a word. I knew that we had to start working on Schnittke's quartet soon, and here they were demanding that I repent and beg for forgiveness, as so many Soviet composers had done before.

I went into the studio, forced myself to say hello, and sat down at my music stand. I tuned my violin and, as always, gave Berlinsky the A. Once he had tuned, I checked all the open strings with him. Then I waited while Alexandrov and Shebalin tuned, and I checked each string with them. This had been our tuning routine for many years now.

Next, I distributed Mozart's Quartet in G-major, K.387, and opened to the first page. We played the quartet from start to finish, and I opened to the next one in D-minor, K. 421, but Berlinsky said, "That's all very lovely, Mozart and music-making, but in two weeks we leave for West Germany."

I played the first few notes of the second Borodin quartet, and everyone opened to it in their music. I made no remarks. Accustomed to painstakingly working on all the details, we all understood that there was no point in simply playing it through. Berlinsky gave up first and put his instrument aside. "This is ridiculous," he said. "Just a waste of time."

"I agree," said Alexandrov.

"I sympathize," I said.

"So what do we need to do to work normally again?" Berlinsky asked.

"What do they do to a person who's dead?" I answered pathetically. "Wash the corpse, put it in a coffin, and organize a funeral ceremony. But it's all the same to the deceased, no matter what speeches are made."

"Well, to hell with all of you!" Shebalin suddenly burst out. "You made this bed, you can lie in it! Tomorrow I'm not coming to rehearsal. The hell with it!"

"I agree with him," said Berlinsky.

"Me too," echoed Alexandrov.

"Well, so do I," I said. "At least we've finally agreed on something."

I walked home feeling certain that I had just left my last meeting with the quartet. Starting from the day when I had first sat down with the original quartet back at the conservatory in October 1946, twenty-one years had passed. In that time, as Berlinsky had so meticulously calculated for us, I had played 2,000 concerts. That was 2,000 appearances before an audience—2,000 times to feel the feverish pulse. Each concert usually lasts two hours. Putting on tails, warming up, and waiting to go on—which is often more nerve-racking than the concert itself—takes another two. Four hours altogether. Thus 2,000 concerts give us 8,000 hours. Divided by twenty-four we get 333 days: 333 days and nights of uninterrupted playing onstage—one month short of a year! And if I totaled up the daily rehearsals and practices? Not less than five to six hours a day. Even underestimating the numbers, it adds up to 1,500 hours per year or 31,500 hours in twenty-one years. Divided by twenty-four that's over 1,300 days. About three and a half years. Plus the other one . . . That means in twenty-one years I played the violin for more than four years without a break!

I started to add up the number of compositions I had played, and lost count past 200. It occurred to me that these dry figures could not re-create the whole picture; each piece, while it is coming to life, means several sleepless nights, because success never comes easily. This was my investment in the quartet, which was rewarded only by the applause of the audience—and this Party meeting?

I felt a lump in my throat.

* * *

I don't know whether the others went to rehearsal the next day. I myself didn't go. Instead, I went to Pushkin Square, where pensioners play chess.

A week later, early in the morning, someone rang my doorbell. It was Shebalin. "I was just passing by," he said casually, although he lived in a new part of Moscow, about ten miles away from me.

"Don't make excuses, come in. Have you had breakfast?"

"I have to admit that I haven't yet."

"Then let's go right to the kitchen."

"With pleasure. The best part of any apartment."

I got out a bottle of wine and two glasses.

"Who's there?" asked my wife, looking into the kitchen. "Oh, hello! Do sit down. I'll fix something."

My wife, of course, had suffered through the recent events in the quartet with me and was dying of curiosity.

Shebalin started chattering. "Excuse me, I can't stay long. They asked me to stop by the conservatory. It seems they're giving me a quartet position. But I haven't made up my mind yet."

"Well, congratulations," I said, ignoring his last words.

"Sveshnikov personally asked me to come by," Shebalin continued carelessly. "If the old man asks, why hurt his feelings?"

Luba and I furtively exchanged glances.

"We must drink to that," I said. "A job at the conservatory—that's just what the doctor ordered. Congratulations again."

"Thanks, old man."

We clinked glasses. He drained his wine while I only sipped, but he wasn't paying any attention to me.

"It smells of a whole department," he went on. "After Borisovsky no one 'measured up' to that position. I suit them in every respect. All the chamber music of the conservatory will be in my hands. But I still haven't decided," he caught himself. "They can wait a little."

I took the bottle and filled up his glass again. "I heard that the conservatory limits its teachers to thirty days per year of travel," I said.

"That's nonsense. And in any case, that has nothing to do with me.

I'm my own boss. Especially since I was appointed head of our delegation to the competition in Geneva."

"Another drink to that?"

"Why not," he said, and drank the whole glass. "They need me. Without me, they . . ."

Ah, so that was it! He was the man! I would never have suspected Shebalin. But why not, after all? He was a simple fellow, with an open Russian face, drank vodka nicely. So it was because of him the quartet went abroad alone without a Fifth. Went? "Had gone" would be more exact.

"What sort of competition?" I asked, so as not to be silent.

"Harps and double basses."

"A bit heavy to drag around."

"I'll manage. I'll arrange everything, transport and the rest."

He raised his glass and we drank the toast, but honestly, it wasn't appropriate to drink to this, because the head of a Soviet delegation spies on his own people, and his main task is to make sure that no one defects to the West.

"There'll be a lot of work there," Shebalin started up again. "It's forbidden to come back to Moscow without the first prize. I already have the list of the whole jury and their habits. Even what their wives like."

"Take along a lot of Russian souvenirs."

"What do you mean! You can't get along with souvenirs alone. Don't you worry, everything has been taken into consideration! That's why they chose me. I'm often abroad, so no suspicions . . . I'm acquainted with a lot of musicians." He glanced at his watch. "By the way, I saw Schnittke yesterday at the Composers' Union."

"Oh yes?"

"There's a splendid restaurant there! They serve carp in sour cream and monastery-style steaks. Nothing like them anywhere! Well, I have to go. Will you excuse me if I run off now? I still have to stop by several places."

I saw him to the door.

"Listen," Shebalin exclaimed suddenly, "I'd completely forgotten! I have a letter for you."

"A letter?"

"Yes, from us. Take it. Well, goodbye! I have to run."

He didn't wait for the elevator but ran off down the stairs. I opened the letter, read it, took it to my wife, and gave it to her to read. Then we read it aloud together. It said:

We, the undersigned, thank our artistic director, R. Dubinsky, for his fruitful work of many years, thanks to which the Borodin State Quartet advanced into the ranks of the finest worldwide collectives of this genre. The selfless labor of Dubinsky, along with his originality of musical thought, allowed us in a relatively brief period to achieve outstanding creative success. We confirm in writing that all artistic work in the quartet, with no exceptions—choice of repertoire, interpretation, conducting rehearsals, and preparation for concerts—are entirely and fully under the jurisdiction of the artistic director on the condition of unlimited creative freedom.

This was followed by their names, signed in blood.

My wife and I looked at each other for a long time without saying anything. Luba was the first to speak.

"Just like Tom Sawyer and Huck Finn. All that's missing is a skull and crossbones."

"So what should I do now?"

"Start working."

"I can't."

"Stupid, you just got back your quartet. Better take your violin and get ready for rehearsal tomorrow. You go to Germany in a week."

Going West
1968

WE LEFT for Germany by train. As usual, Luba didn't come to see me off, since neither of us could stand those last minutes when the train moved slowly away, leaving one of us looking sadly out of the train window while the other stood miserably on the platform. It was so much easier for me to get into the taxi by myself, as if I were going to a rehearsal or a concert and would be returning home soon. Usually I stopped to pick up Berlinsky, but this time I went straight to the train station.

The platform at the Belorussky station was crowded with admirers and students. Berlinsky appeared together with Rostropovich. Two of Berlinsky's students walked behind him, carrying his suitcase and instrument. Both Berlinsky and Rostropovich had been drinking. When Berlinsky saw me he immediately shouted, "Why didn't you pick me up?"

"Someone gave me a lift," I lied.

"You missed a lot!"

"Really, old man." Rostropovich turned to me.

"Why didn't you phone?" I said.

"We wanted to. But we didn't dare tear you away from your lovely wife."

"We drank everything in the house, even the medicinal alcohol!"

exclaimed Berlinsky. "A fine thing, I assure you. Better than any vodka."

Alexandrov and Shebalin appeared, and the crowd broke up into small groups. I led Rostropovich away to the other side of the platform, where no one could hear us.

"I wanted to tell you something. Can you listen?"

"I'm not drunk at all. I'm as sober as a judge. If you mean about Schnittke, then I already know everything. I told Berlinsky, drummed it into his head! Schnittke is a brilliant guy."

"No, I don't mean Schnittke. I mean you."

"Oh, go on, then! I love it when people talk about me."

"Listen. The Soviet all-star team has the finest offensive line in the world."

"Maybe. I'm a complete ignoramus in soccer."

"Let's say that on the forward line we have Richter, Gilels, Oistrakh, Kogan, and Rostropovich. You're the left wing."

"That's interesting."

"We also had other wonderful players: Mandelstam, Tsvetaeva, Pasternak, Akhmatova, and Brodsky. The captain, of course, is Shostakovich. But the referees, they keep whistling! They won't let anyone play! Each one plays alone: Mandelstam begs for a handout on the streets of Vladivostok; Tsvetaeva hangs herself; Brodsky is sent to the North as a parasite; Akhmatova's name, even after her death, isn't officially recognized; Pasternak won't travel to Stockholm for the Nobel Prize because he wouldn't be allowed back in. As to Shostakovich, you know for yourself. We must protect him and save what can still be saved. All the others adapted somehow to the Soviet rules of play and don't notice that they're shooting at their own goalie."

"Well, and me?" asked Rostropovich, his eyes flashing.

"I'm getting to that. You're the only one on the whole team whom the state can neither break nor buy. You fight back! They give you penalties, don't let you abroad, but you still stick in their throats like a sharp bone. The people know that. The people see hope in you. You ceased long ago to be only a musician, you became something like the people's conscience."

He wouldn't let me finish and hugged me with his huge arms. "You can't imagine how important it is for me to hear that. Thank you."

Berlinsky came over to us. "What are you hugging each other for?" he asked jealously.

"Why, we're only talking about soccer," Rostropovich answered cheerfully, quickly wiping away a tear. "It turns out that we root for the same team."

Our departure was announced and I boarded the train. From my window I noticed how Berlinsky couldn't tear himself away from Rostropovich until the train started to move, and then he jumped frantically aboard.

Besides us, our car was empty, but the conductors still kept all the other compartments locked. The prospect of spending two days in one compartment with my colleagues did not excite me, so I timidly asked the conductor whether he could open one more compartment. Without even looking at me, he answered that all the places were reserved and that more passengers would join us along the way. Shebalin, overhearing this, winked at me and followed the conductor into the staff compartment. They soon returned together, and the conductor opened two more compartments for us. Now he was courteous and even offered us some tea.

I gave Shebalin a questioning look, and he smiled complacently and said, "All this pleasure for ten Western D marks. Two-fifty from you. Simple arithmetic."

Berlinsky had yet to appear in the compartment. He was standing on the platform between cars, smoking and staring out the window. Today he might do anything. In the first place, he had drunk a lot. Second, he had been drinking with Rostropovich, who, it seemed, had told him all about Schnittke. And probably more.

Alexandrov raced into my compartment. "The guy's not himself! He just tried to jump off the train. I barely managed to grab his jacket."

"Tell the conductor to lock all the doors."

"I already did. But it's still dangerous. These conductors have special authority. After each trip they make reports on all the passengers. We have to put him to bed right away."

I went to the platform. Shebalin was there already, trying to drag

Berlinsky into the car. Berlinsky was kicking, waving his arms, and shouting that he was going back to Moscow. Both conductors were watching from their compartment.

Berlinsky saw me. "I'll still get off at the very first stop!"

"Why?"

"Don't you understand what has happened? Don't you know who Rostropovich is?"

"A cellist," I said.

"He's our salvation! Our only hope! My place is near him, to help him, and here I am running off to the devil's mother!"

"And what do you plan to do in Moscow?"

"It has nothing to do with you! Your job is to bring Schnittke's quartet to rehearsal." He went on yelling, "Why haven't you handed out the parts?"

"I have the music with me," I said, amazed. "Everything is ready."

"We have to play it right away. And first of all in Moscow."

The great Rostropovich! I thought, and said aloud, "As soon as the trip ends . . ."

"It won't end because it won't begin. To hell with this trip! I'm going back home. And you get out of here. Leave me alone!"

I went to my compartment. Outside the windows it was getting dark. The train went quickly, shaking and swaying. There weren't many stops on this route. The first one was in Smolensk, but that wasn't for a while. It was followed by Minsk, Brest, and the border. I undressed, locked my door, and lay down under the blanket.

A knock on my door woke me. I fumbled in the darkness and eventually managed to unlock the compartment. Shebalin stood in the corridor.

"Sorry I woke you," he said. "Things are bad. The conductors want to throw him off the train."

"What did he do now?"

"Stole the conductor's key and started running up and down the whole train shouting that he's Rostropovich! The conductors threw a blanket on him, brought him back here, and locked him in a compartment. They want to turn him in to the police at the border."

"How is he now?"

"At first he pounded on the door and shouted that he was in prison and they better let him out or he would complain to Rostropovich. Then he quieted down."

"He's never been like this before. When do we reach the border?"

"In the morning."

"Should we go see the conductors?"

"Useless. They're really furious. Mostly because of the key."

"So what can we do?"

"We need plenty of vodka."

"Where can we get it?"

"Only in Minsk. I'll give it a try."

"Should I come with you?"

"It's better with no witnesses."

The train ran on through the darkness. It was good to think to the sound of the wheels; my thoughts somehow rumbled along with the rhythm of the train.

What had that beautiful woman in Cincinnati said? That I belong there, not here. In general, running away would be no problem. We were traveling alone. After the concert I could just get in another car with someone from the Friends of Music, say goodbye at the hotel, even wave to him, and then, as I was in tails and with a violin, take a taxi and off I'd go! There would be a DO NOT DISTURB sign on the door of my room, so no one would come in. And when they did get alarmed the next day, I'd already be far away. They wouldn't find me even with the whole Soviet embassy helping. But my wife was back in the "Communist paradise." If only we were together . . . We had missed our chance. We were abroad at the same time only once, I in England, she in Japan. We bear different names and by some miracle they seemed to have forgotten that we were married. They won't make this mistake again, especially since we have no children, no one to hold hostage.

I fell asleep as the darkness outside the window began to thin, and awoke with the sensation that the train had been standing still for a long time. It was bright in the compartment and a ray of sunlight played on the wall. The train rocked slightly and the spot of sunlight slid down the wall, which meant that we were in Brest and our railroad car was being lifted onto narrower gauge rails.

I dressed and went out into the corridor. At the sound of my door opening, the conductor glanced out of the staff compartment.

"Oh, you're here? I thought you all went to lunch together."

"I overslept. I got to sleep late."

"Well, yes, yesterday there was a bit of a ruckus."

"Yes, there was. And how is he today?"

"Normal. All three came by in the morning. Sat for a bit and talked. They're good guys."

Aha, that meant Shebalin had managed to get some vodka after all!

"Yes, good guys," I repeated automatically.

"And if he drank too much, well, who doesn't," continued the conductor.

"That's good. Someone else might not have been so understanding."

"We understand everything. If he's being sent not to *this*, but to *that* Germany, it means he's valuable."

"That's true. Am I too late to make it to the station?"

"It's a ways from here. Once we move I'll make some tea."

"Will we have a restaurant?"

"It opens an hour after we cross the border. But they don't take our money. In Poland, only zlotys, and farther on marks. I thought you had all gone together. Why did they leave you alone like that?"

"They must not have wanted to wake me. They say that sleeping is as good as eating."

"How d'you like that!"

I went back to my compartment. While I waited I could play the violin a little. Our car moved, clanked metallically, and stopped, then moved again, crossing onto other tracks, jerking and stopping, until it reached the platform on the other side of the station, from where, along a narrower track, the trains set off westward.

At the frontier the border guards chased us out of our compartments and examined the baggage section, the bed, and under the mattress with a pocket flashlight. After the border guards came the customs inspectors. On the way back from Europe they would root through all the suitcases, open the instruments, and, if they wished, check the contents of our pockets, but for now they were interested only in Western currency. I still had ten dollars, but I never would have admitted this even to myself and answered the customs inspector, with all the simplicity that I could muster, that I had neither Western nor Soviet currency. He believed me.

The train slowly passed a bridge, a sentry, the pillar at the border, the neutral strip, and stopped once again. The whole story with the border guards and customs officials was repeated, but this time more softly in Polish—*"Proszu pana"* ("If you please, sir") and *"Dzenkuje bardzo"* ("Thanks very much"). The conductors returned our passports to us, and as all Soviets superstitiously say once they have crossed the border, "This time the danger's over."

My colleagues had vanished into their compartments and locked the doors. Now they would sleep until evening. I waited a half hour or so, looking out the window at the gloomy scenery, then walked back and forth a few times in front of the conductors' compartment, so they would get mixed up and not be sure where I was, then stole into the bathroom and, choosing a moment when the conductors were otherwise preoccupied, crossed into the restaurant car.

The door was open but there were no customers. At the bar two waiters and a plump barmaid were sitting at a table, eating.

"Good day!" I said in Russian, which sounds about the same in Polish.

"Džien dobri," they said. Soviet waiters would most likely not have answered.

"I don't speak Polish," I said apologetically.

"We speak Russian," one waiter answered. "But excuse us, it's still closed."

I made a gesture which Robinson Crusoe and Friday had probably used to communicate to each other: I patted my stomach and opened my mouth. They laughed, and the waiter who spoke Russian said, "We'll open soon. But we don't work on rubles. Only on zlotys."

"We don't work on rubles" sounded magnificent.

"I have a few dollars," I said carefully.

The waiter stood up, ran to the other end of the car, locked the door, and came back. "Please be seated," he told me, and held my chair while I sat down, then bent down and whispered in my ear, "I'll give you forty zlotys per dollar."

"*Dobre*" ("Okay"), I said in Polish, having displayed my entire store of Polish words.

He spread a clean cloth over the table and gave me a menu.

"I can wait," I said. "Finish your dinner first."

"It's all right," he said quickly. "What will you order from the menu?"

"Whatever you recommend," I said, and handed him back the menu. "I'm hungry."

He smiled and vanished into the kitchen. I was playing the millionaire, though I had only ten dollars in my pocket.

The second waiter came up to me. "One dollar—fifty zlotys," he said.

"After dinner, okay?"

He nodded and returned to his table.

The first waiter appeared with a tray and placed several kinds of hors d'oeuvres on the table. "Which wine does the gentleman desire?" he asked.

"I'd rather have beer," I said.

"Good, good." He nodded. "We have German. I'll bring it right away."

I ate an abundant dinner. For my ten dollars I was treated as I never would have been in the Soviet Union, not for any amount of money. The waiters and barmaid sat at their table and chatted. I started calculating in my mind. Everything, including the tip, would total about 250 to 300 zlotys. That was five or six dollars. I'd give him my ten-dollar bill. For his courtesy and for making me feel like a person.

I turned to my waiter. "Thank you very much for everything. It was very pleasant."

"Thank you, sir," he answered, and came over to me. I handed the ten dollars to him.

"Will ten dollars be all right?"

He quickly took the money and shoved it into his pocket. "Come to dinner for free. We close at ten."

"Thank you. I'll come with pleasure."

I turned around. The second waiter and the barmaid were looking at me. I went over to thank them as well.

The barmaid held out her hand to me. *"Pan spricht deutsch?"* ("Does the gentleman speak German?")

"Ja, ein wenig," I answered. ("Yes, a little.")

"If the gentleman should have anything for sale, I give a good price. Dollars as well. For one, sixty zlotys. What do you think?"

"Ich komme am Abend," I said. *"Um zehn Uhr, gut?"* ("I'll come in the evening. At ten, all right?")

"Sehr gut."

"Dobre. Dowidzenia." ("Goodbye.")

"Dowidzenia."

I returned to my car, feeling that I really could go to the Poles in the evening and that they would be glad to see me, and that we would sit down to a bottle of wine and talk about the Soviet Union. But I already knew that I wouldn't go. I had no more Western money, and that could spoil everything.

In the car, as before, there was no one but us. In the corridor I ran into Alexandrov, and since it's not good to push past your colleague without talking, I told him that we could eat on the sly in the restaurant in exchange for Western currency. His face immediately took on a bureaucratic expression, and he answered that such undertakings were categorically forbidden as pure black-market currency speculation.

"I only . . . I'm just bringing it to your attention," I said, apologizing.

"I, also, am just bringing it to your attention," he answered dryly.

"Idiot!" I scolded myself. "You knew he'd answer just that way. What were you trying to do with your stupid conversation?"

I went into my compartment. "Not long ago we were still friends; we'd meet not only at quartet rehearsals and talk without fear. And now he's acting as if he's the boss of the quartet."

I pulled down the blind on the window.

"Okay, then, it's best to limit our contacts only to business. Rehearsals at such and such a time, we're playing this and that, the concert's at eight, and once we've played, goodbye."

I lay down under the blanket.

"The idea that the quartet's a happy family, living with common interests, it's as if that was once in my childhood. Now we're grown-up people, and is it so very necessary to have warmth in our relationships within the quartet?"

I closed my eyes.

"And maybe it's better that way. 'Hello,' 'So long'; you come, you play, you leave. Tomorrow, the day after tomorrow. No emotions. But is that really a quartet?"

I fell asleep.

In the evening and at night there were loud knocks at my door, twice at the Polish-German frontier and once at the border between the two Germanies. I kept my passport under my pillow and held it out, without opening my eyes, even before the border guards opened my door. It seemed a pity to wake up.

We reached Cologne in the morning. Franz Wilnauer, with whom we had become good friends on previous trips, met us. He was standing on the platform, tensely looking into each window of the passing cars. Then he saw us and waved both arms. We came out one by one and Franz hugged each of us.

"*Also, Kinder, wie geht es?*"

"*Am besten, Franz, am besten.*"

Franz seized two of our four suitcases and guided us to his blue Mercedes. As we pulled away, I leaned forward to him from the back seat. "I'd like to talk to you," I said in English.

"Let's have lunch together," Franz replied. "I'll call you."

Berlinsky nervously lit a cigarette. "I hate English," he said through clenched teeth.

Franz quickly glanced at him, then turned to me, obviously waiting for a translation, but I was silent.

* * *

Franz phoned me a few hours later.

"Hi, Franz," I said. "Are you in the hotel?"

"Yes."

"Is there anyone from the quartet around?"

"Why? Do you want them?"

"No. It's better if they don't see us together right now."

"No, there is no one here."

"Okay, then. I'm coming."

"I suggest we go straight to the banquet room," he said when I came down. "We won't be disturbed there."

We sat down together at a big oval table. I ate a little soup, drank a glass of water, but didn't touch anything else. From the other end of the table Franz occasionally glanced at me.

"Some trouble?" he asked softly.

"Things aren't the same anymore."

He nodded. "I felt the tension in the quartet."

"I think I'd better tell you what happened recently. You'll be the first to know." I told him about Schnittke's quartet. With all the details. He listened attentively.

"How strange," he said. "Do you want me to ask them to play Schnittke next time in Leverkusen?"

"No. It would look as if I had complained to you."

"So what can I do?"

"Listen, Franz, I still don't know anything for sure. That's why I wanted to talk with you, to make it clearer to myself. Sort of like visiting a psychiatrist."

Franz smiled. "Go ahead, my patient."

"I think that if the Borodin Quartet is ever going to stop working, then the beginning of that end has already happened. Formally everything's just the same as it was before. I answer for the music, and when we start learning Schnittke's quartet after this trip, I'm sure no one will say a word. And that's the worst of all. We can't talk anymore. Not in the same language, anyway. This could affect our playing, and we'll lose our most important quality: our musical unity, 'the theater of a single actor,' as the critics call us now."

"I call you that, too," put in Franz.

"It seems to me that we need decisive measures, even the most crazy. What would you think if the whole quartet, for example, stayed in the West, in Germany?"

"Are you serious?"

"For now all that's just a supposition. What could we count on here?"

"If you want me to treat the question seriously, I could find out."

"Let's suppose that I inform the quartet of this idea, and . . ."

"Don't you think it's too dangerous for you?"

"There's always a certain risk, but frankly, it's not too big. We're in the same boat, after all."

"Okay, you'll tell them and they . . ."

"And they'll refuse indignantly."

"You see? What's the point?"

"Maybe only that we'll be able to talk about it openly, and it might bring the quartet back together again. If there are any interesting suggestions, we'll start thinking about them, especially now, when we're already in the West and Moscow's far away. To imagine, even for a minute, a free creative life without unceasing terror and all sorts of limitations might have a good effect on the whole quartet."

"Well, well, well."

"I just feel that if I don't do something, we could lose the quartet."

We were silent for a while.

"Maybe you'll try to eat now?" Franz said. "You still have to play tonight."

"I'll eat after the concert."

He got the itinerary of our tour out of his jacket pocket and studied it. At the second page his eyebrows went up. "What!?" he exclaimed. "I didn't realize it at first. You crazy people! You have a concert every night. You will kill yourselves!"

"It isn't us, Franz. It's Moscow."

"I know. But you could do the same twenty concerts, let us say, in thirty days. Five in a week and two days off."

"No way. We're allowed to be abroad only sixty days a year, and not a single hour more. And we have to play in Eastern Europe as well. We have lost the opportunity to make several trips already, just because we had no free days left. Once we played in Italy so successfully that they asked us to give one extra concert in Rome. That meant staying in Italy just one more day. We contacted our embassy, they asked Moscow, and we got a very nice cable: RETURN TO MOSCOW IMMEDIATELY. GREETINGS. GOSKONCERT.''

"Of course I know all these restrictions, but still I can't help wondering."

"Neither can I," I said.

"Well, my friend, I think I understand the situation . . . As soon as I know anything, I'll contact you."

That evening we played our first concert, the next day the second, and so on. Everything repeated itself, as if the same movie were playing over and over, non-stop: alarm clock, suitcase, taxi, station, train, taxi, hotel, pillow, tuxedo, taxi, stage, concert, party, hotel, pillow, alarm clock. Toward the middle of the trip we were exhausted. Our hands got tired; our instruments, too. My colleagues' faces looked paler and older; even their voices changed and sounded a little lower and hoarser. Shebalin swore, but this no longer amused anyone; Berlinsky smoked a lot and bit his nails; and the bags under Alexandrov's eyes were darker. I tried not to look at myself. It seemed to me that the person I saw in the mirror was not me. Or me, but from some other life.

When the last week came, it felt a little easier; we could see the end of the trip. Alexandrov methodically counted off each evening during the intermissions: "Seven more times to take it off, six more to put it on," and the next day: "Six more off, and five on . . ." When there were only three days and three concerts left, Franz phoned me. He came to our hotel, we drove to the concert together, and afterward, when he came backstage to shake everyone's hand, he winked at me and said that he had some interesting news.

Together we went to the Wiener Wald. Franz smiled crookedly. "Are you still alive?"

"No," I said.

"But you played beautifully, all of you."

"I wish they were aware of all that in Moscow."

"Poor fellow! But I have good news for you. Listen, I talked to some people from Bayer, Volkswagen, Siemmens, and some other big firms. They sponsor beautiful quartet series for their workers and are all interested. Very much so. They could offer you, right now, at least six times the whole Beethoven cycle: thirty-six concerts to start with. The fee is all yours and therefore much higher than what you get from Moscow. Second, Bayer could give you a loan of 100,000 Deutsche marks each, which would be gradually repaid from your fees. And third, four good apartments from the beginning, free of charge. They've just built several houses for their people. Is that what you wanted to hear?" he asked triumphantly.

"Franz, it sounds fantastic!"

"I suppose so." He smiled.

We were silent for a while.

"What are you going to do with all this?" he said at last.

"I'll talk to the others. I wonder what their reaction will be."

"Do you think they might agree?"

"No chance. But it will be good for our nerves to dream a little bit."

"Have a nice dream, my friend."

"But . . . who knows?"

"One never does, that's true."

The day of our last concert finally arrived. We were warming up onstage when our German manager, Walter Vedder, appeared, shouting, "Are you still practicing? Haven't you learned to play yet? That's enough. Let's go have a beer. My treat."

"Walter, you're crazy. We have a concert."

"That's not important. The most important thing is that all the tickets are sold by five minutes before the concert. The concert itself is of secondary importance. And what the critics say tomorrow is absolutely unimportant. The house is sold out, so don't worry."

"Walter, be an angel and sit down in the first row. We'll play something for you."

"Are you kidding? I hate music. I'm going out to have a drink. See you later."

A second before we began the final concert, Alexandrov managed to whisper, "Last time to take it off!" And two hours later everything was finished.

Walter took us first to the hotel, where we changed clothes with fabulous speed, and then to a restaurant. It was strange to be without our instruments, as if something anatomical was missing from our hands.

Walter told the waiter to bring us all a beer and leave us undisturbed for half an hour. Then he opened his attaché case and got out a stack of papers. We had to give an account to Goskoncert showing that all the conditions of the trip agreed on in Moscow had been met exactly: so many concerts played; Walter paid us such and such a sum, from which we gave the state so much and not a kopeck less, taking so much for ourselves and not a kopeck more. Moscow was not interested in the creative side of the trip, but we had to hand in the financial report the moment we got home. The money would be carefully counted several times, but I don't recall if we were ever asked how the tour had gone, whether it had been successful or whether we were tired.

I suggested that we add to the report that our intonation had been good and we didn't play too fast.

Walter laughed. "And, in fact, are you taking any reviews back to Goskoncert?"

"Why?" I asked him in return.

"Goskoncert is your impresario and should make sure that its artists play well."

"Walter, don't make us laugh! They send us abroad, we should be glad enough for that. If something fails to please someone, that's it! They'll send other people instead of us. No review will help."

"Yes, I know, Goskoncert has its own way of working."

"They're not to blame," said Alexandrov. "They don't go abroad, they have no personal contacts. How should they know?"

"That's true," said Walter. "They don't know the market at all. I'll tell you about one remarkable incident. Oistrakh was making a record with us, and while he was rehearsing, I was dealing with Goskoncert. Usually we pay an honorarium for the whole recording. We suggested

10,000 marks, of which Oistrakh was to get 500. But in your country they pay per minute of play. Okay, if you want it by the minute, you'll get it by the minute. We figured it out and estimated that it would be the same amount if we paid 300 marks per minute. When they informed Furtseva, the Minister of Culture, she decided to show everyone that she was a financial genius, and without blinking, she told us to add one more zero on the right. Not 300 marks a minute, but 3,000! That came to 100,000 for the whole recording. We'd never heard of anything like it. We tried to explain this to Furtseva, but she told us to pay before she changed her mind and added another zero. I ran to the hall. Oistrakh had just finished the rehearsal and was about to start recording. I told him and the orchestra what had happened. They laughed for a long time. The recording, of course, was canceled. Oistrakh and the world lost the record, and the musicians and Goskoncert lost the money!"

We were quiet for a while, and I told about how, a few years ago, we were to have recorded Tchaikovsky's second quartet for Deutsche Grammophon. The company invited us to West Berlin for three days, with full room and board. We worked on each note. Even a computer would have been satisfied with our intonation. But misfortune was lying in wait on the other side, from the East again. Too many people turned up wanting to "warm their hands" on our recording: the Ministry of Culture, Goskoncert, the Soviet firms Melodiya and International Books. And they all demanded, as a minimum, 50 percent of our honorarium. The telephone war went on for three days. We worked just in case, and in the evening drank beer, paid for by Deutsche Grammophon. Toward the end of the third day, just an hour before the recording, it was canceled.

"Charming," said Walter. "Simply charming. If we worked the way they work at your Goskoncert, we would have gone broke long ago."

"That's why they squeeze all the juice out of the performers."

"Performers shouldn't get rich. It makes them play badly!" joked Alexandrov.

"I don't agree," I joked back. "It's more pleasant to play for a good honorarium. The instruments sound better."

"You have bourgeois ideas."

"Work should be paid for. Why should we wear ourselves out, not eat, not sleep, and then give all our fees to do-nothings?"

"It's all for the sake of great art!"

"I'm speaking seriously now!" I shouted.

"Quiet, *Kinder*," interrupted Walter. "It's true enough that it's crazy to work that way, and all the more so without pay. But enough conversation. Time to get to business. Waiter!"

After dinner, Walter took us to a casino for the first time in our lives, bought 1,000 marks' worth of chips, and divided them among the five of us. We went through the hall and stopped at a roulette table. We sat down, placed our bets, and everyone lost. We tried once more and lost again. Walter said that it was all a matter of chance, so it was better not to think at all. "Put it on whatever catches your eye!"

We put more money down and lost. I decided to walk around the room a little and have a look. It was late and the gambling was at its peak. The faces of the people playing were unhealthily red, and they never tore their eyes from the spinning wheel. At each table two croupiers worked like machines, collecting and moving the chips. I chose a quieter table and stood for a while, watching. There were thirty-six numbered squares on the playing board. You could also bet on color or odd-even, but I didn't know all the fine points of the game. A place opened in front of me and I sat down. Randomly, I chose the squares from 20 to 30, putting each chip on a corner where four squares met. This way the chance of winning was about one in three. The ball stopped at 27. The croupier skillfully collected all the chips from the table except mine, and pushed the whole pile to me. The return wasn't huge, but it was still three times what I had bet. The second time I did the same thing from 10 to 20. The ball stopped at 18. The croupier moved another pile of chips toward me. People started to look at me and wait for me to put down my bet. I stayed out for one round, not putting anything down. Could it really be that there was absolutely nothing here but blind chance? I put double bets from 25 to the end; 30 came up. My pile of chips started to grow anew. I stopped noticing the people around me; only the squares and numbers mattered, along with my barely tangible presentiment of which way I should bet. I played something like twenty rounds and lost only once. And even that time, the winner was the square next to mine. As the croupier moved one more pile of chips toward me, I heard a familiar phrase in a very native language: "Fuck your mother!"

I looked around. Walter and my colleagues were standing behind me, looking in surprise at the mountain of chips in front of me. The croupier had just announced the last turn. I was about to bet, but suddenly I felt certain that wherever I bet, I was bound to lose.

I turned to Walter and offered him several chips. "Put them wherever you want. It's your game."

The croupier spun the roulette wheel for the last time. Everyone followed it with their eyes, as if their lives depended on it. Zero came up.

"But of course!" Walter laughed. "That is a sign from above. Let's go!"

I cashed in my chips and received about 5,000 marks. For a Soviet citizen that was a lot of money, and a heavy burden as well. I immediately felt an inequality in the quartet and subconsciously understood what I should do. I quickly shoved 1,000 marks in each person's pocket. My colleagues protested, but I told them that it was Walter's money and his present to us.

Early the next morning we were on the train to Aachen, a West German border city from where we would leave for Moscow that night. We were all four in the same compartment, and the peacefulness of the day before was still with us. I could see that the easy money we'd acquired yesterday was warming up my colleagues, and from time to time they slipped away to the bar, but they drank moderately because we still had a hard day of shopping ahead.

I knew this was my last chance to talk with the quartet. The closer we got to the Soviet border, the more the possibility of such a conversation would fade.

I started thinking of how to start the conversation. I knew I had to criticize the West and praise the Soviet Union. To reverse the order wouldn't have been hard at all, but it would have instantly created a defensive reaction in my colleagues. "Think, think," I ordered myself. "The whole future of the quartet depends on this. Say something you don't believe. Everyone around you does it, especially the Communists. The more truthfully you lie, the more you'll ripen into a Communist yourself . . ."

I laughed loudly at my joke. My colleagues turned to me. Berlinsky said, "What is it? Already going crazy?"

"Is it noticeable?" I asked.

"Oho!" he said, looking at me seriously and even sympathetically. Alexandrov shook his head. "We really shouldn't work so hard."

"No, no," I said hurriedly. "I'm still all right. I just thought that our homeland's there in the East, but here we are in the West, and if our homeland were in the West, and the West in the East, we would go east, as if to the West, and return west, as if to our homeland."

"Well, brother, it seems that you're really . . ." Berlinsky tapped his temple.

"You said that very well about the homeland," Shebalin interrupted him. "The main thing's clear."

"You see, the days of the West are numbered. It's falling apart and decaying, while at the same time in the East . . ." I started speaking more confidently.

"I agree," said Alexandrov, repeating the phrase that had already become a proverb in the Soviet Union. "The West's rotting, but still, what a smell!"

"The concerts here aren't bad," remarked Berlinsky carefully.

"Ours aren't bad either," I said, trying not to overdo it while still pushing the conversation onto the right track.

We were quiet and looked out the window. The train was going along the Rhine, and we saw vineyards on its far bank, and beyond them, mountains bathed in sunlight and covered with vineyards. From time to time we passed by Rhine cities, their streets full of people, neatly cared-for houses, and shops overflowing with flowers and fruit.

Without tearing himself away from the window, Alexandrov said, "Poor things! We gave it to them so bad in '45 that even now they can't recover."

We were silent again, but it was clear what we were all thinking.

"Yes," added Alexandrov, "we'll still need a long time. Twenty years have passed since the war, and we're still sitting in shit."

"Not twenty, twenty-three," Berlinsky corrected him.

"And many more will go by with the same success," put in Shebalin.

I realized that now was my chance. "But what if . . ." I began uncertainly.

Three heads turned toward me.

"Well, no . . ."

"Say it, since you started."

"Purely theoretically . . ."

"Go on," said Berlinsky impatiently.

"You see, I had a serious talk with Franz."

"Theoretical, I hope?" laughed Alexandrov.

"Oh yes, absolutely."

"Don't interrupt," said Berlinsky.

"It's about our quartet. But only as an abstract possibility, in general . . ."

"Don't beat around the bush!"

"Briefly, we've been offered six times through the Beethoven cycle to start with, four free apartments, and 100,000 marks each, which we'd gradually repay from our fees."

"Seriously?"

"It's only an idea. Simply to know that we have this option."

"We could bring it up carefully in Moscow," suggested Berlinsky. "Maybe they'd let us try it for a year or two."

"You're crazy! They'd close the borders to us forever!"

"So what can we do?"

"The best possibility," said Alexandrov, "is that some sort of commotion would start in Europe, we'd get stuck here, and we wouldn't be guilty."

"There's another way," I said. "To try the Jewish route. The Jews have started leaving quietly."

"Easy for you to say," said Shebalin.

"You mean it's easy to be a Jew?"

"It seems that it's the first time in the whole history of Judaism that it's a plus to be a Jew." Shebalin laughed.

"You don't absolutely have to be a Jew," Berlinsky answered. "Half."

"That's enough. She'll get you out."

"A Jewish wife is not a luxury but a means of transportation."

"Let's add up the chances," I suggested. "Just for fun. I'll have no problem qualifying."

"Me neither," echoed Berlinsky, looking out the window.

"But my wife is Russian, and there's not one Jew in any generation of my family," said Alexandrov seriously, then added, laughing, "No chance!"

"We could think something up," said Berlinsky.

"What?"

"Something. Manufacture some uncle or aunt in Israel who dreams of seeing his dear nephew and begs the Soviet authorities not to ruin the happiness of a family."

"It wouldn't be easy to produce that sort of uncle."

"During the war anything could have happened."

"But seriously," said Shebalin loudly, "I wouldn't object. Germany suits me. I know the language, and the beer's excellent here."

"We'd play concerts, and travel around the world," picked up Berlinsky. "And what would the difference be? We'd be a Russian quartet, just as before."

"And our motherland?" I asked the dangerous question and waited curiously for the answer.

"Don't start using fancy words," said Alexandrov.

I thought that now might be a good time to say that although I generally loved my motherland, it didn't love me. But it was a bitter truth and it could have easily destroyed the atmosphere of unusual sincerity we had now. I could see that the conversation had touched everyone on a sore spot, yet no one wanted to end it.

"Our business is to play!" declared Berlinsky. "For us that's the main thing."

He had said this many times before, but now it sounded entirely different. Now the word "play" meant "live"—and "live," to be free.

"I don't care where I live," said Shebalin. "Just so it's not as insane as this trip."

"That's the point. We could plan our own lives and play only as much as we wanted. Be our own bosses."

"And not have to give anyone what we earned with our sweat and blood."

"Of course, we'd be cursed back at home."

"They'd ban our records."

"Records! If we got away without a car accident, we'd have to be thankful. It's dangerous to joke with the motherland."

"Have you heard the latest joke?" I said. "Two worms crawl out of the ground, father and son, and the little one asks, 'Papa, what's that long and green thing there?'

" 'That, son, is a blade of grass.'

" 'Pretty! And that big yellow-and-green thing?'

" 'That's a tree.'

" 'How pretty! And there, all around, the blue?'

" 'The sky.'

" 'It's so pretty! And that bright red one?'

" 'The sun.'

" 'Oh, what beauty! And why, Papa, if everything around is so beautiful, do we live down there in the dark and muck?'

" 'Because, son, that's our motherland. Let's go home!' "

No one laughed. I realized I had overdone it and escaped to the washroom. When I returned to our compartment, my colleagues were looking out the window pensively.

The Aachen-Moscow train left at night. We gave our passports to the conductors, slipping ten marks in each one "for business"; drank a bottle of vodka with them, "forgetting" two other bottles, unopened, in their compartment; and collapsed into sleep. In Warsaw several Soviets and Poles got on our train, but the conductors kept their word and didn't let anyone into our compartments.

Not long before the Soviet border, Berlinsky quietly tapped on my door. "Are you asleep?" he asked from the corridor.

I turned on the light and opened the door. "Not now, come in."

"The border's soon," he said thoughtfully.

"When you're asleep, time goes fast."

"Blessed is he who sleeps."

My compartment began to smell of cologne. I took a look at Berlinsky. He was sober, cleanly shaven, and painstakingly dressed in his new clothes.

"You want to eat?" I suggested. "I have a few morsels."

"No, thank you. I'll go to the restaurant in Brest."

We were silent. Something was coming, and I gave him time.

"What are we doing in Moscow?" he asked.

"I hope we'll be able to rest for a couple of days."

"It's time to start Schnittke," he said cautiously, and quickly added, "It must be difficult."

I felt uncomfortable, both for him and for myself, and I happily seized on the technical side of the matter. "It's hard. But I think only at first. Then it'll be easier. Easier than Mozart or Beethoven."

"I'm waiting with interest. We have to do it well."

All this sounded as if he was somehow offering me a bribe, to cheer me up and confirm once again that there would be no problem with Schnittke. I waited.

"And what else do we have that's new, besides Schnittke?"

"Stenhammar in Stockholm. And pretty soon."

"And in the Soviet Union?"

"As always, a lot is announced, and some for the first time."

"We'll run out of time again."

"At home that's not important, we can repeat what we've already played and use the time for Stenhammar and Schnittke."

"Listen. I keep thinking about Franz. Our wives probably don't need to know."

"Why not?"

"No need to upset them. It's hard for them as it is."

"Let them dream a little."

"It's dangerous, too. Each extra person who knows is dangerous."

"Even our wives?"

"Even them. Each one has a bosom friend, each friend also has one, and so on. Best of all to decide that the conversation with Franz didn't happen at all."

Oh, so that's what it is, I thought. A simple exchange of favors. I can't be ungrateful. And I said now, for him, "What conversation, what Franz are you talking about? I seem to have forgotten."

He smiled and looked at me with gratitude. "So we've agreed?"

"Sure," I said. "We'll have to tell our colleagues."

"I'll tell them," he said hurriedly. "Better here, before we cross the border."

He went to the door, then stopped and pulled a folded sheet of paper out of his jacket pocket. "Take this," he said. "I turned out to have an extra paper of authorization from the Ministry of Culture. May be handy at the border."

"Thank you," I said.

"And thank *you*," he answered, and left.

I tried to fall asleep again.

At the border everything repeated itself as always: the customs declaration, the border guards, the passports. A customs man came into my compartment, slammed the door behind him, and sat down on the corner of my bunk.

He made himself comfortable for a long visit. That meant there would be a check. But I had nothing dangerous with me this time, besides a Bible. I could stay calm.

"Where are you traveling from?" he asked, even though it was obvious that he already knew me better than I knew myself.

"From West Germany."

He looked at my declaration. "Any foreign currency?"

"A little."

"How much?"

"A hundred and forty-seven marks," I declared.

"Let's see," he said. He slowly counted the money, grudgingly gave it back to me, and started writing out a receipt for it.

I handed him the Ministry of Culture paper, where it said that the Borodin State Quartet, People's Artists and laureates of the State Prize, was on a tour in the Federal Republic of Germany. He read it quickly and gave it back to me carelessly.

"That's good," he said dully, and looked around. "What's this? A violin?"

"A violin."

"Open it."

I opened it.

"Take out the instrument."

I took it out. He started tapping the case and fingering its inside lining. Then, without having glanced at the violin, he turned to the suitcases. He counted them with his eyes and I felt guilty. "Any books?"

"Some," I said simply.

He livened up. "Show me."

I got out the Russian Bible and a few Agatha Christie books. He grabbed the Bible at once.

"What's this?"

"Fairy tales," I said indifferently.

He looked at me attentively. "I'll take this," he said, and quickly shoved the Bible into his pocket.

I wanted very much to tell him that everything written in that book had happened a long time ago, long before the October Revolution, and had no relation to the Soviet Union, but it was better not to irritate him. Even without that, what I had brought back to the Soviet Union considerably exceeded the "norm." He could, if he wanted, take everything away from me. He looked at the other books.

"Take this to room 6. Tell them I sent you. Any magazines with pictures?"

"No," I answered honestly.

He seemed to believe me. Probably because I had given him the Bible right away. "Any sort of songs?"

"No."

"Foreign newspapers?"

"None," I said.

"What do you mean, none? What's that on the floor?"

"Oh, that. I used it to wrap my slippers."

He picked up the newspaper, which was torn in several places, quickly looked it over, and hid it in his pocket, too. "What's in that suitcase?"

"Suit, coat, a dress for my wife."

That was true. The only falsehood was that I should have said them all in the plural. They were the results of our last day abroad, which we, as always, had spent frantically running through shops. This last day abroad was probably the most humiliating punishment that life could come up with for a Soviet artist. How many times had I promised myself that next time . . . Let the money be lost, but the next trip abroad . . .

The customs official brought me back to reality. "And what's in that suitcase?" I didn't answer right away, and he immediately ordered, "Open it!"

"This is bed linen," I stumbled, "towels, yarn . . ."

"Open it," he repeated.

Quickly he reached to the bottom of the suitcase with both hands. "Well, all right," he said. "The ministry paper is clear. As is the fact that you travel abroad alone. You may go to the station."

He went out and closed the door.

What had he said? That the KGB trusts us? Or was he just apologizing for not ransacking all my suitcases?

At the station I found room 6 and knocked on the door. A man in a military uniform opened it.

"I was sent here," I said.

"Books?"

I nodded.

"What language?"

"English."

"Galya," he called to someone.

From the other room appeared a girl about eighteen years old. She leafed through my mysteries.

"All right," she told the officer.

He gave the books back to me. "Everything's in order. You may go."

Oistrakh

1968–1970–1974

"Oistrakh didn't sign!" people told each other with mixed feelings of surprise and exultation. All the leading Soviet Jewish figures of culture and art, whose names everyone knew, had been told to sign a letter replying to the Israeli government's call for all Jews to unite in their historic homeland, Israel. The response from the Soviet Union stated that the U.S.S.R. was the only country in the world whose constitution condemned anti-Semitism as a crime; that the Jews, along with the other free peoples of the country, were devoted to their homeland and were building a society founded on equality and brotherhood between nations; and that all the Jews of the U.S.S.R. angrily condemned this move of the Israeli government as interference in the internal affairs of the Soviet Union. On television they showed a meeting of well-known Jewish artists interrupting each other in their haste to assure the listeners that they were happy in the Soviet Union and would not go anywhere, especially not to Israel. It was absolutely impossible for a Party member not to sign such a statement, but Oistrakh did not.

The campaign began and ended; people made noise about it and then calmed down. One morning, however, a truck pulled up to the house at 15 Chkalov Street. Two men in work clothes jumped out of the back and went inside. They soon reappeared, carrying suitcases and bundles. They threw all this into the truck and disappeared again through the entrance. Onlookers began to gather around the truck. The concierge came outside and went up to the driver.

"What, is someone moving out?"

"Some Oistrakh . . ."

"To another apartment or something?"

"To his summer place, outside the city. For the summer."

"Ah, I understand. For some reason they didn't mention it to me."

"And where is he now?"

"On a trip."

"When does he come back?"

"Tomorrow or so."

"Yes, that's what they told us."

The other two appeared again in the doorway, bending under the weight of a huge trunk. Someone from the crowd went over to help, and then someone else. They loaded the trunk into the truck and watched as it drove out of the courtyard. The crowd dispersed.

The next morning a taxi pulled up to the same entrance. Oistrakh stepped out, violin in hand, followed by his wife, Tamara. The concierge ran out of the entry to meet them. "Welcome back! Well, how's your health?"

"Everything's fine, my dear, thank you."

"Yesterday everything went as you ordered. They came in a truck and took your things to the summer house."

"This year I wasn't planning to go anywhere for the summer," said Oistrakh, perplexed. "Tamarochka, do you know anything about it?"

"No, Dodik, I have no idea."

"And what did they take?"

"All sorts of things: suitcases, a big trunk so heavy that the neighbors had to help them load it . . ."

That evening the Voice of America broadcast the news of the burglary. Nothing was mentioned in the Soviet newspapers. Oistrakh's archive, the whole creative life of the artist captured in programs, posters, photographs, and letters, had been stolen. All his awards had been taken, the Soviet as well as the foreign ones. Records, tapes, books about art. The symbolic key to Jerusalem, Einstein's letter, the film *City Lights* (a present from Charlie Chaplin)—all stolen. Everything that was of great value to Oistrakh but which could have no meaning for the robbers had been taken. The robbery seemed senseless, and thus even more painful. The news flew across the country.

Oistrakh behaved stoically. He didn't cancel a single concert, and his appearance onstage was met with redoubled delight. In the conservatory's Maly Hall he repeated the Chausson concerto, the one he had played with us years before, right after the quartet competition. We met at his home to rehearse. Everything was just the same; only the walls, which before had been covered with photographs, were bare. He played marvelously. It seemed that everything he wished to say but couldn't flowed out from under his bow.

When the rehearsal was over, Alexandrov looked at his watch and said that it was time for him to go. Berlinsky and Shebalin hurriedly got their things together. With their instruments in their hands, they looked back at me. I was slowly wiping off my violin. They said goodbye to Oistrakh and left.

"Why don't we drink some tea?" suggested Oistrakh. "I'll tell Tamara."

The three of us sat down at a table. Tamara Ivanovna, Oistrakh's wife, poured tea for all of us. People said that when the young couple first came to Moscow, she would bake pirozhki at night and sell them at the market in the morning, so that Oistrakh, then still unknown, could practice the violin.

He worked by himself, led by his faultless musical taste and a remarkable natural gift for the violin, but people always added that it was Tamara who had made him a violinist. She was unbelievably devoted to him. He even made jokes about it, occasionally pretending to cough or sneeze, and she would turn pale from fright and ask anxiously how he was feeling.

But now he was in no mood to joke. The strange burglary, which people didn't even mention in his presence, the feeling of unexpected isolation, and the necessity of keeping silent had affected him.

I excused myself for not having left with the others.

"Why, don't apologize!" Oistrakh said hurriedly. "I'm glad that you stayed. It seems we haven't seen each other since Stalin's funeral."

"I wanted to call you, but I couldn't bring myself to talk about this over the phone."

"What do you mean, 'about this'?"

"About this event."

"What event?"

"The robbery."

Oistrakh glanced at Tamara and then at the telephone. His wife got up and unplugged the telephone cord.

"So what were you saying?"

"This burglary, I think it wasn't a burglary."

"Wasn't it?"

"More likely it was a punishment."

"Punishment? For what?"

"For your honesty," I said, as simply as I could.

"I don't understand," said Oistrakh.

"Of course, I can't be absolutely sure, but you refused to sign that letter."

"I didn't refuse. I told them that the letter was signed by only Jewish musicians, and it looked like some sort of Jewish mafia. I'd sign it if I saw the signatures of Shostakovich, Khrennikov, Khachaturian: musicians without regard to nationality. I feel that I am right."

"And how do they feel?"

"I don't know, they didn't come to me again."

"Didn't they?"

"You mean . . ."

"They came when you weren't at home. They stole your archive and letters, in order to check up on you."

"They need to check me? Tamara here can testify: I work like a horse, without vacations or days off. Trips, concerts, students . . . Sometimes I'm forced to practice at night."

"His heart has even started hurting him," put in Tamara. "I tell him all the time that he works too hard."

"We know how you work," I said. "And we know what the name

Oistrakh means for Russian culture and to all of us. But the people who robbed you . . . To those people there's nothing sacred, they have no soul, they're blind police, who . . ." I caught my breath. "Excuse me, I can't talk about this calmly."

"And you think . . ."

"I don't think, I know that they took the idea from Hitler: 'Cultural figures should be threatened from time to time.' They chose you so that no one else would dare to defy them."

"But why me?"

"Because you are Oistrakh. In that way they hit everyone in the mug at once. I think it's just their usual show, and I wouldn't be surprised if they gave everything back to you."

Oistrakh sighed and held his left hand against his heart. Tamara looked at him in fright, and he smiled at her sadly. We finished our tea without speaking. I thanked them and stood up. Oistrakh saw me to the door.

"Thank you, my dear friend!" He held out both hands, but changed his mind and hugged me. We kissed each other goodbye.

He called me two weeks later. "They returned everything," he said.

I gasped. "Everything?"

"Absolutely. Nothing is missing. You are the first I'm telling this to."

"Thank you so much! And . . . congratulations!"

September 30, 1968, had been Oistrakh's sixtieth birthday. Moscow had been surprised and frightened that this occasion had gone officially unnoticed. Not only had the government award, customary on such occasions, not been forthcoming, but it had seemed as if the press, radio, and television of the country were intentionally silenced by some special order from above.

Even so, Oistrakh had received a present. And what a present!

Dmitri Shostakovich had written a sonata for violin and piano, Opus 134, and dedicated it to Oistrakh's sixtieth birthday. In this music, however, there was not one joyful note, not a single cheerful moment. Just deep, unalleviated gloom from beginning to end. In his sonata

Shostakovich expressed deep sympathy for an unforgivably insulted, honest artist, and his support for that lonely courage.

On January 9, 1969, after Oistrakh and Richter first performed the sonata, I stood in line for a long time backstage at the conservatory's Bolshoi Hall to say one word to Oistrakh: "Thanks." Nothing more could be said. Oistrakh understood this better than I. Lowering his voice so that only I could hear him, he said, "I hope very much that you'll play this sonata. Especially after all Shostakovich's quartets."

Oistrakh phoned me again on January 1, 1970. I recognized his voice at once.

"Happy new year, David Fedorovich!"

"Thank you. And happy new year to you. You see, I just sat down by the phone to wish my friends a good new year, but counted only five people I wished to call . . ."

"Thank you very much for calling me. How are you?"

"Not too bad, only my heart sometimes . . ."

"Take some good advice and do breathing exercises."

"Yes, I've heard that you're a great admirer of the yogis."

"You only need to breathe correctly. I could visit you and show you how."

"Thank you, my friend, but today Tamara and I are leaving on a long trip. I'll come back and we'll certainly see each other."

"And play some chess?"

"And play some chess."

"Have a good trip. I wish you good health in the new year."

"Thank you, my dear."

We did indeed meet again, but under unfortunate circumstances.

We were going abroad once more, this time to England. In London all the Soviet performers were booked into the Prince of Wales Hotel. Maybe the hotel gave the manager a discount, or the Soviet embassy had its own people among the staff there. When we flew into Heathrow Airport, the first news we heard was about Oistrakh: serious heart trouble had caused him to cancel all his concerts. He was lying in bed and Tamara wouldn't leave him for a moment. There was a letter for us at the hotel. Berlinsky read it aloud: "Dear friends, I've had a bit of bad luck. Come visit me, I'd appreciate it very much. Yours, D. Oistrakh."

"Let me look . . ." I said, taking the letter. "I don't think it's his writing."

"Really? It's that bad?"

We had a daytime concert in St. James's Church, practically right after the plane landed, and after that, without stopping at our rooms, we went directly upstairs to see Oistrakh.

He was lying in bed. Tamara sat next to him in a chair. The bedside table was covered with bottles of medicine. Oistrakh smiled weakly at us.

"You got my letter? Tamara wrote it at my dictation. They won't let me write yet. Sit down, please. Tamarochka, make them sit down. You just got off the plane and already played a concert? Well, how was it?"

"My ears got blocked up when we landed," I said. "I couldn't hear myself play."

"And I," Alexandrov picked up, "played like a blindman."

"Why is that?"

"I don't see any money in this trip."

Oistrakh laughed quietly and put his hand on his heart. "Under what conditions are you here?"

"Three pounds a day," said Shebalin. "Only beer; it's not even enough for a glass of something better."

Oistrakh laughed again, this time a little more bravely, and looked at Berlinsky. "And you?"

"I forgot my tuxedo pants, but fortunately it was a daytime concert and we played in these suits."

"Tamara always packs for me, so I never forget anything. Right, Tamarochka?"

"Dodik, you've gotten cheerful right away," said Tamara sadly.

"Don't look at me so sorrowfully. Everything will be fine."

Tamara turned away to hide her tears.

"She's upset," said Oistrakh. "Today I was supposed to play the Brahms concerto in Festival Hall, and . . . Menuhin's replacing me. They'll show it on television. Tamarochka, you told them to bring in the TV set?"

She nodded without speaking.

"David Fedorovich," I said, "we'd like to play a little for you, if you're not too tired."

"Oh, I'd be very glad. But only if you're not too tired yourselves."

We got our instruments, set up our music stands, and sat down.

In an artificial voice, as if addressing an audience from a stage, I said, "We shall play the third quartet of Shostakovich in F-major, Opus 73, in five movements, the fourth and fifth to be performed without interruption. The quartet was written in 1944."

Oistrakh looked at us, smiling. We started to play . . .

The Third is Shostakovich's best quartet, written in his wartime period. A lot of sorrow had accumulated for the Russian intelligentsia during these years of Soviet rule, from the 1917 Revolution until the beginning of the war in 1941. And it was only during the war that it found its emotional outlet. This was particularly true in music. Like Shostakovich's Seventh Symphony, this quartet was officially touted as anti-Fascist. But it was in essence anti-Soviet, a disturbing musical tale about the destruction of Russian culture.

The first movement of the quartet is a perfect sonata allegro, the last bright day before an irremediable misfortune.

The second: gathering clouds and the approach of disaster.

The third: the wild triumph of evil.

The fourth: a funeral march, a prayer for those who have perished.

The fifth: a sorrowful, moving story about Shostakovich himself and his pain and anxiety about the future of humanity.

We never played any concert as we did that evening for that one sick man. In the fourth movement Berlinsky, who was seated facing Oistrakh, started making signs to me. I glanced at Oistrakh. He was lying with his eyes closed, tears running down his cheeks. Tamara brought him some medicine, but he gently pushed her hand aside. In the finale, where the last muted chord is like an unearthly choir against whose background the first violin rises higher and higher and disappears, we made a long *diminuendo*, and the silence that followed was just like a continuation of the music. We sat without moving.

"Thank you so much," said Oistrakh very softly. "It's the music of a genius and you play it marvelously."

He closed his eyes again. "Do you think I'll ever be able to play the violin again?" His voice trembled slightly.

"Don't be silly," said Tamara quickly, and started crying again. "Better take your medicine."

"Really, that's silly," we all began at once. "You were just working too hard and your heart told you that it needs a rest. Don't worry, everything will be fine."

He looked at me. "You never did teach me yoga breathing. Isn't it too late now?"

"It's never too late. I could show you right now."

"I'll ask the doctor first," said Tamara. "How long will you be here?"

"Tomorrow we start touring around England, but we'll be in London again."

"I'll talk to the doctor right now." She asked the telephone operator to connect her with a Dr. Gross. It was obvious that she did this often and that the doctor expected her calls. She asked right away what he thought of yoga breathing, and listened silently. Then she said, "I'd better give you Mr. Dubinsky."

She held the receiver out to me.

"Dr. Gross?" I said.

"Yes, Mr. Dubinsky, hello! I've just explained this to Tamara, but I'm afraid I couldn't tell her everything. She's in a state of panic. Please don't tell her, but I feel I would rather separate them for a while. Do stay with David as much as you can, you and your friends. Do you understand? The less those two are left alone, the better it is for David."

"I understand."

"Now, about the breathing. You see, Oistrakh is a special case and we have to be very, very careful. I would personally recommend the breathing exercises, but only a bit later, once the whole picture is clear."

"I understand, Dr. Gross."

"Are you staying in the same hotel?"

"Oh yes, always. We'll be touring in the country but coming back to London a couple of times."

"Very well. Goodbye, Mr. Dubinsky."

"Goodbye, Dr. Gross."

"Well?" asked Tamara. "Are things very bad?"

Oistrakh looked at me without blinking, and there was pain in his eyes. As carelessly and cheerfully as I could, I said, "Dr. Gross asked me to demonstrate the breathing exercises in his presence, once we get back to London."

"Is that true?" asked Oistrakh.

"Yes," I lied. "He said that yoga breathing can work miracles."

"You know, Tamarochka, I feel a little better. Maybe I'll get up and sit in the chair."

"I'm afraid, Dodik," said Tamara.

"But why not?" I asked. "Slowly, *molto adagio* and *legatissimo*. Let's try all together."

We carefully sat him up in bed and all four of us helped him to his feet.

"And now, without the least effort, left foot forward," I commanded.

He barely moved his legs. We brought him to the table and sat him in the armchair.

"Tamarochka, look, I'm walking!" he said happily. "And it doesn't hurt. The boys did everything. I told you that I'd feel better when they got here."

I felt that if I waited one more minute, I might start crying in front of Oistrakh. I quickly went to the bathroom on the excuse that I had something in my eye.

I began crying the moment I closed the door behind me. I ran the water to drown out the noise of my sobs and waited for it all to pass. When I felt better, I washed my face first with cold, then with hot water, but my eyes were still red. In the main room, I heard the telephone ring, then there was a knock at the door and a man's voice.

"Where would you like me to put this, sir?"

I came out of the bathroom. They had brought a large television set into the room. Everyone watched as they turned the screen toward

Oistrakh and plugged it in. A picture of an orchestra appeared on the screen. The musicians were tuning their instruments. Then everything fell silent and after a moment the hall burst into applause. Menuhin appeared onstage, violin in his hands, followed by the conductor, Rozhdestvensky. Menuhin checked his tuning and nodded to Rozhdestvensky. The orchestra began the introduction to Brahms's concerto . . .

I glanced at Oistrakh. He was lying in the armchair, his eyes half closed, his breathing quick and shallow. The fingers of his left hand moved involuntarily to the music. Tamara was also watching him, holding a little medicine bottle in her hand. As Menuhin began to play, Oistrakh opened his eyes, and his face was deathly pale.

"I think I'll lie down," he said.

We four picked him up and carefully carried him to the bed. Tamara turned off the television. Oistrakh breathed heavily.

"Should I call Dr. Gross?" I whispered to Tamara.

Oistrakh overheard and opened his eyes. "No, no, I'm all right . . . It's just too early for me to play Brahms."

He needed rest now; we promised to come back later and quietly left the room.

In October 1974, in Amsterdam, Oistrakh announced a Brahms cycle of four concerts: four symphonies and four instrumental concertos. He was staying in the Park Hotel, there was sunny weather, his heart was not bothering him, and he entered entirely into the music. The members of the orchestra adored him and played only for him. The Amsterdam Concertgebouw Hall was packed with an ecstatic audience, and it was a fantastic success; even the most cynical critic didn't permit himself a single harsh word in the newspapers. After the third evening, Oistrakh allowed himself a day of rest. He rode on the river steamboat along the canals of Amsterdam, went into the Rembrandt Museum, ate a good dinner ("Not too little, not too much," as he would say), napped a bit after dinner, and spent the evening visiting Khukride, the orchestra director. Tamara was with him all the time. They returned to the hotel at eleven and Oistrakh, as always, took a warm bath and soon went quietly to sleep. Tamara, who slept lightly, woke up at four to Oistrakh's uneven breathing. She leaped to his bedside.

"Dodik, what is it?"

"Sharp pain in my stomach."

"I'll call the doctor."

She flew to the telephone, shouting to the operator: "A doctor! Right away!" and returned to the bed. Oistrakh was dead. Tamara gave an inhuman cry of pain and horror and froze. The doctor appeared five minutes later, but could only be a witness to what could not be remedied. Tamara did not move. The doctor forced her to sit down in an armchair. The porter came in, the doctor quietly told him something and picked up the telephone . . .

Half an hour later, Khukride came, walked up to Oistrakh's bed, then to Tamara. She looked into the space in front of her without seeing anything.

At six they phoned the Soviet embassy. The attendant promised to inform the ambassador. At eight they phoned again. The attendant answered that the ambassador was ill, as was the cultural attaché. The first secretary had to leave urgently for someplace, the second still hadn't returned from somewhere, and the third, something else . . . He mentioned that there happened to be an Aeroflot flight to Moscow that day and hung up the phone.

The Soviet plane left at noon. Before boarding, a bus drove along the tarmac right up to the plane. A closed coffin was carried up the stairs, and Khukride escorted Tamara onto the plane, holding her firmly by the shoulders. A section was closed off, and when boarding was announced, all the passengers were directed to take any remaining seats. A smiling stewardess asked everyone to fasten their seat belts, refrain from smoking, and have a pleasant flight. In the Moscow airport the coffin was sent from the airplane straight to the hospital. An autopsy was performed and it was discovered that the cause of death had been a heart attack—Oistrakh's fifth.

In Moscow everything was known by early morning—both that Oistrakh had died and that he was not permitted to be buried in Novodevichy, the best cemetery in Moscow. No one in the government would take responsibility for this "important state decision." The matter dragged on. Moscow prepared to bid Oistrakh farewell, but no one knew where he would be buried. Only on the day of the funeral was it learned that permission had been given to bury him in Novodevichy. It was said that Brezhnev himself had decided.

After Oistrakh's funeral, Tamara went to the cemetery every morning, and in the afternoons to the railroad station to meet him as she had done before. A week after the burial I visited Oistrakh's grave. Tamara was planting flowers. Spotting me, she shouted for me not to come any nearer and, waving her stick, threw herself at me.

On October 24, 1976, just two years after his death, a monument was erected on Oistrakh's grave. Many people gathered for the ceremony. Tamara was calm. That evening, at home alone, she put on the dress Oistrakh liked best, sat in a chair, and, one by one, swallowed a bottle of sleeping pills.

Rostropovich
1974

"Y<small>OU PLAY WELL</small>, old men," said Rostropovich. "Not long ago I was listening to our recording of Tchaikovsky's sextet. It's wonderful! The tempi are just perfect."

We were having dinner together in a restaurant—he, Berlinsky, and I. Rostropovich had recently gone noticeably gray, and bald spots had appeared near his forehead, but he had let the rest of his hair grow long.

"There's something not quite right with your hair," Berlinsky told him.

"Yes, old man, you're absolutely correct! Here"—he slapped his forehead—"I'm catching up with Lenin, and in back with Marx."

Our dinner was just a few months before Rostropovich left the Soviet Union. Solzhenitsyn had already been sent out of the country, and Rostropovich, because he had given him shelter, had been dismissed from the Bolshoi Theater. He now gave very few concerts, and he had to get permission from the authorities even for these.

At dinner he tried not to seem upset, but we could tell how much it had cost him. He had just been forbidden to complete his recording of Puccini's opera *Tosca*, and he was very unhappy about it.

"You know me, I don't like to brag, but believe me, it could have been the recording of the century! I even invited people into the hall to inspire the singers. The orchestra played as if it were their last concert on earth! And all of a sudden the door bangs open, some thugs come in, clap their hands, and stop the recording. Can you imagine? Then they run into the sound studio and demagnetize all the tape. Well, what do you say to that? They're just bandits! But the eighteen minutes that I managed to record—it was the best work I've ever done."

He drank his vodka and went on: "Yesterday I had a day off and I flew to Moscow specially to see Prokofiev's *War and Peace* at the Bolshoi. It's my performance to the last note, to the last rest. Here's the ticket. I bought it myself for two-fifty. When I stopped backstage, the musicians couldn't look at me . . . It's hard, brothers! Let's have one more! A little cognac?"

"But aren't you performing *Don Quixote* tonight?"

"One more and that's all. What time is it now? Five . . . We'll make it just in time for the concert. Yes, all this isn't easy. Not long ago a couple of guys came to me from the Bolshoi. They wanted me to sign a letter against Solzhenitsyn, like everyone else. Promised that they'd roll out the red carpet for me to come back to the Bolshoi Theater! Just sign. I sent my wife to them. She didn't waste any words. Told them, 'We have two daughters and we want them to respect their father.' How about that? What a girl! My wife's wonderful. Sometimes, when things get too hot, she says she'll give such an interview that events in Czechoslovakia will pale in comparison. At times like that I lock myself in the bathroom in fear!"

The cognac came. Rostropovich poured for everyone.

"You know, guys, people have started bringing me letters. They bring them to concerts, at hotels . . . Ask me to help with a pension, an apartment, a job. They ask why it's hard to get food. Well, just like a government official! But I should tell you about Richter. You know that we were friends and played together. Well, he's been begged to talk with me, to influence me, so to speak. Richter, as always, started making them look stupid: 'I don't know . . . what if Rostropovich won't listen to me? If Solzhenitsyn's the problem, well, fine, let him live at my place.' "

We laughed loudly.

"He said that?"

"Cross my heart! When Solzh was living in my garage, what things he was writing! The world'll go crazy when it finds out! He worked for days on end! And during breaks he made babies. And the surprising thing is—the more there are, the more they look like him. This last one, the third, is his spitting image. Just glue a beard on him and they could put him in jail at once."

We laughed again, so much that people started looking at us.

"Quiet. Quiet, boys! Well"—he glanced at his watch—"now for some coffee and then we'll go. I'll just tell you one more story. Recently I was allowed to make a trip along the Volga with a second-rate orchestra. We played Tchaikovsky's Sixth Symphony, and Galya sang Tatiana. And you know what the bastards wrote in the papers? They didn't even mention our names. It went like this: 'The conductor gave an interesting reading of the great Russian composer's score.' And about Galya: 'Scenes from *Eugene Onegin* were also performed at the concert.' . . . I saw for myself how on the day of the concert in Ulyanovsk they pasted other posters on top of mine. But I have a long name, and either *Ros* would stick out on one side, or *vich* on the other. But the most striking: We're on a steamboat going down the Volga with the whole orchestra. At night we get to Saratov and they won't let us dock! Understand? They change the schedule and send us right along! Won't let us into the city, and we have a concert there! Then the brass section comes out on the upper deck of the boat and plays Chopin's Funeral March. Can you imagine? Nighttime, the city all lit up, and the funeral march thundering in the silence. Galya and I stood on the deck, crying like babies. Oh, brothers! . . ."

Shostakovich
1975

THAT SHOSTAKOVICH was constantly thinking about death we already felt from his late quartets, the first of which, No. 12, appeared in 1968. The following year, right before the first performance of his Fourteenth Symphony, he suddenly began to speak to the audience: "I was advised to make the finale of this symphony comforting, to say that death was only the beginning. But it is not a beginning, it is the real end; there will be nothing afterward, nothing."

That Shostakovich himself was dying we could read on his face. And the inevitable happened on August 9, 1975.

In the Moscow Conservatory's Bolshoi Hall people stand in the Guard of Honor. The great Shostakovich's face—his sharp nose, the curved line of his compressed thin lips, the eyelids unnaturally glued together—is very close. The sight makes an indelible impression on people. The memory imprints it forever. Death . . . it is the end of life. Life has gone, death remains. How wise are the nations which at funerals don't open the coffin's lid! They want to remember their people alive.

When was it that our paths crossed for the first time? Oh yes . . . back in 1948, when that ill-fated ideological storm swept over Soviet music and Shostakovich, perhaps the greatest composer of the twentieth century, was banished from the Soviet musical scene. Expecting arrest, he locked himself in his home and wrote the fourth string quartet, the score of which, wrapped in a copy of *Pravda*, was given to us secretly by his wife.

We worked on it at night with muted instruments. It was not just music: something else was there, a truthful account of our existence, narrated to us by musical sounds instead of words.

The quartet, of course, could not be performed.

The following year, however, when the Soviet government was busy preparing its next blow, and music seemed to be less controlled, we wrote a letter to the Ministry of Culture, asking permission to perform the quartet in public. Strangely enough, we received an answer: They wanted to audition it first. The date was set, and when that day arrived, we crossed the mysterious threshold of the ministry with a mixed feeling of fear and hope.

We put our hearts and souls into that performance. We emphasized everything that socialist realism requires to be concealed. We spoke the truth!

When we had finished, silence fell. Was it more eloquent than any praise? Or was it an ominous silence that could become a death sentence?

We looked at each other, and I hastened to say, "Will you permit us to play it once more?"

We were given a nod of assent.

This time we played it differently. The tempi were faster, the sound lighter. We removed all possible "anti-Soviet" insinuations from the music. Even our faces tried to look optimistic. We lied! We presented the foreboding mood of the first movement as hope for a brighter future; the plaintive lyricism of the second as a pleasant little waltz; the sinister muted scherzo became a cheerful dance; and the tragic Jewish themes of the finale took on traditional Oriental coloring.

The tension eased. There were smiles. We were thanked, even praised.

The music was still banned.

The Guard of Honor is changed every five minutes. More and more people are coming to say goodbye. The hall is overcrowded. Perhaps at the very top of the second balcony there are still some free places. From there the stage looks small, the coffin even smaller, his face barely visible.

It is quiet. Only the music of Shostakovich is heard. His music will never die. Through it, Shostakovich will live forever.

He was so animated that evening when we played the quartet by Yuri Marutaev in the Composers' House. The concert went well; we called the composer to the stage. He bowed and shook our hands.

"Don't go yet," he whispered to us.

After the concert we all sat in the restaurant at a large table. Everyone toasted the composer and he toasted the performers. It became noisy as everyone talked at once.

Shostakovich looked into the restaurant. Immediately a place was cleared for him, and vodka poured. It grew quieter. Revol Bunin, a former student of Shostakovich's who worshipped him, raised his glass and offered a toast. Everyone at the table joined in. Several people rose and drank to him standing.

Shostakovich, embarrassed, nervously bit his lips.

The bulky Otar Taktakishvili, the Georgian composer, addressed Shostakovich from the other end of the table.

"Dmitri Dmitrievich! I'm working on a symphony now. To tell the truth, nothing comes out. Could you teach me, maybe?"

Chewing, Shostakovich answered rapidly, spitting out the words, "Yes, yes, sure thing. Definitely, I'll teach you. I'll just finish this piece of chicken and teach you right away."

Everyone at the table laughed. Shostakovich drank his second shot of vodka, and his eyes began to twinkle behind his glasses.

"The other day I went to the movies to hear my music in *Young Guards*," he said. "There were, of course, no tickets. I was standing in the street like everyone else, hopelessly asking, 'Have you a spare ticket by any chance?' Somebody told me to go to . . . No, not to hell, but to the manager, you know . . ."

Pleased that he was relaxed, his listeners hung on to every word.

Shostakovich continued: "I'm led to a little window. Such a small, low one . . . I bend down one way, another . . . Can't quite adjust to it, it's so low, seems especially done to humiliate people . . . Finally somebody's head appears in the window.

" 'What d'you want?'

" 'Well, a ticket. Just one for myself.'

" 'Who are you?'

" 'I am Shostakovich, forgive me . . .'

" 'Shostakovich? So what? You're Shostakovich, I'm Rabinovich. Why do I, Rabinovich, have to give a ticket to you, Shostakovich?'

" 'I don't know,' I said.

" 'Neither do I,' he said, and slammed the window shut."

No one could restrain himself any longer, and laughter shook the table. Shostakovich resumed biting his lips.

Marutaev, the composer whose quartet we had just played, asked for quiet.

"Dmitri Dmitrievich! I'm so happy that you heard my quartet and I would like . . ."

"A fine quartet," said Shostakovich.

"I would like to ask you for some criticism."

"An excellent composition."

Marutaev was beaming. "Please be more specific."

"No, no, everything is marvelously written."

"Please, I ask you . . ."

"Well, if you insist. The first movement—allegro, isn't it? So the theme, you see, also has to be in allegro. Otherwise it doesn't work and there's neither theme nor allegro. Then the scherzo—everything goes up, up, up . . . Too much on the surface, you see. The slow movement—any ladies around?—crap, you see. And the finale—it's generally difficult with the finale. The so-called problem of the finale. Here's Mr. Kabalevsky, he has even written an article about it, where he says that with finales Ludwig van Beethoven had some success, you see. But congratulations—an outstanding quartet!"

Everyone was laughing loudly again, even Kabalevsky and Marutaev. Only Shostakovich was not laughing. He was nervously biting his lips.

The official speeches begin. They are very carefully thought out, so as not to refer to dangerous moments of recent history. "The music of Shostakovich reflects the fight between good and evil, light and darkness . . ." Well, that is true—could easily be said about Beethoven as well. "The music of Shostakovich helped the Soviet people in their struggle for peace." We had already heard that many times before. They

usually say that when they don't know what else to say. "We, his
compatriots, are proud that his music was born on Soviet land." Pro-
paganda, of course, but yes, we are proud.

If only once someone would dare to speak the truth: "Dear comrades!
There were people who made Shostakovich's life shorter. Some of them
are still alive. They didn't come here today to say goodbye to the cou-
rageous man who was not afraid to tell us that Russian music and
Russian culture were in danger!"

Shostakovich wrote his eighth quartet in 1960. Two scores were
hastily copied at the Composers' House. One, as always, was for the
Beethovens, whose performance of the quartet was to be the first and
had already been announced in the chamber-music section. As for
the second score, Shostakovich told his secretary, "Give it to those,
the young ones, you know, let them play it." The secretary phoned
Berlinsky and urgently asked him to stop by. Handing him the music,
he said, "This is for you from Shostakovich. Personally." Berlinsky
brought the score to our rehearsal like a banner. We wrote out the
parts ourselves, in four nights, each writing out his own. I sat over the
score another few days and nights. I didn't exactly work on it; rather,
as I worked, I prayed. In the music was the composer's life, bitter and
tormented.

The eighth quartet is dedicated to the victims of the war and Fascism.
The very first notes of the quartet spell out Shostakovich's initials in
German:

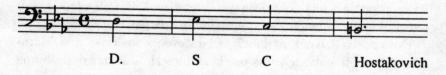

D.   S   C   Hostakovich

When, at the first performance at the Composers' House, the chairman announced the quartet and started talking about the war and the
heroism of the Soviet people and the Communist Party, Shostakovich
jumped up and shouted, "No, no . . . that is, you see, I, I myself,
personally, so to speak, am protesting against any sort of Fascism . . ."

A silence fell. The Beethovens started playing the quartet. Everyone sat there, stunned. "Someday we'll play it, too," I whispered to Berlinsky.

A few days later Berlinsky ran into a rehearsal, beside himself, and told us that he had phoned Shostakovich's secretary, just to thank the composer for the music, when suddenly Shostakovich himself took the telephone and quickly said, "Hello, hello, how are you?"

"And before I could answer," Berlinsky went on, "Shostakovich invited us to come to his house and play him his eighth quartet."

"When?" I asked.

"Tomorrow."

"We aren't ready yet . . ."

"What could I do? You know how he talks! He said in one breath, 'We're all set, I'll expect you tomorrow, thank you very much,' and hung up the phone."

"Well, the only thing to do is declare martial law and work all day, and even all night . . ."

We went to see Shostakovich the next day, without having eaten or slept. He was expecting us and opened the door himself.

"Hello, how are you? Thank you for coming," he said rapidly, convulsively shaking all our hands. Four music stands were waiting in the room. Shostakovich sat down in an armchair and waited impatiently. We quickly opened our cases, took our places, and immediately began playing.

The five-movement Quartet No. 8 in C-minor, Opus 110, is played without interruption. The slow fugato, with its theme, "D-S-C-H"; the furious scherzo, with the Jewish melody from his own second trio, Opus 67; the agitated waltz; the requiem for those who perished; and once again the original bitter fugato con sordino, with his initials.

As he listened, Shostakovich picked up the score and a pencil, and then put both aside, his head bent.

What he must have felt at this moment, we could only guess. Having openly said at the beginning of the quartet, "This is myself," he sat before us, tormented, listening to his story about himself, his musical confession, the sorrowful cry of a soul, where each note weeps with pain.

We tried not to look at him. We began the fourth movement, which imitated either bombs falling from above and exploding on the earth or just hearts breaking. Then came the old Russian song "Tormented by Heavy Bondage," and finally the culmination of the quartet, which came from his opera *Katerina Izmailova*. In the last scene, when the prisoners are being moved across a Siberian river, Sergei, for whose sake Katerina has sacrificed everything on earth, betrays her with Sonetka. The impact of the scene is that the entire audience, the orchestra, and all the characters see this; even the gendarme spits at Sergei and Sonetka; only Katerina alone knows nothing and is happy to meet Sergei. The insolent Sonetka appears, and slowly the irremediable catastrophe reaches Katerina's consciousness. She throws herself into the icy water, pulling Sonetka with her. Thus it happens in the opera. The same melody sounds different in the quartet: here, it is the loneliness of the composer himself and his premonition of his inevitable end.

We finished the quartet and looked at Shostakovich. His head was hanging low, his face hidden in his hands. We waited. He didn't stir. We got up, quietly put our instruments away, and stole out of the room.

The speeches are over. The largo from Shostakovich's Fifth Symphony is played. The coffin is carried through the hall and down the long stairs, then outside and into a bus. It starts moving slowly along Gertsen Street to the Novodevichy cemetery.

The End?
1975

IN THE SPRING of 1975, Haydn's *Seven Last Words of Christ on the Cross* was performed for the first time in Moscow. Its effect on the public was stunning: people did not conceal their tears, and the State Concert Office was deluged with letters requesting a repeat performance. We were asked to give an additional concert and were even given permission to perform the composition by candlelight.

"We have no objection," the Director of Concerts, Kuznetsov, told us. "But it seems to me that the full name of the work should not be printed. Simply say *Seven Words*. Or even better, just use the opus number. Yes, we'll agree on that."

We were left with no alternative but to nod our heads and mumble, "Yes, yes. Of course. We understand."

And indeed, we understood. But we also knew how fast news spreads in Moscow. Something like an oral *samizdat*. We were certain that everyone would know what was concealed by the words "Opus 51."

The director rose from his chair and politely held out his hand. "Well, what else is to be on the program?"

"Something for contrast," I said. "We'll give it some thought."

In the corridor, I told the others, "I have a great idea, but I didn't want to propose it without general agreement. Haydn and candles, naturally, for the second part. For the first, it would be good to have Berg and Schönberg, with voice."

"And a scandal!" Shebalin said.

"Why? Not necessarily," Berlinsky said unexpectedly. "Schönberg's *Verklärte Nacht* has been played in Moscow. And besides, Kuznetsov is a good man. I'd try it. The program is splendid!"

"Well, now? Does it pass?" I asked.

"Let's do it!" Berlinsky answered.

At the secretary's table I carefully wrote out the following program and handed it to the typist:

A. BERG	Quartet, Opus 3
A. SCHÖNBERG	Quartet No. 2, Opus 10, for two violins, viola, cello, and soprano
	INTERMISSION
J. HAYDN	Quartet, Opus 51

The next morning, the editor of programs called me. "Your program was returned to me unsigned. The director does not accept the first part. It is too concentrated. He suggests that one composition be changed."

"One?"

"Yes. That's what he said."

It could have been worse. When I reported the results of my conversation at rehearsal, Berlinsky said, "There, you see? I told you. He understands everything, better than we do. He's right! Why tease the bull with red?"

"Shall we leave the Berg in?" I said. "It's a good work to start the concert. And I suggest Schnittke. It's contemporary, it's Soviet, and, most important, it's good. And it's been performed, so they can't knock it! Okay?"

"Okay!"

I sent the new program upstairs.

At the end of rehearsal a message came: "Report to the program editor. Urgent." I went right over.

"The director asks what sort of music Schnittke's quartet is and whether it has been performed. And he also has objections about Berg. Mr. Kuznetsov is in his office now. You may talk it over with him personally and decide."

The director, however, did not receive me, but his substitute had already been informed.

"Here is your program," he said from his desk, neither rising nor offering me a seat. "The Schönberg is weak music. The Berg, I don't know it, but we shall not be hearing it. We await other proposals."

"Thank you. Thank you very much!" I said angrily.

I repeated his words in the rehearsal room. "To tell you the truth," I added, "I've lost the desire to perform. What can we play? Borodin again?"

"It's not as bad as that," Berlinsky said. Luckily, just as I thought I might lose my temper, the program editor walked in.

"Fellows, I urgently need a program."

"And where can we find one?" I countered. "Everything we propose is unacceptable. Perhaps we could get a list of forbidden composers so we'd know?"

"We don't have any forbidden composers," the program editor said quickly.

"No, of course not!" Berlinsky said. "That was only his temper talking!"

I didn't wait to hear more. I grabbed my violin and left.

The next day the director of the conservatory's Maly Hall called me. "I just spoke with Kuznetsov. He said that if I took the responsibility upon myself, he would allow Schnittke. But Berg, never. Better tell me what kind of music this Schnittke is."

"Very interesting, and very listenable. Bear in mind that the quartet has been performed abroad. Critics have even written that such Soviet music 'serves to strengthen peace and friendship among nations.' That's somewhat idiotic, but the composition is splendid."

"So be it! I'll take the fire upon myself! It's my last season, anyway. And what will the second composition be?"

"That still requires some thought. I'll talk it over with the quartet and call you tomorrow."

The next day, however, we never began our rehearsal. An argument on the theme of the day before started on its own.

Berlinsky said, "Kuznetsov is not to blame. He has his instructions, and it would be a risk."

"That means there is suppression, after all?"

"What's the matter with you? Were you born yesterday?"

"I'd simply like, at this time in my life, to stop lying."

"But no one's lying! To tell the truth, I'm not so excited by Schönberg. We can play Beethoven or Shostakovich. It would be even better!"

"It all works out for you so cleverly!"

"And you, don't act like Don Quixote! Do what everyone else does and everything will be all right."

"What about your earlier comments—'a splendid concert!,' 'What a program!,' and other gushing?"

"Does the world end with Schönberg and Berg? What's wrong with Debussy or Ravel?"

"They're performed every season for the same audience. I wanted to make this concert an event."

"It seems to me we should be grateful that he has allowed Schnittke. And Debussy."

"I still don't understand why Debussy can be performed while Berg can't be."

"Go see Kuznetsov. He'll explain it to you."

"You know, I think I will. For the last time. And I'll tell him everything that's on my mind."

"And then what? He'll report to the Vice Minister of Culture. And, at best, we'll be banned from travel abroad."

"Listen, do you believe yourself that we aren't right? You, speaking for yourself?"

"They're also right."

"They're right, and they forbid us. We're right, and we have to agree with them and say thanks as well. For once, I have to fight it. For myself. So it won't all be so nauseating."

"Well, try it, try it."

"Oh, to hell with you!" Shebalin said. "What difference does it

make what we play? I'm going. I can't stand it anymore!" He turned
to Alexandrov. "You seem to be sick of it, too!"

"Wait, I'll go with you," said Berlinsky, and they all left.

We hadn't even opened our instrument cases.

When, a while later, I left the room, I saw the director surrounded
by his colleagues in the foyer. I had to walk past them.

"There he is!" the program editor said. "Now we can decide everything on the spot. And at the same time the repertoire for next season."

"Come into my office!" said Kuznetsov.

The two of us sat alone in his study. It was quiet, the end of the
workday, and I felt like talking seriously.

"Our quartet is thirty years old," I began. "Almost a whole lifetime
has passed since the day we first sat down with our instruments. We
have performed all the best music composed for string quartet. We
always keep returning to the classics. Recently we've started to play
cycles. Each cycle, especially Beethoven, Shostakovich, and Bartók,
raised us a step higher, and now we've come right up to the basic gap
in our development: contemporary music and its classics, especially
the new Viennese school. We want to be familiar with it, but more
than that, we feel that without it our continued development will stop.
It seems now that our natural direction as musicians is coming into
conflict with certain conditions, and I'm making things unpleasant for
you. We're confused . . ." I fell silent.

"Have you finished?" asked Kuznetsov. "I'll repay your frankness
with frankness. The composers you call the 'new Viennese school,' or
whatever that was, are a movement with worthless sources. They have
nothing in common with music in general, and Soviet music in particular. It's just grist for the mill of ideologically unsound elements. I
understand that if you include the likes of Schönberg in your program
you'll have a sold-out house, but what sort of people are they? Bourgeois
elements, with various decadent tendencies!"

I couldn't understand his last phrase. I understood the separate
words, but together their meaning eluded me. Such large words are
spoken with the intention of entrapping the person they are spoken
to, so that any objection would be impossible, even dangerous.

Kuznetsov, pleased with himself, went on. "Don't think I'm afraid of unpleasantness, or that I could lose my position because of you. I myself don't allow this music! Does that satisfy you?"

"Oh yes! Completely. Thank you for a frank conversation. Now at least everything is understood." I got up and, very calmly, without realizing what my words could lead to, said, "Will you forgive me if I look for other ways to perform this music?"

He rose abruptly, and said dryly, "It's your business."

I had the next season's repertoire in my hands. "Now, this evidently has no meaning. There's Haydn, and the new Viennese composers. But after our talk . . ."

"Not at all, why? It's very interesting. Leave it. We'll study it."

Two days later we left on a two-week tour.

"He'll never approve the repertoire," Berlinsky said. "It would mean he'd have to whip himself. He'll inform the ministry as a matter of course, and we'll find only enemies. And what enemies! It was stupid to bring it up."

"Should we go on with nothing but restrictions?"

"Well, what an idealist we have here! Better men than you have been broken!"

When we returned from the tour, our wives and friends met us at the railroad terminal. In the taxi, my wife whispered in my ear, "Interesting news. After you left, Kuznetsov ran to the Ministry of Culture. Reported everything: about the concert, the program, next season's repertoire, and you. They cursed and canceled the concert. And then he said you threatened to leave for Israel. You know what they called you? A bastard and a cheat!"

"How do you know all this?"

"Let's just say that all of Moscow talks of nothing else but you and Kuznetsov."

"Looks like the Tatars are near. Our time has come."

As soon as we walked into our apartment, Berlinsky phoned to say that he was to appear before the Party Committee.

"Call me immediately afterward," I asked him.

The next day he came by my house late at night, tormented and drunk.

"What's this?" I asked. "Why did they call you and not me?"

"Because I'm the one in the quartet . . ." He trailed off.

"Are you hinting at your Party privilege?"

"I'm not hinting at anything!"

"What about Alexandrov?"

"An old fox! Knows how to get away with things . . ."

"And Shebalin?"

"That's another department. You have any vodka?" He poured some for himself and gulped it down. "Yes, I must tell you," he went on, "our goose is cooked, we've really done it this time! Kuznetsov didn't even talk to me. He was shouting about your repertoire. He said he would write at once to the Central Committee about our 'anti-Soviet activity and ideological diversion'! Understand? And I have a wife and children! And they want to eat!" He poured himself more vodka.

"Don't get so upset," I said. "I have another repertoire: Haydn and Shostakovich. Show it to them tomorrow and everything will be all right. Put all the blame on me! It's my fault, after all. Tell them that we all thought it over and we acknowledge our mistakes. What else do they say on such occasions? That we'll prove ourselves with our deeds—but this time it will be without me."

He looked at me grimly. "And what is that supposed to mean?"

"Just what I said: without me. I'm off. I'm going to use my Jewish origin and get out of this shit."

"Oh hell, I'm not thinking very clearly right now. I haven't eaten, I haven't been able to sleep. Tomorrow . . . I'll call you tomorrow . . ."

Epilogue

BERLINSKY didn't phone me tomorrow, or the next day, or on any day. Neither did my other colleagues.

Instead, all sorts of unfamiliar people started to phone constantly. Not trusting the phone, they didn't tell us their names but asked permission to visit us for a minute. My wife and I would say that we were very busy, but they kept coming anyway. Almost all of them were Jews who wanted to leave the Soviet Union. They asked about life in the West. There were Russians, too, who were married to Jews. They shook our hands warmly and looked deeply into our eyes as they said the unfamiliar word "Shalom."